NAMELESS PERSONS

NAMELESS PERSONS

Legal Discrimination Against Non-Marital Children in the United States

Martha T. Zingo and Kevin E. Early

PRAEGER

Westport, Connecticut
London

Library of Congress Cataloging-in-Publication Data

Zingo, Martha T.
    Nameless persons : legal discrimination against non-marital
  children in the United States / Martha T. Zingo and Kevin E. Early.
        p. cm.
    Includes bibliographical references (p.   ).
    ISBN 0–275–94711–4 (alk. paper)
    1. Illegitimate children—Legal status, laws, etc.—United States.
  I. Early, Kevin E. II. Title.
  KF543.Z56 1994
  346.7301'35—dc20
  [347.306135]   94–8550

British Library Cataloguing in Publication Data is available.

Library of Congress Catalog Card Number: 94–8550
ISBN: 0–275–94711–4

First published in 1994

Praeger Publishers, 88 Post Road West, Westport, CT 06881
An imprint of Greenwood Publishing Group, Inc.

Printed in the United States of America

The paper used in this book complies with the
Permanent Paper Standard issued by the National
Information Standards Organization (Z39.48–1984).

10 9 8 7 6 5 4 3 2 1

Contents

Preface

In 1968, the United States Supreme Court recognized children born outside of wedlock as "persons" under the Equal Protection Clause. Since then the Court has slowly expanded the legal rights of non-marital children. The Court has not, however, provided total relief for these children. Nor has it adequately protected the rights of single parents or non-marital family units.

In this book we analyze the Supreme Court's equal protection birth status decisions from 1968 to 1992 and suggest that those affected by birth status classification might obtain relief and protection through the utilization of feminist jurisprudence and international normative standards. Through a case-by-case analysis, we trace the development of the Court's rulings, examine the pattern of the equal protection tests utilized, and evaluate the consistency of its position.

The Court's reluctance to declare birth status a suspect category deprives non-marital children and single parents of life, liberty, and property. For the Court to properly protect the Fourteenth Amendment rights of non-marital children, single parents, and alternative family units, it should alter its approach to birth status cases and focus on the needs and rights of all persons affected by birth status classifications. Feminist jurisprudence provides the Court with a methodology to address the underlying issue at the crux of birth status distinctions. Further, international normative standards, with their unambiguous recognition of human rights, could then inform the Court's interpretation of the Equal Protection Clause. By these means, the Court would be able to guarantee the substantive rights of non-marital children and their parents.

Chapter 1 begins with notes on nonsexist language usage and the terminology employed throughout this book. It also traces the historical foundations for discrimination against non-marital children and single mothers and outlines the authors' methodological framework. Chapter 2 contains an in-depth analysis of conventional case law regarding Equal Protection claims of non-marital children at the Supreme Court level from 1968 to 1992. It also examines the Equal Protection standards employed, the justification offered by the Supreme Court in support of its decisions, and its use of the constitutional tests. The third chapter examines the Court's "bricolage" approach to Equal Protection theory. This chapter attempts to answer such questions as: What constitutes equality? What method does the Court employ to reach its equal protection decisions? What methodology does and should the Court use to reach its birth status decisions? Are the Court's birth status decisions consistent? Is the Court's method adequate? Finally, Chapter 4 speculates on the theories that could be utilized to challenge and restructure the Supreme Court's decisions regarding non-marital children and single parents. It argues that the Court could guarantee the substantive rights of non-marital children and their parents if it based its birth status decisions on a feminist analysis of the issues underlying birth status distinctions and then used international normative standards to inform its interpretation of the Equal Protection Clause.

Acknowledgments

I thank my co-author, Martha, for conceptualizing and facilitating this project. To my parents, I owe a debt of gratitude for their direct and indirect contributions, their support, and their love. Above all others, I wish to thank my wife, Bonnie, who continues to be a source of support.

—Kevin E. Early

A debt of gratitude is owed to both Evelyn Torten Beck and Richard P. Claude at the University of Maryland and to Leslie F. Goldstein at the University of Delaware for their valuable suggestions, criticisms, and advice on the original version of this manuscript. This current volume constitutes a substantive restructuring and rewriting of the original; the conclusions drawn here supersede those I articulated earlier. I am indebted, as well, to the Reference staff at Widner University Law Library, who facilitated my acquisition of necessary legal materials, and to my co-author, Kevin, for remaining calm despite numerous computer difficulties.

I would like to offer recognition and appreciation to my family for providing encouragement along the way—my father, Pasquale A. Zingo; my sisters: Margaret R. Bachofen, Mary B. Emery, Michele A. Baray, Marie A. Gula, and Marcella C. Bonsall; and my brother, Michael A. Zingo. Honor is also paid to the memory of both my mother, Elizabeth H. Zingo, and my stepmother, Ruth Rhinehart Zingo.

This book could not have been written without the numerous meals, loving rituals, and patient nurturing I received from William Truxton Boyce, Donna Donato, Dorothy Hirsch, Barbara T. Gates, Akasha Hull, Geraldine MacIntosh, Faith Queman, Joe Rose, Stacey Schlau, Subee, and the women in my Detroit feminist reading group. Special gratitude is extended to Susan Klimist Solomon for help in maintaining well-being and trust in the final stages of this project.

Finally, my deepest appreciation—a world of *verde*, "the force that through the green fuse drives the flower" [Dylan Thomas, 1934]—goes to Electa Arenal (City University of New York and the University of Bergen/Norway), whose unconditional support and interest from original to final manuscript helped bring this whole project to fruition.

—Martha T. Zingo

We would like to thank John K. Urice, Dean of the College of Arts and Science at Oakland University, Rochester, Michigan, for making resources available for the initial manuscript revisions, Sandra Williamson for editorial assistance, and Darlene Roach and Patricia Petry for photocopying assistance. Special thanks to all of the staff at Praeger Publishers for making this project a reality.

—Martha T. Zingo and Kevin E. Early

NAMELESS PERSONS

1

Some Truths Are Not Self-Evident: Birth Status—Historical Foundations and Feminist Critique

INTRODUCTION

Various interests and concerns motivated us to undertake this study of U.S. Supreme Court decisions with regard to children born outside of wedlock. They include issues that have captured the attention of feminist scholars and activists worldwide: the powerlessness of women and children within patriarchal society; the inferior economic position of women and those economically dependent upon them; the perpetuation of legal, educational, political, cultural, physical, and social barriers that restrict women's growth and development (especially of those who defy the conventions of traditional motherhood); the endowment of women with privileges instead of rights; and the resistance faced by women who endeavor to participate in society as full, independent, rational, adult persons.

The simple thesis of this book is that it is impossible to gain full equality for children born out of wedlock unless equality is also gained for their family unit; it is necessary to rectify the preferential treatment currently accorded only those families consisting of two opposite-sexed parents united by a legally recognized marital ceremony and the corresponding rejection and unequal status conferred upon alternative family models— for example, the disparate treatment bestowed upon families headed by a single mother or a homosexual parent. In this book we discuss feminist challenges to traditional thinking and develop themes essential to understanding the legal status of non-marital children and their parents in a historical context, highlighting the contrast between masculinist and feminist perspectives. The historical overview provides a sampling of those aspects of Western patriarchal thinking which carried over into contemporary United States attitudes and have had an impact on policies and law concerning the rights of non-marital children and their parents. The sampling is not meant to be comprehensive, but to emphasize the consistency over several centuries of prejudices regarding women and non-marital children.

TERMINOLOGY

Language embodies and reflects the values of society. The individuals who speak it have inherited the encoded thought and reality of their forebears. As we utter and write sentences, few of us are conscious that what we think or say is circumscribed by the words and symbols at our disposal. Language is a system that allows us to classify—but which also classifies us. Nelly Furman points out: "One is born into a language, and must adopt its functioning system in order to produce meaning, to communicate with others. We may wish to make our language our own, but we must first recognize that we are molded into speaking subjects by language, and that language shapes our perceptual world" (Furman, pp. 69–70).

In the Western world, language has been officially structured and legitimated by an educated elite. The resulting codification—based on the perceptions, experiences, and beliefs of a narrow though most vocal segment of the population—has been neither inclusive nor neutral. Linguists point out that reality cannot be embodied in linguistic terms if it encompasses only fragments of an entire people's consciousness. It becomes difficult, if not impossible, for those who are excluded to articulate their own perceptions, experiences, or beliefs about the world; their language proves inadequate to their own needs. Dale Spender explains one of the consequences of this state of affairs: "Trying to articulate the meanings of names which do not exist is a difficult task and yet it is one which feminists are constantly engaged in. Trying to reveal the falseness of patriarchal terms while confined to those false terms themselves is also difficult" (Spender, pp.182–183).

Awareness of the problem is helpful but does not guarantee a definitive solution. It may be that language must remain in a state of transition to be fully inclusive. For whenever any group of individuals is denied the power to name their own reality, doubt arises (at both an individual and a social level) regarding the validity of their observation, experience, or perception. Regarding language in general and our own tongue in particular, Casey Miller and Kate Swift have argued that "[e]very language reflects the prejudices of the society in which it evolved. Since English, through most of its history, evolved in a white, Anglo-Saxon, patriarchal society, no one should be surprised that its vocabulary and grammar frequently reflects attitudes that exclude or demean minorities and women" (Miller & Swift, 1980, p.3).

Nor should anyone be surprised by the common pejorative and stigmatizing terms almost inevitably encountered, whenever the social or legal condition of non-marital children are considered. It is inconceivable that any person's existence should be deemed "illegitimate." What is outside the bounds of a society's framework is the sexual union that produced the offspring. While the justifiability of society's stipulations regarding the *type* of sexual unions that will be officially recognized is debatable, the devaluation of an innocent person's existence can never be justified. In the United States of America, as in England before it, the concept of "illegitimacy" reinforces the patriarchal structuring of society, since historically only males were deemed essential for legitimation. The fact that biologically nothing differentiates "legitimate" from "illegitimate" children is irrelevant, for "illegitimacy" is a social and political construct. Of prime importance in most male-dominated societies is the state's recognition that the unions are sanctioned and the male "owner's" acknowledgment that the progeny belongs to him.

The concept of "illegitimacy" serves no positive social purpose. It stigmatizes the labeled children, making them the object of scorn and malice, and it devalues their worth as persons (Bodenheimer, p.53 fn.228; Hamilton, p.949 fn.2). "Illegitimacy," "illegitimate," and "bastard" are concepts that have yet to become obsolete enough to disappear from society's active vocabulary and frame of reference. These concepts will *not* be used in this book, however, *unless* an author who is being quoted has employed them.

Even when alternative terms are used (such as "non-marital children" or "children born out of wedlock") in an attempt to move beyond unacceptable value judgments inherent in such labels as "illegitimate" or "bastard" and to state the legal condition of the parents at the time of their offspring's birth, the substitutes prove inadequate. These expressions do not challenge archaic patriarchal modalities in familial relationships. "Non-marital children" and "children born out of wedlock" lend credence to the persistent notion, analyzed by Scarlett Pollock and Jo Sutton, that "ideologically, a family should contain two parents: a female who is a mother and a male who is a father to the child/ren [this notion in turn perpetuates the legitimacy of fatherhood]. Attempts to describe other arrangements are couched in language which expresses deviation and social deviance from this model" (Pollock & Sutton, p.593). In order to overcome the impression of deviance conveyed by designating the birth status of only certain children, the terms "marital children" or "children born in wedlock" will be used in addition to the alternative terms noted above.

Similar problems arise with the usage of the term "single mother/single father." As employed in this book, the terms "single mother" and "single father" do *not* include divorced or widowed mothers or fathers, but instead are used synonymously with "unwed mother"/"unwed father," and "non-marital mother"/"non-marital father." It is recognized that since these terms are juxtaposed to marriage, the latter term becomes the embedded perspective. Thus, the unstated assumptions contained within seemingly neutral terms—"mother" and "father"—are revealed by the necessity of a modifier—"unmarried" or "non-marital"—to indicate deviation from the assumed norm. The same is true with regard to the term "female-headed household," which signals, through its qualification, that it is not the norm. Indeed, it should be noted that the qualification "male-headed household" is seldom found in the literature, for it refers to a situation still considered the societal norm.

With regard to the capitalization of the word "Black," we are in agreement with the explanation provided by a prominent feminist theorist and legal scholar Catharine MacKinnon:

Black is conventionally . . . regarded as a color rather than a racial or national designation, hence is not usually capitalized. . . . [However,] it is as much socially created as, and at least in the American context no less specifically meaningful or definitive than, any linguistic, tribal, or religious ethnicity, all of which are conventionally recognized by capitalization. (MacKinnon, 1982, p.516).

While the term "African American" eliminates the problem of nonconventionality of capitalization, it falls prey to problems similar to those discussed for the concepts of "mother"/"father"—that is, the hyphenation signals that the unstated normative standard for "Americans" is someone who is not of African descent.

It should be noted that in our text the term "man" does not include *all* individuals who are biologically male, but rather refers to those males who constitute the "dominant" group within society—those who are white, culturally and economically privileged heterosexuals. While not all males who fit this description endorse the attitudes ascribed to them, they still benefit from the laws and norms that discriminate on the basis of race, gender, class, and sexuality.

When referring to or criticizing marriage in this book, we follow Robin Morgan, who speaks "of marriage *as an institution*, in its legalistic, religious-fundamentalist, and sexual-fundamentalist terms, not of marriage as a freely chosen and affirmed commitment between two persons (of either sex) living as sexual lovers in an emotional bond and sharing of resources" (Morgan, p.9 fn.8).

Finally, while the grammatical rules of English dictate that: "a personal pronoun referring to a singular antecedent should be singular; one referring to a plural antecedent should be plural" (Perrin, Smith, & Corder, p.94), this rule will *not* always be followed—most notably, when the gender of the subject is not specifically or exclusively male or female. For example: "A child born out of wedlock is stigmatized by the circumstances of their birth." Although the word "child" is singular, according to the common rules of English grammar, and requires a singular personal pronoun, the gender of the referenced person is undisclosed.

Casey Miller and Kate Swift urge the adoption of "they" as a singular indefinite pronoun, in light of the "confirmed inadequacy of the 'generic' he" (Miller & Swift, p.58), noting that the grammatical rule which made "they" exclusively plural was an imposed rather than a naturally developed linguistic device (Miller & Swift, p.45). In support of their proposal, Miller and Swift cite antecedents in the writings of George Eliot, Ronald Reagan, George Bernard Shaw, William Makepeace Thackeray, Walt Whitman, and others (Miller & Swift, pp.47–49). They note, however, that opposition to nonsexist language persists "because changes in a language . . . signal widespread changes in social mores" (Miller & Swift, p.4).

In an effort to express both personal and political dissent from *all* that the false generic entails, third-person singular pronouns are double-constructed (s/he, her/him, her(s)/his). In our attempt to avoid the awkwardness of repetition, we alternate them with the third person plural pronouns (they, them, their[s]). It will be clear from the context whether the pronouns "they," "them," or "their(s)" are singular or plural.

MASCULINIST AND FEMINIST PERSPECTIVES: THE FEMINIST CHALLENGE

In 1981, Myra Jehlen published an essay that has become a reference point in the quest to "rethink thinking itself" (Jehlen, p.601). She suggests that to critically examine unstated social presuppositions and values we must, of necessity, "focus on points of contradiction as the places where we can see the whole structure of our world most clearly" (Jehlen, pp. 600–601). In order to do this, Jehlen seeks "a terrestrial fulcrum, a standpoint from which we can see our conceptual universe whole but which nonetheless rests firmly on male ground" (Jehlen, p.576). She finds a solution to the seeming impossibility of standing simultaneously on and off the world in "devising a method for an alternative definition . . . as the investigation, from women's viewpoint, of everything, thereby finding a way to engage the dominant intellectual systems directly and organically" (Jehlen, p.577). Jehlen's metaphoric vantage point allows for the study of pivotal instances of social inequity. The aim of such study is to illuminate what had been invisible and to hold people accountable for the perpetuation of the inequity.

Jehlen's proposal can be likened to ideas expressed by the noted and prolific social critic Michael Walzer in *Interpretation and Social Criticism* (1987) and *The Company of Critics* (1988). He asserts that a social critic "needs to find a place to stand, close to but not engulfed" by the people being criticized (Walzer, 1987, p.26). Indeed, according to Walzer, "social critics 'firmly anchored' in the world of women seem more likely to see the mistake [of insisting that only women's imitation of men and male achievements can count as liberation] than critics already assimilated into the world of men" (Walzer, 1988, p.165).

The difference between Jehlen and Walzer is more a question of degree than of substance. The form of social criticism advocated by Walzer, and implicitly agreed to by Jehlen, entails "the identification of public pronouncements and respectable opinion as hypocritical, the attack upon actual behavior and institutional arrangements, the search for core values (to which hypocrisy is a clue), the demand for an everyday life in accordance with the core" (Walzer, 1987, p.87; Walzer, 1988, p.232). Both critics allow for the use of "a comparative viewpoint as an alternative footing at the critical distance needed for re-vision. It also [allows for] the joining rather than avoiding [of] the contradiction between ideological and appreciative criticism on the supposition that the crucial issues manifest themselves precisely at the point of contradiction" (Jehlen, p.600).

As Jehlen intuited, the resolution of contradictions is sometimes only possible through paradox and the exposure of paradox. To David Cole, reliance on the power of paradox has aided those who would challenge the values, assumptions, and norms inherent in prevailing ideological frameworks. Paradox can neither be ordered nor "fit into a hierarchy. The articulation of paradox leaves traditional categorizations bereft of their sharp lines, and thus calls into question their very meaning. Paradox refuses to let us rest in the illusion of a compartmentalized order; it forces us to re-think our position by alerting us to another position that is irreconcilable with our own" (Cole, 1985, p.82).

MacKinnon is part of the growing number of authors whose radical discourse has attempted to supersede traditional ways of thinking. A controversial figure even within feminist circles, she has spurred an ongoing debate regarding the function and operation of law in the United States. Her primary epistemological contention is that insofar as males possess the power to universalize their perspective—by labeling it objective, neutral, and/or rational—a male viewpoint dictates how

individuals apprehend the world: The perspective from the male standpoint enforces woman's definition, encircles her body, circumlocutes her speech, and describes her life. The male perspective is systematic and hegemonic. The context of the signification "woman" is the context of women's lives. Each sex has its role, but their stakes and power are not equal. If the sexes are unequal, and perspective participates in situation, there is no ungendered reality or ungendered perspective. And they are connected. In this context, objectivity—the non-situated, universal standpoint, whether claimed or aspired to—is a denial of the existence or potency of sex inequality that tacitly participates in constructing reality from the dominant point of view. (MacKinnon, 1982, pp.538–539, fn.56)

MacKinnon takes exception to the facade of "aperspectivity" embedded in the formal and substantive dimensions of the legal system. Where male supremacy is the rule, "the task of legal interpretation . . . is to ensure that the law . . . reinforce existing distributions of power" (MacKinnon, 1983, pp.644–645, 658). In her estimation, a male perspective is synonymous with an institutionalized frame of reference that legitimates the status quo. Its definitions, as the standard for judging society, describe what constitutes true, valid, or rational evidence and ignore or fail to recognize non-male rationality. Ultimately, its epistemological and ontological stance is deemed to represent all human experience and opinion.

MacKinnon is convinced that the institutionalized primacy of a male perspective in law enforces the subordination, limits the options, and ensures the social inferiority of women. She is just as convinced that the only way to counter the "reality," "truth," and "objectivity" codified by a male perspective is "to uncover and claim as valid the experiences of women" (MacKinnon, 1982, pp.637, 638, 639, 640). The problems encountered by women must be addressed on their own terms—from the viewpoint of women—unconstrained by the traditional legal paradigm that recapitulates patriarchal interpretations.

What Jehlen, Cole, MacKinnon, and other writers who share their discourse have in common, then, is distrust for the so-called "neutral," "objective," "universal" rules and methodological analysis of nature and history that are a primary source of legal and other textual interpretations. As Lucinda Finley observes:

Throughout the history of Anglo-American jurisprudence, the primary linguists have almost exclusively been men—white, educated, economically privileged men. Men have shaped it, they have defined it, they have interpreted it and given it meaning consistent with their understanding of the world and of people "other" than them. As the men of law have defined law in their own image, law has excluded or marginalized the voices and meanings of these "others." . . . Law . . . has exalted one form of reasoning and called only this form "reason." Because the men of law have had the societal power not to have to worry too much about the competing terms and understandings of "others," they have been insulated from challenges to their language and have thus come to see it as natural, inevitable, complete, objective, and neutral. (Finley, 1989, p.892)[1]

Tacit assumptions, perspectives, and biases inherent in legal language, and their presence in legal cases involving non-marital children, must be made explicit.

Wide reading in the fields of feminist jurisprudence and critical legal theory have persuaded us that the application of a feminist analysis would facilitate the study of birth status classifications and their impact on non-marital children and single parents. Indeed, the designation of individuals or family units as "illegitimate" could be repudiated if one were willing to employ the paradoxical reasoning suggested by Jehlen, Cole, or MacKinnon, for instance. Critical feminist approaches provide a refutation of the racial, sexual, and class discrimination that the label "illegitimate" effectively conceals.

It should be noted that there is no unified, universal theory of either feminism or feminist jurisprudence. The definitions available point to the diversity of meaning inherent in the concepts "feminism" and "feminist jurisprudence" and reveal the truth of Caroline Ramazanoglu's contention that "defining feminism is . . . clearly a question of taking a political stance. The way in which feminism is defined is contingent upon the way the definer understands past, existing, and future relationships between men and women" (Ramazanoglu, p.7). According to both Leslie F. Goldstein and Patricia Smith, some characteristics or elements that seem common to all feminism are: "the presumption that a patriarchal world is not good for women" (Smith, 1990, p.3); "the promotion of equality between women and men, and a description of the world . . . to identify the social transformation necessary for equality" (Smith, 1990, p.3); and the commitment to "change the legal structures so that they do justice to women's lived experiences, which are different from men's experiences" (Goldstein, 1992, p.28). Finley believes that in order to look at the multiple voices and experiences of women, feminist legal theory requires (at a minimum) a critical perspective—that is

to ask constantly and critically who has been involved in shaping law, in selecting and defining its terms, and in deciding what is and is not one of those terms. Whose understandings, philosophy, and world view are imprinted on law? Consequently, how neutral and how inclusive is the structure of legal reasoning? (Finley, 1989, p.890).

METHODOLOGICAL FRAMEWORK

An opportune critical feminist approach to legal issues can be found in a set of seven questions devised by Heather Wishik (1985, pp. 72–77). We quote Wishik's questions below and model our answers on her exposition, as an example of the theoretical perspectives that underlie this study.

1. *What have been and what are now all women's experiences of the "life situations" addressed by the doctrine, process, or area of law under examination?*

While the law defines the problem as one of the legitimacy of children, feminist jurisprudential inquiry might describe it as one of the legitimacy of the (alternative) family unit and of the economics of intimacy and parenthood. Widening the definition of the inquiry would necessitate the inclusion of mothers of all races, sexual preferences, classes, and ages; the inquiry would then, necessarily, encompass *all* women who choose to become mothers but not to marry (regardless of the reason) or who *cannot* marry (because of legal rules or life circumstances).

Others have addressed this issue. Kenneth Karst, for example, observes that "the constitutional problem of [birth status] is not just a problem of the status of [non-marital] children; it is intimately connected with the relation between men and women, and with racial discrimination" (Karst, 1984, p.501). Alice Wallach and Patricia Tenoso maintain that "discrimination against the children, the mothers, and taken together, the family units themselves, is an effort of social control of *female* behavior. In order to reach the person responsible for the undesirable conduct . . . the law has branded unlawful the entire family" (Wallach & Tenoso, p.25). They assert that to grant equality to some members (children), but not all members (mothers) of a family unit, or to "a particular substantive incident of the parent-child relationship" is meaningless (Wallach & Tenoso, p.23). Removal of the inferior legal status requires the granting of status equality to both the individual members of a non-marital family unit and to the unit itself.

2. *What assumptions, descriptions, assertions, and/or definitions of experience—male, female, or ostensibly gender neutral—does the law make in this area?*

Through this second question, Wishik seeks to show not only what the law actually says about women but also the sociopolitical operation of the law. Keeping this explanation in mind, we can initiate an inquiry into *Caban v. Mohammed* (1979), for example. This case challenged the consent policy in New York's adoption laws pertaining to non-marital children. The statute required the consent of a single mother, but not a single father, for the adoption of a non-marital child. In overruling New York's distinction between unwed mothers and unwed fathers, Supreme Court Justice Powell asserted that the state relied upon overbroad generalizations regarding gender distinctions that failed to promote its purported objective of ensuring the adoption of non-marital children.

In addition to examining Justice Lewis F. Powell's assertions regarding gender distinctions, Wishik's second inquiry would examine the social conditions of women and men to ascertain whether they were in fact "similarly situated" in relation to their offspring. These conditions might include prevalent attitudes, beliefs, and assumptions regarding the parent-child relationship and the economic and gender realities of single parenthood. It might also include an analysis of how the judicial decisions fit into the larger social and political context.

3. *What is the area of mismatch, distortion, or denial created by the differences between women's life experiences and the law's assumptions or imposed structures?*

Wishik maintains that the answer to this question should uncover the interests served by existing laws and the ways in which women's reality is both distorted and rendered invisible by the law. In order to answer this question using the *Caban* case, we need first to look to the life situation of women. This might be described as the plight of mothers who, because of social prejudice, have less economic and social autonomy than men. Such information might refute Justice Powell's assumptions, suggesting that by placing unwed fathers on equal footing with single mothers the Court is perpetuating the patriarchal oppression of women. As Ann Ginger points out, "[i]n 1987, 814,000 women (aged eighteen to forty-four) had a family income under $10,000, and 614,114 of these women had a baby that year" (Ginger, p.407). Although many states mandate that single fathers support their offspring, such laws are difficult to enforce; as a result, non-marital fathers frequently fail to render the support. According to Ginger:

In 1985, 61.3% of women seeking child support for their own children under twenty-one years of age were awarded such payments, but 1,138,000 did not receive payments due, and the 3,243,000 who received payment received only 74% of what was due. Payment was not awarded to 3,411,000 women. The mean child support was $2,215. Women who did not receive payments had a mean money income of $10,837. Among women below the poverty level, 1,130,000 were awarded a mean income of $1,383. These are figures for a year, not a month. (Ginger, p.407)

The federal government has tried to guarantee support payments "through mandatory income withholding, incentive payments to States, and other improvements in the child support enforcement program" with passage of The Child Support Enforcement Amendment of 1984 (Public Law 98–378). The federal Family Support Act of 1988 (Public Law 100–485) mandated tougher child support enforcement by including a federal requirement for state child support enforcement programs. While this act, according to Timothy Casey, "should increase child support collections to some extent, the key changes [which became effective between 1989 and 1993] do not alter the basic fact that a single mother must support her children on her own when the absent parent is unable to contribute or is able but no collection is made" (Casey, p.942). Because problems in enforcement of child support orders still persist, the U.S. Commission on Interstate Child Support drafted a series of recommendations in 1992 to facilitate the collection of support payments (p.2001).

Moreover, the social reality of institutionalized sexual discrimination, which bestows upon males more rights and authority than upon females, places the state's *puissance* at the disposal of the unwed father should he ever decide to undermine the single mother's efforts at self-determination and self-control. An unwed mother's choices, under the *Caban* decision, may have force only when the unwed father chooses to forgo male prerogatives in familial affairs.

4. *What patriarchal interests are served by the mismatch?*

Wishik's query would encompass the social, political, economic, and cultural events that have surrounded both the acceptance of, and changes in, the law or legal action. According to Harry Krause (1967), birth status classifications are first and foremost a creation of law; their original purpose was to control the sexual activities of women and to insure male dominance. The shift in the Court's treatment of non-marital children occurred in 1968—a time when the United States was awash with social concerns for those individuals and groups viewed as "politically powerless" and thus in need of protection. More specifically, people who practiced, studied, and wrote about law, seeing only the impact on "blameless children," declared that birth status discrimination constituted injustice writ large.

Birth status laws are predicated on the following ideas or beliefs: the nuclear family unit; heterosexual marriage; the idea of "fathers' rights"; the partial recognition of women's rights as human rights; denial of women's right to self-determination, thereby restricting and condemning women to passive roles; the discouragement of free choice for women in matters of procreation, lifestyle, and personal association; the right of males to dictate/conrol the sexuality of females; institutionalized sexism; the right of the state to regulate morality; the regulation of the inheritance of male property; and the abdication of fatherly responsibility for the care of children. Like the language in which they are written, birth status laws embody male-oriented assumptions/stereotypes. The doctrinal categories were designed by men to serve a public world organized around the values of "the ladder of achievement."

As a consequence, the interests and needs of women have not been met in the past and are not yet met in the present, in part because birth status laws continue to draw distinctions between children on the basis of their parents' marital status. Birth status laws focus narrowly on which children are legally entitled to the benefits and protections granted by statute. In so doing, these laws remove themselves from the contextual lives of those individuals who are affected by the distinctions. No fundamental alteration has been enacted to modify the original purpose of these laws: to establish and enforce a hierarchical ordering of family units, limit the claims of accidental offsprings against their fathers, and guarantee that reproduction and socialization of the young take place exclusively within the bounds of a patriarchal family.

5. *What reforms have been proposed in this area of law or women's life situation? How will these reform proposals, if adopted, affect women both practically and ideologically?*

Two United Nations documents, *The Study of Discrimination Against Persons Born Out of Wedlock* (Saario, 1967) and *European Convention on the Legal Status of Children Born Out of Wedlock* (Council of Europe, 1975), focus specifically on the rights of non-marital children. However, these publications overlook the rights of single mothers and alternative family units. In so doing, they reflect the continuing prioritization of patriarchal values in many nations. Since both U.N. documents affirm the legitimacy of fatherhood, whereby the privileges and power of fathers are extended beyond marriage, some feminist juridical scholars might argue that the U.N. authors fail to understand the difference between fatherless families and "illegitimacy." As a result, the U.N. authors seek only to abolish the first concept—but not the second. By assuming that men are intrinsic to a family unit, the theory of "father-right" is repackaged; by labeling children "illegitimate," the stigma and burdens associated with that concept adhere to both the individuals and the family units existing outside of marriage, thus accentuating the powerlessness of women to direct their own personal and family life.

   6. *In the ideal world, what would this woman's life situation look like, and what relationship, if any, would the law have to this future life situation?*

In the ideal world, women would participate fully in society. The law would assist in the establishment of new institutions to accommodate the needs and life choices of all citizens. It would no longer regulate sexual behavior between consenting adults. Insofar as the legal status and legal relationships of all persons would be deemed equal and independent of marriage, the concept and institution of birth status would be obsolete.

   7. *How do we get there from here?*

On the road from here to there, the very perception of the nature and order of things would need to be transformed. The route to ontological changes might come through the following: the reconceptualization of gender away from an either/or (bipolar) construct and toward a multidimensional scale; the identification, understanding, and elimination of all forms of oppression experienced by women, and by extension all other human beings (regardless of race, age, sexual preference, religion, ethnicity, physical condition); and the elimination of reproductive capacity as a delimiting factor for women. The world would be viewed from the perspective of a web, from which no one should be left out (Karst, 1984, p.462). The focus would shift from the individual parties before the Court to the context of the actions of the parties before the Court, from a zero-sum game (winners/losers) to balance and networks (cooperation/sharing). Consciousness raising would be practiced as a strategy helpful to women and men. The idea of domination would be replaced with the notion of interdependence.

As Karst has observed, "if the Court should ever decide to widen its doctrinal inquiry, seeking more inclusive ways of looking at these issues, the constitutional problem of [birth status] will be seen clearly as a problem of responsibility and care in the web of connection" (Karst, 1984, p.501).

THE NUCLEAR FAMILY AND THE DEPENDENT STATUS OF WOMEN

It is impossible to thoroughly examine the socially prescribed importance of birth status without simultaneously scrutinizing the institutionalized (sexual) double standard perpetuated by the nuclear family.[2] Three factors—presumed inferiority, gender bias, and private property—are ultimately entangled in society's attempt to preserve the traditional family unit and to regulate the reproductive activities of its members. They echo the moral, social, and economic customs upon which the legal system of the United States is based (Eisenstein, 1981; Eisenstein, 1984; Baer), and provide a philosophical foundation for birth status discrimination. But birth status itself emanates from the inferior social and legal position of women in patriarchal society.[3]

The traditional nuclear family consists of a man and a woman legally bound in a monogamous, monandrous relationship wherein children are conceived, born, and raised in a single-family unit. As part of this unit, children are socialized with reference to the dominant culture; a complex and subtle gendering process trains them to live within the culturally approved limits of masculine and feminine behavior (Rubin). Each individual is patterned for gender-appropriate responses to either general or specific situations encountered during childhood and adulthood. Indeed, the gendering process shapes everyone's expectations regarding both themselves and others, throughout their lifetime. The more strictly an individual adheres to the gender stereotypes implanted during the process, the better the patriarchal society and the nuclear family thrive.

The nuclear family, which in its modern form is a product of nineteenth-century industrial transformations, serves many functions.[4] It embodies the spirit and structure of a society in which males are dominant and females are subordinate. The nuclear family confines women to the home symbolically, and often physically, through the socially reinforced mechanisms of dependence and subordination. Both men and women learn to accept, unthinkingly, that the family-head is destined to confer property rights, lineage, and status upon women and children; regulate reproduction; foster hegemonic ideology; and socialize children to accept hierarchical relationships and authority within the social order.[5] Kate Millet in her ground-breaking 1970 book, *Sexual Politics*, claimed that the nuclear family:

is both a mirror of and a connection with the larger society; a patriarchal unit within a patriarchal whole. Mediating between the individual and the social structure, the family effects control and conformity where political and other authorities are insufficient. . . . Serving as an agent of the larger society, the family not only encourages its own members to adjust and conform, but acts as a unit in the government of the patriarchal state which rules its citizens through its family heads. (Millet, p.55)

The relationship between the nuclear family and the social order is reciprocal insofar as each supports and perpetuates the values, structure, and power of the other—the former through socialization; the latter through law—for its own survival and, by extension, for the survival of male authority. To refute or reject the dominant male rule means to question the basis of both the nuclear monandrous family and the existing social order, including the laws, which maintain that dominance. One such law concerns an individual's birth status—that is, whether an individual's birth is "in accordance with law." While the distinction is inconsequential if the primary focus is upon familial equality and the protection and maintenance of the human rights and dignity of *all* persons in a family, it has crucial consequences for patriarchy.

The institutionalization of power relationships within the family legitimated those social, religious, and political practices which perpetuated male domination. The historical prejudices related to the evolution of the family in the early modern period have been emphasized by the feminist historian Joan Kelly:

State legislation in the fifteenth and sixteenth centuries strengthened the household as an instrument of social control. Laws concerning the poor and laws against vagrants, prostitutes, witches, and even religious orders in Protestant countries herded people into households for their livelihood and placed unpropertied males—and *all women*—under the governance of the household "master." Both these processes weakened traditional support for female authority *and subjected women to patriarchal power in the family and the state.* (Kelly, p.23; emphasis added)

Marilyn French ventured a study titled *Beyond Power: On Women, Men and Morals* (1985) in which she elaborates on the institutionalization of male power and control:

Patriarchal cultures control women, exclude women, and attempt to control all those things women produce—from children to manufactures. They attempt to take over as their own the very physical functioning of women's procreation, by assigning children to men and diminishing the role of women in procreation. They do this through *the word*: that is, by decree and institutionalization—the setting up of independent hierarchical structures devoted to control in a particular field or area. Not only unequal degree of status but also the ideas that sustain and perpetuate male control over females, are institutionalized in patriarchy. (French, p.72)

Pollock and Sutton and others[6] who have delved into the issue of women's unequal place in the social scheme agree that once the subordinate status of women is codified into law, it reinforces and perpetuates their "otherness"—that is, the childlike position of women legitimates the notion that they are less than men, less than human, and less than persons. The symbolic disassociation of women from the realm of persons, becomes acutely obvious through the dictionary definitions of these terms.

Using typically "man-made" language, *Black's Law Dictionary* defines the word "person" as: "A man considered according to the rank he holds in society, with all the right to which the place he holds entitles him, and the duties which it imposes. . . . The word in its natural and usual signification includes women as well as men" (Black, p.1299). Women are designated persons as an afterthought, while children are totally excluded. First and foremost, persons are men, and as such they possess both rights and duties denied to non-males and non-adults. While male children eventually become men, and by extension persons, women and female children, exempted from metamorphosis into either men or adults, remain forever inferior persons, subsumed under a gendered rubric.

To concede the point that the word "man" encompasses members of both sexes, as evidenced by the second part of the definition, does not negate the above observations. Such a concession merely strengthens them, giving evidence of how women are rendered invisible in an androcentric society. Men, *the* representative humans, are the standard against which the norm is designed and measured.

Black does not provide a definition of the word "human," but *Webster's New Collegiate Dictionary* does. "Human," according to Webster, means that which is "[o]f, relating to, or characteristic of man; consisting of man; having human form or attributes; susceptible to or representative of the sympathies and frailties of man's nature" (*Webster's*, p.556). Implicit in this definition is the equation of human with man.[7] Maleness is consistently deemed the authoritative standard of humanness. The unacknowledged notion that women, when independent of men, are legally neither persons nor humans, as evidenced by the respective definitions of Black and Webster, is firmly embedded in the political and legal traditions of the United States.

HISTORICAL OVERVIEW

Birth Status: The Problems of Classification and Marriage Laws

For nearly nineteen centuries, Western society has labeled persons born outside the bonds of a legally recognized marital unit "illegitimate";[8] their birth is not "in accordance with law." Such persons are deemed a serious threat to the traditionally defined family which relies, as has been shown, upon institutionalized patriarchy—with its concepts and practices of monogamy, monandry, private property, heterosexuality, and legitimacy—for survival.[9] Those born out of wedlock symbolize a violation of societal norms. Products of unsanctioned unions, the infant issue have historically borne the stigma of a condemnatory label.

The identity of the biological father is crucial to the concept of legitimacy, since in a patriarchal society women and children are recognized only in relation to men. To say that a child is fatherless is to place her/him outside the power of a specific male and notes the presence of a mother/woman who is not directly controlled by a man. A non-marital child and an unwed mother are both perceived as a menace to the social status quo. They represent a violation of the community's familial and reproductive norms. Both are "unlawful" (or outside the law), since they transgress moral and civil convention by their very existence. Inherent in the idea of illegitimacy is the existence of laws that define the legitimate character of any heterosexual relationship that produces offspring. These laws, commonly referred to as "marriage laws," embody a society's concept of legitimacy, without which the concept of illegitimacy cannot exist.

Virginia Sapiro, writing in 1986 about women in America, notes the appeal made to biblical authority in juridical defenses against nontraditional sexual liaisons. In the eyes of the state, according to Sapiro, marital laws and policies are

viewed in part as a commitment by a couple to carry on their lineage by conceiving and raising children. As the Minnesota Supreme Court argued in 1971 in explaining why homosexuals could not be legally married, "The institution of marriage as a union of man and woman, uniquely involving the procreation and rearing of children within a family is as old as the book of Genesis" (*Baker v. Nelson*). Further, the institution of marriage is the primary means the state has to regulate the distribution of property within and across generations. (Sapiro, p.325)

In contemporary as in premodern times, marriage laws establish and organize the family as a social institution; dictate the rights and responsibilities of parenthood; determine the legal status of all progeny resulting from both natural and artificial insemination; prescribe sexual preference; and impinge upon all economic and domestic arrangements affecting the coupling adults and/or their offspring. Theoretically monogamous, monandrous marriage assures the existence of a blood relationship between a man and his children. Winfred Hooper, reviewing legislation on this issue early in this century, discussed the European origins of conventional monogamy and monandry: "The wife is singled out from other women by being appropriated to one man, and, when she becomes a mother, the presumptive paternity of the husband, though never so conclusive as maternity, has a strength about it that no other form of marriage can give. The demarcation between legitimate and illegitimate offspring arose in Europe primarily from the certainty of parentage established by the monogamous union" (Hooper, p.3).

Frank Haskins, in the 1939 edition of the *Encyclopedia of the Social Sciences*, describes the role of religion in sanctioning sexual unions. Beginning in the second century, the valuation of monogamous, monandrous marriage was enhanced and strengthened by orthodox Christianity. By attaching sin to unsanctioned reproduction, Christianity sought to eliminate sex outside marriage. Women and non-marital children bore the brunt of the ecclesiastical condemnation of illicit behavior, since the culpability of a specific man was difficult to prove. Acknowledging gender inequity, Haskins describes the cruel treatment and unmerited punishments meted out by religious authority: "In medieval and early modern times the mother was often required to confess her sin before the congregation . . . she was sometimes fined, sometimes publicly whipped, sometimes placed in stocks, and the child was neglected and socially ostracized, while the father suffered little or no penalty" (Haskins, p.579).[10]

From the times of Roman Law, legal policy regarding inheritance and property centered on males, while policy determining non-inheritance centered on females; property rights passed patrilineal. Under English common law, persons born outside the bonds of marriage were *filius nullius* (a child of nobody) or *filius populi* (a child of the people). In the nineteenth century William Blackstone, whose interpretations of English common law were to influence early American legislators, explained: "The incapacity of a bastard consists primarily of this, that he cannot be heir to anyone, neither can [he] have heirs, but of his own body; for being *nullius filius*, he is therefore a kin of nobody and has no ancestor from whom any inheritable blood can be derived" (Blackstone, p.485; Bysiewicz, p.403). Histories of the period indicate that such persons were considered the lawful children of neither their father nor their mother. Prior to passage of the Elizabethan Poor Laws, no living person or governmental unit had a civil responsibility to support their non-marital children.[11] Society felt economically compelled, however, to attach these children to someone—if not legally, at least socially. The logical persons to encumber were the women who bore them,[12] since, as Kingsley Davis observed, women were not important with regard to lineage: "When the system of descent revolves around the male, the principle of non-descent revolves around the female. By placing the illegitimate child's relationship, if any, on the shoulders of the woman, the male line—and hence the family system—is protected" (Davis, 1939, p.224).

Persons whose birth was not in accordance with law were traditionally denied not only their right of inheritance and paternal support but also their father's name. The inheritance of property was intimately tied to the subject of personhood and non-personhood. Without a legally recognized surname, a person was no one; a nameless person was stigmatized (Teichman, p.96) by the circumstances of their birth—scorned, condemned, and discriminated against. To perpetuate its social dominance, the patriarchy established and legally protected such institutions as marriage, legitimacy, and the male-led households; all of these institutions intensified the importance of male surnames, transforming them into a symbolic branding iron. Nineteenth-century feminists such as Lucy Stone saw that the naming process, in effect, reduced women and children to chattel, denying them an existence independent of the men whose names they bore.[13]

Surnames are essentially property titles, proclaiming the alleged owner of every woman and child. Though women and children are extremely dependent upon a man's surname for both identity and status, however, the acquisition of a name is *not* guaranteed. Ultimately, whether a woman or a child acquires a name depends upon male self-will. Women and children whose surnames did not accurately reflect the identity of their societal owner were rendered legally and socially invisible. This category included women who became mothers outside marriage and any children resulting from an unsanctioned sexual union. While single mothers and their non-marital children constituted a family, they were not legally recognized as such.[14]

Bronislaw Malinowski, in a 1929 study of kinship, delineated "Principles of Legitimacy" and influenced subsequent thinking on the matter of the patriarchal family structure. According to his central principle, "No child shall be brought into the world without a man, and one man, assuming the role of sociological father, that is, a guardian and protector, the male link between a child and the rest of the community" (Malinowski, p.403 as quoted by Teichman, p.89). This legitimacy principle lays bare the elevated importance of the adult male in the family. Insisting upon the male presence, it insures male social and legal dominance to the detriment of unmarried mothers and their children. Indeed, Krause's historical study of "illegitimacy" verified the anthropological observations of Malinowski. Krause noted that

the basic self-interest of the father . . . may . . . have been most directly responsible for the situation of the illegitimate. It was natural that men, as legislators, would have limited their accidental offsprings' claims against them, both economically and in terms of a family relationship, especially since the social status of the illegitimate mother often did not equal their own. Moreover, their legitimate wives had an interest in denying the illegitimate's claim on their husband, since any such claim could be allowed only at the expense of the legitimate family. Against these forces have stood the illegitimate mother and the helpless child. (Krause, 1971, p.403)

The statutes, rules and mores governing the lives of children born out of wedlock are in turn the institutionalized expression of vested self-interests.[15] Rules delimiting the legitimation process reflect not only the presumed inferiority of non–wedlock born children[16] but also the inherent gender bias of legitimation proceedings[17] and the primacy of private property.[18]

John Locke and William Blackstone: Their Influence on Law in the United States

The devaluation of women is based on prejudices fed by centuries of misogynist convention. It is most often rationalized through biblical authority and reference to the law of nature. One of the primary scriptural justifications offered to substantiate the continued subordination of women to men is found in Genesis 3:16 when God curses Eve: "Unto the Woman he said, I will greatly multiply thy sorrow and thy conception; In sorrow thou shalt bring forth Children, and thy desire shall be to thy Husband, and he shall rule over thee" (Locke, I, 47:16–20).[19]

John Locke, the seventeenth century philosopher whose writings greatly influenced the authors of both the Declaration of Independence and the federal Constitution of 1787 (Beitzinger, pp.7–11), subscribed to this injunction. He summarized and codified previous thinking regarding women and children, and his works served as the basis for subsequent beliefs and convictions. While Locke was not the first (nor the last) political theorist to embrace as "God's command" that men rule over women, his acceptance of this biblical passage is important (Locke, II, 1:4).[20] Melissa Butler points out that "while the subjection of women carried no political import . . . Locke largely accepted the empirical fact of women's inferiority and saw it grounded in nature as ordered by God" (Butler, p.142). Carole Pateman pushes this point further by asserting that "the contract theorists' aim was theoretical patricide, not the overthrow of the sexual right of men and husbands" (Pateman, p.39). Thus, according to Pateman, "Locke had no quarrel with Filmer about the *legitimacy* of sexual, patriarchal right; rather, he insists that it is not political" (Pateman, p.39).

Locke relies upon Genesis 3:16 to anchor important ideas in Books I and II of the *Two Treatises of Government*. First, he uses it to strengthen his refutation of Sir Robert Filmer's theory of divine rights (Locke, I, 47:20–23; I, 49:1–14, 42–57)—a necessary precondition for legitimating a social contract theory. By attacking Filmer's absolute monarchy, Locke challenges the validity of a government possessing arbitrary power over individuals (Locke, II, 119:6–24). Locke argues that the only form of government consistent with the law of nature is that to which individuals freely consent.

Feminist critics including Jean Elshtain, Teresa Brenner and Carole Pateman, Melissa Butler, and Susan Okin point out that although either express or tacit consent is required in order to bind an individual to the social contract envisioned by Locke (Locke, II, 95:1–10; II, 112:15–17; II, 118–121), he "is silent on the question of women's participation in that mutual act of consent which brought political society into being" (Elshtain, p.121).[21] It can be inferred that Locke's silence is not accidental. His conceptualization of women's sphere mirrored the attitudes and prejudices of his times. According to Butler,

the audience Locke was addressing was essentially an audience of fathers, household heads and family sovereigns. Locke had freed them from political subjection to a patriarchal superior—the king. He did not risk alienating his audience by clearly conferring a new political status on their subordinates under the patriarchal system, this is, on women. (Butler, p.147)

Looking back, Locke saw that the original commonwealths were historically patriarchal (Locke, II, 105–106), their chief end was the preservation of private property (Locke, I, 92:1–9; II, 3:1–3; II, 123:15–19; II, 124:1–3), and the primary property holders were men (Locke, II, 25–76; Elshtain, p.122; Donovan, p.5).[22]

Secondly, Locke used Genesis 3:16 both to ground his denial that a woman is obligated to accept domination by her husband and then to undercut the strength of his denial (Locke, I, 47:1–15, 33–39; I, 67:11–17; II, 4:13–18; II, 82:1–8; II, 86:1–4, 10–18). While Locke grants that women who endeavor to avoid God's curse upon Eve are not remiss, he maintains that women are bound by Law to subjection—that the lot of women is ordained by divine providence, the foundation of nature, the laws of men, and the customs of nations (Locke, I, 47:33–39; I, 48). This subversion of positions is crucial. In conjunction with his understanding of Genesis 1:28–29,[23] Locke's formulation of women's circumstances implies the conditions for excluding most women from actively participating in the formation and perpetuation of civil society (Locke, I, 75–77; I, 84; I, 92; II, 3; II, 50; II, 94–95; II, 124; II, 124n; II, 127; II, 137–138).[24] Only individuals who are free and who own property are granted full citizenship within society (Locke, II, 95:1–4; II, 119:1–6, 15–24). A prerequisite for being free is that an individual possess and utilize reason (Locke, II, 57:1–2, 6–12; II, 58:1–7; II, 59:5–12; II, 60:1–10; II, 61:1–5; II, 63:1–5), since all freedom is derived from the law of nature that is reason (Locke, II, 6:6–11; II, 63:1–5). Theoretically, "[t]he *Freedom* then of Man and Liberty of acting according to his own Will, is *grounded on* his having *Reason*" (Locke, II, 63:1–3) [original emphasis].

Consequently, anyone who adheres to the rule of reason is allowed to freely exercise their will, while anyone who is incapable of reason, either temporarily or permanently, is subject to the will of someone who is governed by nature's law (Locke, II, 58). Children (or more accurately, *male* children) are primary examples of individuals whose ignorance of reason results in their temporary governance by another—a condition that ends with nonage (Locke, II, 55; II, 58–63; II, 69:16–22). On the other hand, Locke consigns women (and female children) to that group of individuals who are *always* bound by the political will of another. According to Pateman,

although [Locke] argued that sons, when adult, were as free as their fathers and equal to them, and hence could only justifiably be governed with their own consent, it is usually "forgotten" that he excluded women (wives) from this argument. His criticism of the patriarchists depends upon the assumption of natural individual freedom and equality, but only men count as "individuals." Women are held to be born to subjection. (Pateman, p.213)

The argument for denying women's rationality begins with Locke's assertion that all should be equal "without Subordination or Subjection, *unless* the Lord and Master of them all, should by *any* manifest Declaration of his Will set one above another" (Locke, II, 4:14–16; emphasis added).

If one individual comes under the dominion of another, it is necessary to demonstrate that such is the will of God. Locke does this through his understanding of the divine punishment inflicted upon Eve. According to his interpretation of the Bible, "God ... foretells what should be Womans Lot, how by his Providence he would order it so, that she be subject to her husband" (Locke, I, 47:33–36). He also contends that her husband's "will take place before that of his wife in all things of their common Concernment" (Locke, I, 48:12–18). Locke thus lends credence to societal conventions that exclude women from the realm of "free and equal individuals" since, according to Pateman, "a natural subordinate cannot at the same time be free and equal. Thus women (wives) are excluded from the status of 'individuals' and so from participating in the public world of equality, consent, and convention" (Pateman, p.121).

The "natural differences" between males and females legitimate the idea that a woman follows not her own will but, rather, submits to the will of another. As a child, she is under the dominion of her father. Because she is deemed incapable of ever reaching nonage, she remains subject to her father's will until she marries. If she engages in sexual relations with a man, she remains under the domain of her father until such time as she eventually "consents" to marriage. At that point, she is transferred—along with any potential or actual offspring—from her father's household to her husband's. Under such societal conventions, it is irrelevant which man actually exercises control over her; femaleness makes her the quasi-property of a male. She can never be free to the same degree as a man; she can only be free indirectly in the manner of "[a] Child [who] is Free by his Father's Title, by his Father's understanding, which is to govern him" (Locke, II, 61:6–8).

In his Treatises, Locke stresses the primacy of the father within the family despite his observation that the term "Paternal Power" is incorrect insofar as it infers that the father has complete control/power over his children. He suggests that a more accurate term is "parental power," since it indicates that the mother and father share their power (Locke, II, 52:1–11).

No sooner are these words written than Locke reverts to his preference for paternal domination. He locates the executive power of the law of nature *solely* in the father (Locke, II, 74:22–38), hence familial protection remains the duty of the father; according to his own disclosure and in real experience, once the mother is invested with parental authority she is excluded from this responsibility. Moreover, the husband's will and understanding always takes precedence over that of the wife in matters pertaining to "their common interest and property" (Locke, II, 82:6–7). The family dynamic that Locke establishes is such that the father/husband alone represents the interests of the entire family. The mother's/wife's voice has been effectively silenced, albeit with her "consent."[25] It is the father, and by extension men in general, with whom the children associate power, and to whom the children customarily defer. The social message implicitly conveyed by such a family model—which the children are socialized to replicate—is that women are powerless, voiceless, and subordinate to men. As a female child ages physically, she has the "choice" of remaining under her father's jurisdiction or acquiring a new master. Generally, the latter occurs.

Locke's conviction that individuals of both sexes are driven into marriage or conjugal society (Locke, II, 77:1–6) implies that non-married individuals were considered the exception rather than the rule. In his worldview, the conjugal state is entered because "God planted in Men a strong desire . . . of propagating their Kind, and continuing themselves in their Posterity" (Locke, I, 88:20–24). The motives of men and women for remaining in the conjugal state, however, differ. A man remains in conjugal society in order to solidify his paternal power[26] and to discharge his moral responsibility for the nourishment, support, and education of his children (Locke, II, 80:16–19). A woman, on the other hand, remains in conjugal society because of economic insufficiency—she cannot adequately maintain herself and her child without material assistance and protection (Locke, II, 80:1–8).

Hence, although both parents are responsible for the mutual support and assistance of their offspring, the mother's primary role is to bear the young; the father's, to provide for the child's present and future necessities. He does this through his power "to bestow [his] estates on those who please him best" (Locke, II, 72:12–13). Since the father generally controls the inheritance, it is his duty to determine the "rightful" heir of all the interest and property held in common by himself and his wife. For this reason, the father has a vested interest in guaranteeing that the heir apparent is the heir entitled.

The supremacy of the patriarchal family encoded in the political philosophy of Locke[27] is echoed in the legal writings of Sir William Blackstone, who uncritically embraces the principle of male authority. Blurring the distinction between natural and positive law, Blackstone relies upon secular rationalizations for the devaluation of women and non-marital children and for the double standard that governs the sexes. For Blackstone a woman's proper sphere is the family, wherein she is expected to serve the male who heads the household and to conceive only *his* children. The blood of the father, with few exceptions,[28] *must* course through the veins of the designated (male) heir if his line is to be perpetuated and not defrauded. This certainty, however, is contingent upon each man's ability to accurately identify his offspring—a problem seldom encountered by women.[29] In order to alleviate, or at least significantly reduce the possibility of an "uncertain mixture," men have attempted to control the sexual activity of women. Through the concepts of monogamy and monandry, each man is promised exclusive sexual access to the woman he selects to conceive his children. He thereby obtains a reasonable measure of assurance that his property will remain with his *male* blood children—or those he has legally recognized—who will carry on his genetic line and his family name.

According to Blackstone, within marriage a husband becomes his wife's master. He has the power to deprive his wife of her liberty, "administer chastisement," determine the conditions and availability of divorce and separation, and settle the disposition of child custody and inheritance questions. Blackstone thus submerges a female's identity into the male's. In the *Commentaries on the Laws of England*, he explicitly states his understanding of the precise legal ramifications of the marriage contract: "By marriage, the husband and wife are one person in law; that is, the very being or legal existence of the woman is suspended during the marriage, or at least is incorporated and consolidated into that of the husband: under whose wing, protection, and cover she performs everything; . . . and her condition during her marriage is called her coverture" (Blackstone, pp.442–445).

The significance of Blackstone's interpretation of the marriage contract cannot be overstated. Susan Okin designates it the "legal fiction of coverture" (Okin, p.249); for all practical purposes a married woman ceases to exist—she is civilly dead. In almost every sense of the word she is legally a non-person. Her very essence is absorbed by her husband—she is infused in him; he is the embodiment of her. Power and control are wielded by the male head of household, under whose perpetual tutelage a woman is destined to remain. His needs delimit her function, for she is a legal non-entity within the family devoid of weight, worth, and influence. A woman's inseparability from a man makes her the ideal breeder of his property and of his heir. Her body is in law his body. He exercises virtual control over her body: he defines the conditions under which her body will be sexually accessible to him; he dictates that her body may appropriately house only his fetus; he devises the punishment, within legal limits, to be inflicted upon her body should she transgress his will.

In 1938 Grace Abbott underscored how devastating the status of legal non-entity could be for a woman. She gathered documents pertaining to the children of unmarried parents. The seventeenth century statute to which Abbott refers below may well have influenced Blackstone's own formulations:

The dependant status of the married woman at the common law resulted not only in the absolute dormancy of any legal rights of the mother during the lifetime of the father but exerted its influence even after his death; for the father had power by deed or will to appoint a guardian for his minor children, and the statute granting or confirming this power (1670) ignored any rights of the mother. With such an attitude toward the rights of the lawful mother it is not surprising if we hear little of the rights of the illegitimate mother. She is first recognized in criminal legislation. (Abbott, p.5)

More than thirty years after Abbott, female historians and feminist writers, such as Diane DeWar (1968), Adrienne Rich (1976), and Jenny Teichman (1982) have added to our understanding of the history of single mothers

and non-marital children. They have shown that if married mothers were
at the mercy of the man to whom they were attached, single mothers were
in an even more precarious situation. While married mothers legally dis-
appeared, single mothers were legally suspect. A mother whose non-marital child died as a result of any form of accidental or deliberate infanticide
was guilty of murder. In addition, the entire burden of support fell on a
mother's shoulders, *unless* she could establish beyond a reasonable doubt
"clear, convincing, and satisfactory" proof of paternity in a court of law.[30]

Prior to the development of scientific methods such as blood or genetic
tests, a paternity hearing (assuming that one even occurred) could well be
decided on the preponderance of presumptions, conjectures, or circum-
stantial evidence available to the court, and/or on the strength of the
putative father's denial. When his word contradicted the mother's, especially where no other evidence corroborated her story, two approaches were
employed: in the earlier epoch, the man alleged to be the child's father was
ordered to maintain the child until such time as a conclusive decision could
be rendered (Rich, p.264fn; DeWar, p.20; Teichman, p.65); in later times, the
putative father's innocence was upheld (Dewar, p.20; Teichman, p.65).

This dual attitude toward paternity cases reflected the conflicting interests of various segments of society at differing historical moments. The
Bastardy Act of 1576 addressed one set of concerns; centuries later, in 1832,
the Poor Law Commissioners responded to popular criticism and resent-
ment aroused by the earlier act. In the sixteenth century, there had been a
pragmatic concern lest the non-marital child became an economic burden
on the community's resources; the community feared being forced to
assume financial responsibility for the child's maintenance if the mother
were unable to support her child. Because support of non-marital children
could quickly deplete the treasury, it seemed to be in society's best interest
to locate the putative father and have him assume the burden. The Bastardy
Act of 1576 stated that unless a man "could prove his innocence, the 'father'
was liable upon the mother's word alone to indemnify the parish for the
cost of the child's support" (DeWar, p.20).

DeWar traces the reaction to acceptance of a mother's word regarding
the identity of her non-marital child's father. She cites the Poor Law
Commissioners' 1832 allegations against the Bastardy Act, which, they
claimed, allowed too easily "for the punishment of innocent men if unmarried mothers were unscrupulously determined to name 'fathers.' More
importantly, [the Poor Law Commissioners] felt that the just investigation
of these accusations were overridden by concern to find men to assume the
financial burden of the illegitimate and so relieve the local ratepayers"
(DeWar, p.20).

At this juncture in the nineteenth century, the primary societal fear in
paternity cases was that spurious claims would be lodged against innocent
men as a means of harassment or extortion. In an effort to protect a man's

wealth, property, and family from demands made by someone who was not *legally* attached to him, the parishes established procedures to ensure, to the degree possible, that the named father and the biological father were the same person. The New Poor Laws of 1834, required, for example, that "the mother's word as to the identity of the father of the child had to be corroborated by other evidence" (Teichman, p.65).

Three major concerns were obvious: society did not want to support non-marital children; putative fathers did not want to be harassed; society did not want to punish innocent men. Both the alleged fathers and the community at large feared that single mothers would endanger their respective resources. The last two concerns thus became enmeshed and male self-interest dominated. Any resolution to the problem of establishing paternity had to simultaneously grant men the benefit of the doubt regarding their sexual activities and shift the economic burden for non-marital children away from society. As a result, single mothers were once more ensnared and sacrificed on the altar of androcentricity. Like the ancient mythological Lilith,[31] the unwed mother was designated the culprit who alone produced children and alone was required to suffer the consequences of her "crime."[32]

Single mothers continued to be characterized as sinful, immoral, and untrustworthy—a projection of the larger social and legal definition of women. Male culpability in the making of non-marital children was conveniently ignored. Kenneth Karst, taking a feminist approach to the issues, describes how, in an effort to control the sexuality and maternity of women, men in power narrowed the sphere of life within which women could move and shifted the entire onus to women: "The non-bearers of children wanted to control the bearers of children. . . . [They wanted] to define a breeding territory from which other men were excluded, and which would guarantee at once both their having offspring and their being able to identify them as their own. Women can by nature be confident about both these matters; men cannot at all, as long as women are on the loose" (Karst, 1984, p.457). Women possessed a power that men did not; it was a power men perceived as threatening. Men devised a means of neutralizing the threat by controlling women's capacity to bear children and to speak for themselves.

Abigail Adams Defeated: Women's Place in the United States

Almost two hundred years after the Bastardy Act of 1576 and fifty-nine years before the New Poor Laws of 1834, Abigail Adams protested the subjugation of women to laws which were designed exclusively by men for the benefit of men. In a 1775 letter to John Adams, who was then a delegate to the Continental Congress of Philadelphia, she warned: "Remember all men would be tyrants if they could. If particular care and attention are not paid to the ladies, we are determined to foment a rebellion and will not hold ourselves bound to obey any laws in which we have no voice or representation" (Adams, pp.10–11). Her warning was answered with laughter—and a retort from her husband that reminds American women, in their search for legal justice, of the expressions of chauvinism current in the early years of the Republic. Rarely does one currently hear such bald statements uttered any longer, but the same sentiments and assumptions fuel the persistence of sexual inequalities: "Depend upon it, We know better than to repeal our Masculine systems. . . . We have only the Name of Masters, and rather than give up this, which would completely subject us to the Despotism of the Petticoat, I hope George Washington, and all our brave Heroes would fight" (Adams, p.11).

Obviously, these "brave heroes" were fearful. The founders firmly believed in and adhered to the model established most cogently by Locke and made more narrow by Blackstone. Women were excluded from the political and legal framework that confined rights to white property-owning men.

Fear of women reared its head again in Thomas Jefferson's justification for denying women access to the public sphere. In his opinion:

Were our State a pure democracy, in which all the inhabitants should meet together to transact all business, there would yet be excluded from their deliberations: 1. Infants, until arrived at years of discretion; 2. Women, who, to prevent depravation of morals, and ambiguity of issues, could not mix promiscuously in the public meetings of men; 3. Slaves, from whom the unfortunate state of things with us takes away the rights of will and of property.[33] (p. 295 as quoted in Martineau, p. 126)

Jefferson's words justified the systematic and deliberate ostracism of women (among others) from the public sphere. They also echoed the Western tradition as it became codified in the subsequent legal, economic, and political policies of the new country: women were granted legal personhood in only a qualified sense and deemed dependent upon men. Indeed, as Okin points out:

these "persons" of the Constitution, like the consenters to the original contracts of Hobbes, Locke and Rousseau, did not include every adult individual, but only the male heads of families, each of whom was understood to represent the interests of those who constituted his patriarchal entourage. . . . The state and federal constitutions . . . were written with the understanding that in many important respects, women were not, legally, persons, but subordinate members of patriarchal households. (Okin, p.249)

Neither the term "person" in the Fourteenth Amendment of the U.S. Constitution nor the term "men" in the Declaration of Independence, included women. The main argument of the Declaration of Independence is grounded on "the laws of nature and of nature's God." In the words of the Declaration, "[w]e hold these truths to be self-evident: that all men are created equal; that they are endowed by their Creator with certain inalienable rights; that among these are life, liberty and pursuit of happiness; that to secure these rights governments are instituted, deriving their just power from the consent of the governed." Jefferson and the authors of the Constitution followed Locke, and indeed Western tradition as a whole, in assigning only to men executive power in the laws of nature. The socioreligious and political definitions of females, transplanted by the European emigrants to their new country, made it nearly impossible for men to consider women equal or to endow women with the same inalienable rights bestowed upon men. Voiceless by imposition, women neither established the new government nor formally consented to be subjects of that government.

If Abigail Adams's words had been taken seriously, the centuries-old denial of women's natural rights might have been rectified. References in the Constitution (1789), the Bill of Rights (1791), or the Fourteenth Amendment (1868) to "the people" and/or "all persons" might have been different if the same shift in thinking that had occurred regarding monarchy and the landed aristocracy had been applied to the power imbalance between the sexes. Earlier than Abigail Adams, Locke had momentary flashes of insight that might have provided ground for a shift: his recognition of parental as opposed to paternal power, his belief that the biblical subjection of women carried no political importance, and his abstract grant of formal property rights to women. But they were unavailing because he himself retracted them. In the eyes of America's founders, women were deemed to be almost entirely outside the scope of these concepts. Only male heads of families were protected, since, as James Mill noted, "all those individuals whose interests are indisputably included in those of other individuals may be struck off from political rights without inconvenience. . . . In this light also women may be regarded, the interest of almost all of whom is involved either in that of their fathers, or in that of their husbands" (Mill, 1983, p.122). Okin, covering this period of American history, terms women in effect "subordinate members of patriarchal households" (Okin, p.249) whose role as wives, mothers, sisters, or daughters preempted their right to legal personhood. The framers of the country's basic documents excused themselves by seeing women's rights as individual rights.

WOMEN AND SUPREME COURT DECISIONS

Almost a hundred years after the Declaration of Independence, in *Bradwell v. Illinois* (1873), the Supreme Court intimated assent to the continuation of women's second-class citizenship status. It was the first Fourteenth Amendment case to challenge a sex classification—or any other legislation. As Leslie Friedman Goldstein notes, by a quirk of history, although *Bradwell* was argued at the Supreme Court a couple of weeks before the *Slaughter-House* cases were argued, the Supreme Court handed down the *Slaughter-House Cases* decision one day in advance of the *Bradwell* decision. This timing rendered the *Slaughter-House Cases* the historic first official interpretation of the Fourteenth Amendment. (Goldstein, 1988, p.66)

In *Bradwell*, Justice Lawrence of the Illinois Supreme Court denied Myra Bradwell's application for a license to practice law on the grounds that "[the court] should not admit any persons or class of persons who are not intended by the legislature to be admitted, even though their exclusion is not expressly required by the statute. . . . [thus] when the legislature gave to this court the power of granting licenses to practice law, it was with not the slightest expectation that this privilege would be extended equally to men and women" (*Bradwell*, Transcript of Record, p.11).[34]

Why would this expectation not exist? Perhaps because neither members of the judiciary nor of the legislature could tolerate the idea of equality between the sexes. Were it not for that, then in the words of John Stuart Mill, "almost everyone . . . would admit the injustice of excluding half the human race from the greater number of lucrative occupations" (Mill, 1970, p.181). The Court, instead, perpetuated "a relic of an old world of thought and practice" (Mill, 1970, p.146) when it refused to allow Myra Bradwell an equal opportunity to participate in the legal profession on the same terms as her male counterparts. The Court, in effect, denied her equality before the law, considering it outside their judicial capacity to reach beyond the unspoken intentions of the legislature. By failing to counter what it interpreted as the legislative expectation, the lower court essentially denied the legal personhood of women, without expressly doing so.

When *Bradwell* reached the United States Supreme Court, the only acknowledgement of the lower court's opinion was the Court's passing comment that "[t]he supreme court [of Illinois] denied the application apparently upon the ground that it was a woman who made it" (Goldstein, 1988, p.70). The Court bypassed the underlying sexism of the lower court decision and concentrated instead on whether "the right to control and regulate the granting of license to practice law in the courts of a state . . . [was] governed or controlled by citizenship of the United States" under the Privileges and Immunity Clause of the Fourteenth Amendment (*Bradwell*, p.139). Ruling that it was not, the Court affirmed the lower court's decision.

The Court accepted the suggestion of Matthew H. Carpenter, Bradwell's attorney, that the Privileges and Immunity Clause of Article IV of the 1789 U.S. Constitution and the Fourteenth Amendment safeguarded the civil liberties of citizens from oppressive state legislation. It rejected, however, the argument in Carpenter's legal brief that:

If [the privileges and immunities] provision does protect the colored citizen, then it protects every citizen, black or white, male or female. (*Bradwell*, Brief for Plaintiff in Error, p.136)

· · · · ·

I maintain that the 14th Amendment opens to every citizen of the United States, male or female, black or white, married or single, the honorable professions as well as the servile employments of life; and that no citizen can be excluded from any one of them. . . . [A]ll of the privileges and immunities which I vindicate to a colored citizen, I vindicate to our mothers, our sisters, and our daughters. (*Bradwell*, Brief for Plaintiff in Error, p.137)

The Court, however, asserted that the Privileges and Immunity Clause did not guarantee to any citizen the right to practice law in a state's courts.

While the Court's response was not surprising in light of its decision in the *Slaughter-House Cases* (1873), Justice Bradley's opinion was. In his *Slaughter-House Cases* dissenting opinion, Justice Bradley had affirmed "the right of any citizen to follow whatever lawful employment he chooses to adopt . . . [as] . . . one of his most valuable rights, and one which the legislature of the state cannot invade, whether restrained by its own Constitution or not" (*Slaughter-House*, pp.113–114). After defining the inalienable rights of man, Justice Bradley declared that

[for] the preservation, exercise and enjoyment of these rights the individual citizen, as a necessity, must be left free to adopt such calling, profession or trade as may seem to him most conducive to that end. Without this right he cannot be a freeman. This right to choose one's calling is an essential part of that liberty which is the object of government to protect; and a calling, when chosen, is a man's property and right. (*Slaughter-House*, p.116)

In *Bradwell*, however, he drew a sharp distinction between the citizenship rights of women and men in his concurring opinion:

the civil law, as well as nature herself, has always recognized a wide difference in the respective spheres and destinies of man and woman. Man is, or should be, woman's protector and defender. The natural and proper timidity and delicacy which belongs to the female sex evidently unfits it for many of the occupations of civil life. The constitution of the family organization, which is founded in the divine ordinance, as well as in the nature of things, indicates the domestic sphere as that which properly belongs to the domain and function of womanhood. The harmony, not to say identity, of interests and views which belong or should belong to the family institution, is repugnant to the idea of a woman adopting a distinct and independent career from that of her husband.

· · · · ·

It is true that many women are unmarried and not affected by any of the duties, complications, and incapacities arising out of the married state but these are exceptions to the general rule. The paramount destiny and mission of woman are to fulfill the noble and benign offices of wife and mother. This is the law of the Creator. And the rules of civil society must be adapted to the general constitution of things, and cannot be based upon exceptional cases. (*Bradwell*, pp.141–142)

While this opinion was not the official position of the Court, J. Ralph Lindgren and Nadine Taub argue that it illustrates how "[t]he separate sphere ideology affected every aspect of the lives of women and men in the nineteenth century. It also affected the interpretation of their rights under the federal constitution. Few segments of that pattern of thinking are as clear as the one issued by Justice Bradley . . . in the [Bradwell] decision" (Lingren and Taub, pp.11–12). Justice Bradley's opinion voiced the tenet that the majority decisions in both *Bradwell* and *Minor v. Happersett* (1875)[35] implied regarding women, but which the majority left unarticulated until *Muller v. Oregon* (1908).

This is not to suggest that the Court neglected to pay lip service to the legal personhood of women, for indeed it did not. In fact, the Court affirmed in *Minor* that "there is no doubt that women may be citizens. They are persons" (*Minor*, p.165). This pronouncement, however, did not invest women with the political, legal, or social power to make their citizenship meaningful. In *Bradwell* it allowed the legislature to prohibit women from practicing law; in *Minor* it allowed the legislature to deny women the vote. Both decisions indirectly infringed upon the right of women to be treated as legal persons, since the Court—with the exception of Justice Bradley in *Bradwell*—declined to address the sexism inherent in the challenged statutes. As a result, the Court permitted the disparagement of women thereby implicitly precluding women from the Fourteenth Amendment's protection of *all persons*.

Given the Court's concession that "women may be citizens" and that women are persons, a literal reading of the Fourteenth Amendment's Privileges and Immunities Clause would necessarily grant equal citizenship rights to women. The clause in question explicitly states that "*All persons* born or naturalized in the United States and subject to the jurisdiction thereof, are citizens of the United States and of the state wherein they reside. No state shall make or enforce any law which shall abridge the privileges or immunities of citizens of the United States" (emphasis added). Nina Morais presents evidence suggesting that as early as the 1870s the first section of the Fourteenth Amendment was considered applicable to sex discrimination claims [Morais, p.1153].[36] Yet beginning with Justice Samuel Miller's majority opinion in *Slaughter-House Cases*, judicial interpretations of this amendment emphasized that it was intended to protect racial minorities. By narrowing the amendment's scope to racial discrimination, Black women—and by extension any woman regardless of race—were forestalled from extending the equality argument to gender.

By failing to accept a broad reading of the Fourteenth Amendment in *Bradwell*, and by relying on the *Slaughter-House Cases* decision[37] it had delivered the preceding day, the Court rejected any attempt to infuse the Privileges and Immunities Clause with a "radical" interpretation. Thus, indirectly and through omission, the Court prepared the foundation for continued discrimination against women. Its decisions in *Bradwell* and *Minor*, in conjunction with Justice Bradley's concurring opinion, served as a cornerstone for its *Muller* decision.

In *Muller*, the Court explicitly accepted the type of sexual differentiation evident in Justice Bradley's *Bradwell* opinion. It upheld the constitutionality of a statute which restricted the hours of women's labor only. In language reminiscent of Justice Bradley's, the Court issued a classic statement of traditional beliefs regarding the "weak, fair sex" and deserves to be quoted at length:

That woman's physical structure and the performance of maternal functions place her at a disadvantage in the struggle for subsistence is obvious. This is especially true when the burdens of motherhood are upon her. . . . as healthy mothers are essential to vigorous offspring, the physical well-being of woman becomes an object of public interest and care in order to preserve the strength and vigor of the race.

Still again, history discloses the fact that woman has always been dependent upon man. He established his control at the outset by superior physical strength, and this control in various forms, with diminishing intensity, has continued to the present. . . . Though limitations upon personal and contractual rights may be removed by legislation, there is that in her disposition and habits of life which will operate against a full assertion of those rights. . . . Differentiated by these matters from the other sex, . . . legislation designed for her protection may be sustained, even when like legislation is not necessary for men, and could not be sustained. . . . the denial of the elective franchise in the state of Oregon, . . . rests in the inherent difference between the two sexes, and in the different function in life which they perform. (*Muller*, pp.412–413)

The Supreme Court, as a political institution of liberal reform, overtly maintained that there existed a need to protect women legislatively against the abuse of male power, while it covertly defended the male-dominated power structure with this Fourteenth Amendment decision regarding women. Indeed, its decision is a direct product and reflection of traditional patriarchal attitudes. The Court neither exists nor functions in a vacuum, and must necessarily be sensitive to "the times" in which its decisions are rendered. Public acceptance of its decisions is predicated on the public's belief in the legitimacy, fairness, and timeliness of the Court's opinions.[38] If the Court were or remained unsynchronized with society's beliefs and values, it would soon discover its own limitations and powerlessness; either "idle law" would become the norm or the Court would be bypassed altogether. The Court's initial decisions symbolically denied women's personhood by neither permitting women to make choices nor responding to their choices with respect. It thus perpetuated the fiction that the subordination of women was natural.

A possible justification for the Court's implicit and explicit acceptance of the protective legislation in early twentieth-century Fourteenth Amendment cases lies in the Court's recognition of the legislature's right to classify citizens. Exceptions to this occurred in economic, substantive due process cases such as *Lochner v. New York* (1905). But the Court's ruling in *Muller* left gender discrimination, which seemingly violated the Due Process and Equal Protection provisions of the Fourteenth Amendment, standing. Inherent in this posture was an attitude of judicial deference toward the legislature since the Court considered only the legislative means for classifications, not the legislative ends. As a result, discriminatory classifications were usually upheld, despite their invidious effect, since a rationale could always be provided. Laws subjected to this minimum standard of review were inevitably deemed constitutional, thereby precluding a confrontation between the judiciary and the states or federal legislatures' interpretation of the Fourteenth Amendment.

In the non-racial Equal Protection cases heard prior to 1940, the Court accorded every conceivable latitude to the challenged legislation. The "reasonableness" standard permitted (and indirectly encouraged) the legislatures to pass unequal or oppressive laws with impunity, since the Court judged any reason conjured up by the legislatures to be an adequate justification for the codified discriminations against women and against non-marital children. This placed the burden of proof regarding the unreasonableness of the law firmly on the shoulders of the challengers—especially if the Court adhered strictly to its four rules for applying minimum scrutiny articulated in *Lindsley v. Natural Carbine Gas* (1911):

The equal protection clause of the Fourteenth Amendment does not take from the State the power to classify in the adoption of police laws, but admits of a wider scope of discretion in that regard, and voids a legislative classification only when it is *without any reasonable basis* and therefore is purely *arbitrary*. A classification having some reasonable basis does not offend against the clause merely because it is not made with mathematical nicety or because in practice it results in some inequality. When the legal classification [in such a law] is thus challenged, if *any* state of facts reasonably can be *conceived* that would sustain it, the existence of the state of facts must be assumed. One who assails the classification in such a law must carry the burden of showing that it does *not* rest upon *any reasonable basis* but is essentially arbitrary. (*Lindsley*, p.78; emphasis added)

Nowhere in its guidelines does the Court clearly define the term "reasonable." The closest it comes to a definition is its assertion that classifications cannot be arbitrary, while noting that "if *any* statement of facts reasonably can be conceived that would sustain it," then such facts will be assumed to exist. But what nine Supreme Court justices or legislative representatives consider "reasonable" might not be viewed as such by the women, men, and children who suffered the consequences of legal discrimination. Indeed, as numerous decisions made clear,[39] often the motives accepted as adequate justification for statutory classifications were blatantly unreasoned. Indeed, classifications were only rejected by the Court if *absolutely* no reason at all could conceivably be ascribed to them.

CONCLUSION

The Supreme Court's commitment and adherence to liberalism—the basic philosophical cornerstone of the U.S. legal tradition (Blackstone; Baum; Gunther, 1980)—led to the reaffirmation of repressive social, cultural, and legal structures that shaped women's lives. Because the Court accepts liberalism's sexual hierarchy, the relative position of women and men vis-à-vis their non-marital offspring is significantly different. A nonmarried women can never give birth to a child in accordance with the legitimation principle, while a non-married man can render that birth legitimate. Indeed, the patriarchal and paternalistic values contained in the principle of legitimation provide the traditional theoretical underpinnings of American policy (Teichman; Levitan & Belous). The implication of this pro-male bias produces inevitable consequences regarding the legal, political, and economic status of single mothers and their non-marital children (Hirsch; Eisenstein, 1979; Eisenstein, 1984).

Since the social position of children born outside wedlock is inseparable from considerations of paternity, it is difficult, if not impossible, to alleviate the stigma of birth status without simultaneously eradicating the unequal distribution of power, property, and privilege between the sexes. Without a sexually balanced distribution of these assets, the privileging of paternity can never really be eliminated; the concept of paternity currently enhances male control over women and children in both the public and private spheres. The systematic denial of women's rights to self-determination and reproductive freedom, which arises from the sexist, racist, heterosexist, marketplace biases ingrained in liberal ideology (Eisentein, 1979, 1981, 1984), and the resulting policies governing non-marital children perpetuate men's socioeconomic control of women (Millett, p.85). The mere act of acknowledging responsibility for a non-marital child allows men legally to define and control a fundamental aspect of women's lives.

The interconnection between sexual equality and reproductive freedom cannot be ignored. Women cannot fully exercise their rights and freedoms if men (individually or collectively) possess the right to legally control pregnancy and childbirth. As long as this patriarchal control remains intact, biology and destiny remain synonymous for women. As Sylvia Law expressed it, "although both men and women seek to control reproduction, only women become pregnant. Only women have abortions" (Law, p.981).

Unless women are accorded the same opportunity to plan when and under what circumstances they will become pregnant, they can never plan their lives to the same degree as their male counterparts. Without complete control over their reproductive capacity and reproductive decisions, women are held hostage by archaic legal restrictions.

By allowing the state to define the parameters within which women are permitted to make their reproductive decisions, the Court frequently ignores or negates the indisputable fact that *only women become pregnant*. Although the Court seemed cognizant of the reality regarding pregnancy in *Roe v. Wade* (1973), it appeared to negate this fact one year later in *Geduldig v. Aiello* (1974). At issue in *Geduldig* was the constitutionality of California's Disability Fund, which paid medical disability and hospital benefits for "virtually all disabling conditions without regard to cost, voluntariness, uniqueness, predictability, or 'normalcy' of the disability" (*Geduldig*, p.499), but which excluded from coverage normal-pregnancy-related disabilities (*Geduldig*, p.500). Justice Potter Stewart, who delivered the majority opinion, asserted that

[t]here is no evidence in the record that the selection of the risks insured by the program worked to discriminate against any definable group or class in terms of the aggregate risk protection derived by that group or class from the program. There is no risk from which men are protected and women are not. Likewise, there is no risk from which women are protected and men are not (*Geduldig*, pp.496–497).

Justice Stewart pointed out in footnote 20 that "the program divides potential recipients into two groups—pregnant women and non-pregnant persons. While the first group is exclusively female, the second includes members of both sexes" (*Geduldig*, p.497). The Court relied upon a physical difference to uphold the discriminatory statute—only women can become pregnant—without analyzing the cultural and social ideology that elevates pregnancy from a mere biological occurrence to a legally significant fact.

In light of *Geduldig*, the sex bias implicit in any restriction of a woman's reproductive rights becomes all too apparent. Such restrictions reenforce and indirectly uphold sexual double standards. Since men cannot become pregnant, their sexual independence is guaranteed *even* in those instances when the chosen contraceptive method fails. The same guarantee is *not* available to fertile women who engage in sexual activity with sperm-producing men.[40] The risks and burdens associated with pregnancy are assumed by women. Despite "the technological developments of the twentieth century, there is today no contraceptive method which provides 100% reliability and has neither adverse effects upon health nor interferes with 'normal' heterosexual intercourse" (Arditti, Klein, & Minden, p.141). Women bear the primary responsibility for pregnancy and are intimately affected by this state of affairs. Removal of reproductive decisions from women to the state enables the state to resurrect traditional sex roles in the area of sexual conduct. As long as women are dependant upon male permission to control even a single aspect of their being, they are deprived of their right, in the words of Harry D. Krause, "to take responsibility for choosing [their] own future. . . . For to be a person is to respect one's own ability to make responsible choices in controlling one's own destiny, to be an active participant in society rather than an object" (Krause, 1977, p.58).

It is no exaggeration to say that women are treated neither as full human beings nor as complete persons, for they are still prohibited from making independent personal choices and from having their choices consistently respected (Morris, p.127; Karst, 1986). If Herbert Morris's conceptualization of a person is correct, such prohibitions cannot be justified. He claims that "[w]e treat a human being as a person provided: first, we permit the person to make the choices that will determine what happens to him[/her] and second, when our responses to the person are responses respecting the person's choices" (Morris, p.127). Morris maintains that "the right to be treated as a person is a fundamental human right belonging to all human beings by virtue of their being human. It is a natural, inalienable, and absolute right" (Morris, p.127). Aleta Wallach and Patricia Tenoso expand this point by observing that "[t]his sense of being a person is vitiated by illegitimacy classifications that create a subordinate and inferior class of individuals by burdening self-determination for women and impairing achievement of equality among persons" (Wallach & Tenoso, p.29).

The designation of individuals or family units as "illegitimate" inherently denies the personhood of the designated individuals. The very act of saying or trying to prove that the designated individuals are persons assumes a Kafkaesque dimension of absurdity, since the utterance automatically implies the possibility that they are not. The repudiation of this conceptualization might create the possibility of addressing the racial, sexual, and class discriminations from which the label "illegitimate" diverts attention. Such a challenge, however, would necessitate serious consideration of several pressing questions: Does a woman have a right to herself? Is a woman's body her own property? Since a woman's body is the fetus's sojourn, does a woman have a right to choose whether and when to conceive, or whether to bear a child in conformance with society's rules?

Answers to these questions require the acceptance of an alternative perspective, similar to that proposed by various feminist scholars—for example, Cole (1985), Jehlen (1982), MacKinnon (1987, 1989, 1991), and Minow (1990). Such a perspective, which is essential to a feminist legal standard, must reject, at a minimum, subordination on the basis of gender, race, sexuality, or birth status of any group or individual to any other group or individual. It must eradicate the powerlessness of women and the supremacy of men through the valuation of women's experiences. Ultimately, this standard must transform the current system by altering reality and demanding a new way of thinking and communicating. Women must be empowered and given voice; they must be elevated from their current status of less-than-human to a status that recognizes them as being fully human. They must be viewed as they view themselves—that is, from a woman-centered point of view. Women would be guaranteed control over their reproductive capacity and access to their sexuality. Indeed, they would have access to that which they are currently denied, not on patriarchal terms, but on their *own* terms.

Before a feminist legal standard can come to fruition, however, the existing legal standard must be radically transformed. A thorough examination of the Supreme Court's systematic discrimination against single mothers and non-marital children, as well as an analysis of its justifications for the continuation of such practices, is a necessary preliminary to the establishment of a feminist legal standard.

NOTES

1. See also: Finley, 1986; Finley, 1987; MacKinnon, 1982; MacKinnon, 1983.

2. The American nuclear family is a political institution. Historically, the government has exercised the power to recognize/not recognize the union of a man and woman. Its decision regarding who could/could not legally unite in marriage adversely affected the children produced by such unions, since children born outside legally sanctioned unions were deemed "illegitimate" by the government. The group in American society most obviously affected by the government's regulations were persons who lived as slaves, non-colored women who chose to procreate with men of color, and non-colored men who raped slave women or who were chosen by free women of color. See: "Bastard," p.297; Vincent, 1968, p.85–89; Chesler, pp.4–6, 16; White, 1981, pp.6–8; Giddings, pp.35–39; Auwers, p.232 fn13; "Marriage . . .;" "Bastards," pp.844–847; Laslett, Oosterveen, & Smith, p.376.

The "plight" of the Black family within the United States has been the subject of renewed interest since Moynihan's publication (1965). According to his report, "[a]t the heart of the deterioration of the fabric of the Negro society is the deterioration of the Negro family. It is the fundamental cause of weakness in the Negro Community. Unless the damage is repaired all the effort to end discrimination, poverty and injustice will come to little" (Moynihan, p. 5; emphasis added). The problems within the Black family, according to Moynihan, are exacerbated by "the tangle of pathology"—that is, a matriarchal structure which results in "the reversed roles of husband and wife" (p.30). Within his worldview, the patriarchal nuclear family is the norm and the ideal form. It should be remembered, however, that this ideal does not exist even in non-colored families, and as Angela Davis and Fania Davis point out,

[Black] families, of course, have never corresponded in structure to the prevailing ideal. First of all, original African cultural traditions defined the family as much more expansive than biological parents and their progeny. Especially during the earlier phases of the African presence in the Americas, the extended family was a vital tradition. Secondly, the brutal economic and political pressures connected with slavery and continuing throughout subsequent historical eras have inevitably prevented African-American family patterns from conforming to the dominant family models.

Finally, black people, during and after the slave era, have been compelled to creatively and often improvisationally build a family life consistent with the dictates of survival. Yet, because the African-American family does not reflect the norm, it has been repeatedly defined as pathological in character. (Davis and Davis, p.36)

See also: Gutman; Staples, 1971; Frazier; Davis, 1971; Giddings; Stack; Smith, 1970; Ladner.

3. Wallach and Tenoso; Wallach; Rich, 1976; Corea; Arditti, Klein, and Minden; Brophy and Smart; Krause, 1971; Millet; Krause, 1967; Pollock and Sutton; Standard; Eisenstein, 1979.

It is impossible to discuss the inferior social and legal position of women in society without noting that the status accorded to non-colored women is greater than that accorded to women of color. The concept of whiteness within American society, rather than being merely a biological characteristic, is a sociopolitical construct—a point often (conveniently) forgotten/ignored by many non-colored women. In an attempt to improve their status within society, non-colored women concentrate on conditions that are peculiar to their own situation. Reliance upon white skin privilege allows non-colored women to remain unmindful/ignorant of the needs of women who are different from them—women who suffer from double or triple discrimination; women who are systematically excluded from the remedies pursued by non-colored women. Consequently, whenever discrimination against women is discussed, it is imperative to understand that the discrimination tends to have an even greater impact on those women who possess neither economic nor skin privilege.

4. Works extolling the value and function of the traditional nuclear family include: Blustein; Fuchs; Noonan, Jr.; Viguerie; Kramer; Berger and Berger; Pines; Westin; Lasch; Nicholi, Jr.; Reagan; Felsenthal; Otto.

5. Teichman; Sapiro; Rich, 1976; Wallach and Tenoso; Millett; Freeman, 1971; Miller & Swift, 1976; Thorne; Rifklin. For a further discussion of hegemonic ideology, see: Kellner.

6. For example: Williams, 1983; Rich, 1976; Ginsburg; MacKinnon, 1982; MacKinnon, 1983; MacKinnon, 1991.

7. Note that the term "man" does not include *all* individuals who are biologically male. It refers to a very specific group of males—that is, those who are white, economically privileged, heterosexual, and Christian, who constitute the "dominant" group within society.

8. In some matrilineal societies in which descent is traced through the mother and her clan—the Hopi of Arizona, the Ashanti of Ghana, the Truk of the Caroline Islands, the Atjehnese of Java, the Choctaw of the Southeast United States, the Nayar of Northern India, the Polynesians, and the Iroquois of New York—the identity of the biological father is not important, or at least less socially significant, since *all* social attributes are inherited through the female bloodline. See: Leavitt; Rosaldo and Lamphere; Schneider & Gough; Eisler; Whitelegg.

9. Rich, 1976, pp.24–25, 44; VanZile III; Davis, 1939–40; Wallach; Comer.

10. See also: Hooper, p.27; Werner, pp.24–27; Friedmann, p.281; Robbins and Deak, p.312; Krause, 1971, pp.1–2; MacFarlane, pp.71–85.

11. Clark, 1957; Breckinridge, 1934; Douthwaite; Hooper; Zuckerman, p.69; Stone; Note, 1966; Notes; *Doughty v. Engler; Pfeifer v. Wright; Houghton v. Dickinson; Kotzke v. Kotzke's Estate; Baugh v. Maddox; Martin v. Claxton; Turnmine v. Mayes.* Although each of these articles and cases maintained that children of non-marital unions were not entitled to paternal support prior to passage of the Elizabethan Poor Laws, Helmholz disputes this contention. According to Helmholz, in A.D. 1234 courts of the Western Church began enforcing the right of non-marital children to support. As the power of the Church declined, civil law was enacted to supplement, and eventually replaced, canon law. Once the old ecclesiastical juris-diction was forgotten, the secular law was viewed as imposing no legal duty of support on the father of a child born outside marriage. See also: Ayer, Jr.

12. Robbins and Deak explain the importance of Roman law regarding the inheritance rights of non-marital children:

[F]irst, because of its influence on U.S. legislation and second, because it is over a thousand years of legal development. . . . Because of the structure of the Roman family the illegitimate child was particularly unfortunate. Not only had he no father but he had no mother. . . . The Roman family was an agnatic one. . . . Cognatic relationship is . . . the relationship arising through common descent from the same pair of married persons, whether the descent be traced through males or females. . . . Agnates are all the cognates who trace their connection exclusively through males. . . . A woman could *legally* have *no* descendants. The attachment of the illegitimate child to its mother's family . . . is explained by the rise of the *jus naturale,* or the law of nature, in Roman jurisprudence. Under this philosophy cognation came to be regarded as the natural basis of kinship and the natural basis of the family. As such, the law began to accord the cognate the right to succession and aliment. But while the natural child remained a stranger to its father, all children, whether legitimate or illegitimate, became cognates of their mother. . . . The accordance of any property rights to the illegitimate child was not the result of any legislation directed towards his betterment but merely the logical and necessary consequence of the structure of the Roman family. (Robbins and Deak, pp.312, 310–311; this information is also in: Jacobs, pp.582–586; Krause, 1971, p.3 fn.7)

13. For a detailed discussion of the significance of surnames and the naming process see: Standard.

14. This also would be true for unmarried couples with children—even if the father is known.

15. Teichman; Pogrebin; Krause, 1971; Davis, 1939–40; Robbins and Deak; Hooper; Vincent, 1961.

16. Teichman; Cohen; Krause, 1971; Dwyer.

17. Krause, 1971; Davis, 1939–40; Teichman; *Stanley v. Illinois*; Pogrebin; Rich, 1976; DeCrow; Vincent, 1961.

18. Teichman; Krause, 1971; Friedmann; Vincent, 1961; Locke.

19. All citations to Locke will be referenced in the following manner—roman numerals I and II refer to the texts of the First and Second Treatises, respectively; the numbers immediately following them refer to sections of the specified Treatise, respectively; and the numbers appearing *after* the colon refer to line numbers in the cited section(s) of the designated Treatise. Hence, the reference to Book I, section 47, lines 16–20 appears as Locke, I, 47:16–20. It is noteworthy that under English common law, women and children were the property of men.

20. Locke states at II, 1:4 that the story of Adam does not give "the least shadow of authority" to political arrangements in post-biblical times. It would be a misreading of the text, however, to suggest that this passage removed Adam's

jurisdiction over Eve. The four premises that Locke is specifically challenging in II, 1:4 all concern the legitimacy of Adam's political dominion over his children and over the right of succession.

21. See also: Brennan and Pateman, p.195; Butler, p.146; Okin, p.249.

22. See also: Okin; Clark 1979.

23. *The New World Translation of the Holy Scriptures* renders Genesis 1:28–29 as: "Further, God blessed them and . . . said to them: 'Be fruitful and become many and fill the earth and subdue it, and have in subjection the fish of the sea and the flying creatures of the heavens and every living creature that is moving upon the earth.' And God went on to say: 'Here I have given to you all vegetation bearing seed which is on the surface of the whole earth and every tree on which there is fruit of a tree bearing seed.' " (See also: The Holy Bible, King James Version (New York: New American Library, 1974); Locke, I, 86:20–21; I, 92:1–9; II, 26:1–18; II, 27:1–3).

24. Butler points out that "[Locke] registered no protest over the rule of Queens Elizabeth or Anne or Mary; but he never stated whether he, like Tyrrell and Sidney, would have excluded the 'whole multitude of women' from any form of political life" (Butler, pp.149–150).

25. Patemate observes that "[t]he most intimate relations of women with men are held to be governed by consent; women consent to marriage, and sexual intercourse without a woman's consent constitutes the criminal offense of rape. To begin to examine the unwritten history of women and consent brings the suppressed problems of consent theory to the surface. Women exemplify the individuals whom consent theorists have declared to be incapable of consenting. Yet, simultaneously, women have been presented as always consenting, and their explicit non-consent has been treated as irrelevant or has been reinterpreted as 'consent' " (Pateman, p.72).

26. Locke states that "there is *another Power* ordinarily *in the Father,* whereby he has a tie on the Obedience of his Children: . . . it passes into the World for a part of *Paternal Jurisdiction.* And this is the Power Men generally have to *bestow their Estates* on those who please them best" (II, 72:5–19).

27. See: Brennan and Pateman; Okin; Pateman.

28. Exceptions to the rule of blood are made by rules of law that allow a male to accept legal responsibility for a non-blood-related child through adoption or marriage to the child's mother.

29. The ability of women to accurately identify their offspring may become increasingly difficult, without the assistance of genetic testing, as reproductive technology encroaches upon "the female *control* of reproduction" (Chesler, p.248). See also: Corea; Arditti, Klein, and Minden.

30. Helmholz (p.440) disputes this contention. See also: Teichman, p.108.

31. The Lilith character is found mainly in the literature of the Middle East (Arabia, Assyria, Babylonia, Iran, Israel, etc.), although there is mention of her character in other cultures (England, Greece, Mexico, Russia, West Africa) as well. While each civilization has its own variation of both the myth and the character of Lilith, a common thread runs throughout almost all of the stories—she was the first woman created and the first person to challenge male authority. Some of the stories associated with Lilith are found in The Alphabet of Ben Sira, The Talmud, The Tergums, The Kabala, and The Zohar.

32. For commentary on the ignorance of male culpability in the creation of non-marital children and the shifting of the entire onus onto women, see: Wallach and Tenoso, p.29; Teichman, p.66; DeWar, p.20; Clark, 1987, pp.12, 14, 74, 88, & 92; Petchesky, pp.46–47.

33. A slightly different version of Jefferson's remarks is provided by Okin (p.249), who quotes Gruberg, p.4.

34. *Bradwell v. Illinois* Transcript of Record, Opinion of the Court Denying the Application, p.11.

35. In *Minor*, the Court ruled that "(2) the word 'citizen' in the Constitution of the United States conveys the idea of membership of a nation and nothing more; women are citizens of the United States. (3) The right of suffrage is not one of the necessary privileges of a citizen of the United States. . . . (7) The Constitution of the United States does not confer the right of suffrage upon anyone, and the constitutions and laws of the several States which commit that important trust to men alone, are not void" (Headnotes to *Minor*. See: Claude for an incisive commentary on *Minor*).

36. See also: Kay; Maltz.

37. "In the *Slaughter-house Cases*, the Supreme Court laid down the basic rules of the game for future Fourteenth Amendment rules effective, to some extent, today. The basic impact of those cases was to decimate the privileges and immunities clause as a potential grounds for attacking state statutes" (Goldstein, 1988, p.4). "In summary, then, the legacy of the *Slaughter-house Cases*, the first Supreme Court interpretation of the Fourteenth Amendment, was as follows: (1) the privileges and immunities clause was emptied of any real meaning; (2) the idea that the due process clause might create a limit on the substance of legislation, requiring that the mandate of a statute be 'fair,' was summarily rejected. . . ; (3) the equal protection clause was interpreted to focus narrowly on the evil of racial discrimination" (Goldstein, 1988, p.8).

38. See: White, 1976; Baum; Goldman and Sarat; and Murphy, 1964.

39. Note the language of the Court in: *Bradwell, Lockner, Muller, Quong Wing, Nolan Breedlove, Goesaert, and Hoyt*.

40. "The chances a woman faces each year that she will inadvertently become pregnant while using some form of contraception have been placed at 2.4 percent from oral contraceptives, 4.6 percent from an IUD, 9.6 percent from condoms, 18.6 percent from diaphragms, 17.9 percent from foam, and 23.7 percent from rhythm" (see: Schrim, p.68).

2

Burdening the "Nameless" and Their Parents: Case Analysis

INTRODUCTION

Between 1968 and 1992 the U.S. Supreme Court adjudicated over twenty cases[1] involving equal protection claims of non-marital children. In each case, it has had to determine whether discrimination against individuals deemed "illegitimate"[2] by law constituted a denial of equal protection. When these decisions are analyzed, two points become apparent: the decisions mirror the male thinking[3] evident in the dominant society; and the Court's difficulty in determining the appropriate constitutional test to apply to statutory classifications affecting children born outside wedlock, resulted in inconsistent rulings. In order to ascertain the Court's position on the question of equal protection for non-marital children, its decisions, as well as the justifications offered and the constitutional tests employed, must be considered at length.

Before 1968, the Supreme Court never appraised any statute concerning non-marital children in terms of equal protection (Krause, 1971; LEXIS Search). Since that time, it has utilized both the Due Process Clause of the Fifth Amendment[4] and the Equal Protection Clause of the Fourteenth Amendment. If a federal statute is the subject of the constitutional challenge, the Fifth Amendment is utilized.[5] If the constitutionality of a state statute is questioned, the Fourteenth Amendment applies.[6]

Equal protection cases challenging the constitutionality of statutory disabilities imposed on non-marital children (and their parents) fall roughly into seven categories: wrongful death,[7] the rights of fathers,[8] financial assistance–state benefits,[9] financial assistance–federal benefits,[10] inheritance,[11] paternity and support actions,[12] and immigration.[13] While the Supreme Court has succeeded in eliminating *many* of the legal barriers encountered by non-marital children, it has been unwilling to remove *all* legal obstacles faced by non-marital children and their families.

WRONGFUL DEATH

The first two cases involving non-marital children that the Court subjected to equal protection consideration were *Levy v. Louisiana* (1968) and *Glona v. American Guarantee & Liability Insurance Company* (1968). Both cases centered on two issues: the Louisiana Wrongful Death Statute, which allowed heirs of an injured party to recover damages if the injured party died;[14] and the decisions of the appellate courts that only "legitimate" children were covered under this statute.[15]

In *Levy* the appellant sued on behalf of five children, born outside wedlock, to recover damages for the wrongful death of their mother. Justice Douglas, who delivered the majority opinion reversing the appellate court's decision, prefaced his arguments with the observation that "illegitimate children are not 'nonpersons.' They are human, live, and have their being. They are clearly 'persons' within the meaning of the Equal Protection Clause of the Fourteenth Amendment" (*Levy*, p.70). Since children born outside wedlock are covered by the Equal Protection Clause, Justice Douglas set out to determine whether the statutory exclusion of non-marital children was invidious or rational. He noted that while the legislature is accorded wide latitude when making classifications, the Court is not averse to striking down invidious classifications. In *Levy* the Court found no inherently rational basis for the invidious discrimination against non-marital children in the questioned statute: "Legitimacy or illegitimacy of birth has no relation to the nature of the wrong allegedly inflicted on the mother. . . . We conclude that it is invidious to discriminate against [non-marital children] when no action, conduct, or demeanor of theirs is possibly relevant to the harm that was done the mother" (*Levy*, p.72).

The Court came to a similar conclusion in *Glona*, where under the Louisiana Wrongful Death Statute a mother was barred from recovering damages for the wrongful death of her non-marital son. Louisiana's courts interpreted the phrase "the surviving father and mother of the deceased" to mean that "a decedent must be legitimate in order for an ascendent or sibling to recover for his death" (*Levy*, p.74 fn.3). Although this interpretation may have been in keeping with English common law, the Supreme Court viewed it as irrational. The Court majority was unable to discern how precluding recovery for a wrongful death would deter the "sin of illegitimacy." According to the Court, "[i]t would . . . be farfetched to assume that women have illegitimate children so that they can be compensated in damages for their death" (*Glona*, p.75). Because the Court could find no rational basis for the discrimination created by the state court's interpretation of the Wrongful Death Statute, it maintained that the mother was being denied equal protection of the law by the State of Louisiana.

Much to the consternation of the dissenters in both *Levy* and *Glona* (Justices John Harlan, Hugo Black, and Potter Stewart), the Court utilized the language of the strict scrutiny approach in *Levy*,[16] while purportedly applying the rational basis approach in both *Levy* and *Glona*[17]—without explaining whether a fundamental right had been infringed or whether birth status constituted a suspect classification.[18] Justice Harlan, writing for the dissent, decried the Court's "brute force" process. He believed that basing recovery on a legally recognized relationship was just as "rational" as basing it on a biological relationship. Indeed, Justice Harlan considered the legal distinction posited by the lower court to be valid and justified. In his view, it was in the interest of the state to promote legitimate family relationships. Since the state was empowered to require such formalities as marriage and the acknowledgment of children born outside marriage, it seemed reasonable for a state to demand adherence to these formalities in order for any person to recover damages under the Louisiana statute.

Justice Harlan argued that the challenged statute differentiated among many relationships "in terms of their legal rather than their biological relationship to the deceased."[19] It was irrelevant whether an individual denied recovery by the Wrongful Death Statute was capable of altering their legal condition. The "obvious justification" for Louisiana's distinction between marital and non-marital children and family units, according to Justice Harlan, was to enforce the state's purpose: to require "that people who choose to live together should go through the formalities of marriage and, in default, that people who bear children should acknowledge them" (*Glona*, p.80). Since only the nuclear family and families recognized by the legislature constituted formal units in his eyes, they were the only types of families he deemed "legitimate."

Perhaps if the Court's composition had remained unchanged, it would have declared birth status to be a suspect classification, thereby removing any ambiguity from the status of non-marital children and their parents. Under such circumstances, future decisions would necessarily have been based on the strict scrutiny approach rather than on a loosely constructed, rational basis standard or on the hybrid standard used without acknowledgment by the Court in *Levy* and *Glona*. But by the time a third case arose challenging a wrongful death statute, *Parham v. Hughes* (1978), the Court's membership was significantly altered,[20] and the Court seemingly retreated from the looser rationality and hybrid tests it had used in *Levy* and *Glona*, relying instead upon the traditional rational basis test. Justice Stewart, writing for a plurality of the Court, conferred upon state laws "a presumption of validity against attack under the Equal Protection Clause, [since] legislatures have wide discretion in passing laws that have the inevitable effect of treating some people differently from others, and legislative classifications are valid unless they bear no rational relationship to a permissible state objective" (*Parham*, p.350). If the Court found that the discriminatory treatment of unwed parents in §105-1307 of the Georgia Code[21]—allowing mothers, but not fathers, of non-marital children to recover for their child's wrongful death, unless there was no mother and the father had legitimated his child—bore no conceivable relationship to any legislative purpose, then the Court would invalidate the statute.

The state professed that this statute advanced three interests: it avoided the problem of proving paternity in wrongful death actions; it promoted a legitimate family unit; and it set a standard of morality. In evaluating these interests, the Court observed that the distinction drawn between unwed parents under §105–1307 did not invidiously discriminate against the father. This observation was grounded on §74–103 of the Georgia Code,[22] which mandated that only the father could unilaterally petition the court to legitimate his non-marital children. In this respect the unwed parents were not similarly situated. Unlike the Louisiana statute challenged in *Glona*—which permitted either or both parents to legally acknowledge their children—under the Georgia statute at issue in *Parham*, only a father could act to change his child's birth status. Another difference between unwed parents was related to identity—while the mother's identity was rarely in doubt, the father's could easily be unknown.[23] The Court specifically distinguished the *Glona* decision, noting

that [the] Louisiana statute [in *Glona* which] did not allow a natural mother of an illegitimate child to sue for its wrongful death violated the Equal Protection Clause. That case was quite different from this one. The invidious discrimination perceived in [*Glona*] was between married and unmarried mothers. There thus existed no real problem of identity or of fraudulent claims. . . . Moreover, the statute in *Glona* excluded every mother of an illegitimate child from bringing a wrongful-death action, while the Georgia statute at issue [in *Parham*] excludes only those fathers who have not legitimated their children. Thus, the Georgia statute has in effect adopted "a middle ground between the extremes of complete exclusion and case-by-case determination of paternity." (*Parham*, pp.355-356 fn.7)

In order for an unwed father in Georgia to make his identity known, he merely needed to file a motion under §74–103. If he did this, he was eligible to sue for the wrongful death of his child in the same manner as wedded fathers. Georgia law also granted an unwed father the opportunity, prior to the death of his child, to officially identify himself. By filing the appropriate motion, he changed not only the status of his child but also his own status. Through his own action, he could be accorded the same rights as a father who had children inside marriage or a father who had filed a motion under §74–103. The unwed father in *Parham* was denied the right to sue for his child's wrongful death as a result of his personal behavior and his own inaction. The Court emphasized that

[t]he appellant, as the natural father, was responsible for conceiving an illegitimate child and had the opportunity to legitimate the child but failed to do so. . . . Unlike the illegitimate child for whom the status of illegitimacy is involuntary and immutable, the appellant here was responsible for fostering an illegitimate child and for failing to change its status. It is thus neither illogical nor unjust for society to express

its "condemnation of irresponsible liaisons beyond the bonds of marriage" by not conferring upon a biological father the statutory right to sue for the wrongful death of his illegitimate child. (*Parham*, p.353)

The Court was unable to establish to its satisfaction that §105–1307 invidiously discriminated against fathers as a class. All the statute did, according to the Court, was distinguish "between those fathers who [had] legitimated their children and those who [had] not" (*Parham*, p.356).[24] The Court affirmed that by means of the statutory classifications in §74–1307, the state was able to maintain an efficient system for the disposition of property at death, for the avoidance of fraudulent paternity claims, and for the settlement of wrongful death litigation. In its opinion, the Georgia solution, embodied in §105–1307, was "a rational means for dealing with the problem of proving paternity" in wrongful death actions (*Parham*, p.358).[25]

Although Justice Powell affirmed the judgment of the Court, he arrived at that conclusion by using the sex discrimination test of *Craig v. Boren* (1976) rather than the rational basis test. He asserted that §105-1307 recognized real differences between mothers and fathers in the difficulty of proving parenthood:

[the] law is substantially related to the State's objective. . . . It lies entirely within a father's power to remove himself from the disability that only he will suffer. The father is required to declare his intentions at a time when both the child and its mother are likely to be available to provide evidence. The mother, on the other hand, is given the opportunity to appear and either support or rebut the father's claim of paternity. The marginally greater burden placed upon the father is no more severe than is required by the marked difference between proving paternity and proving maternity—a difference we have recognized repeatedly. (*Parham*, p.360, quoting *Lalli*, pp. 268–269)

Justice White, in conjunction with Justices Blackmun, Brennan, and Marshall, attacked both the state's contention that its interests were served by §105–1307 and the Court's casual acceptance of the blatant sex discrimination inherent in the statute.[26] He argued that "[t]here is a startling circularity in [the Court's] argument" (*Parham*, p.361). The sex discrimination in the wrongful death statute, which *required* unwed fathers to pursue the legitimation procedure, was not alleviated by resorting to the fact that under Georgia law only fathers *may* legitimate their non-marital children:

The plurality not only fails to examine whether required resort by fathers to the legitimation procedure bears more than a rational relationship to any state interest, but also fails to even address the constitutionality of the sex discrimination in allowing fathers but not mothers to legitimate their children. It is anomalous, at least, to assert that sex discrimination in one statute is constitutionally invisible because it is tied to sex discrimination in another statute, without subjecting *either* of these classifications on the the basis of sex to an appropriate level of scrutiny. (*Parham*, pp.361–362, fn.2)

Justice White directed attention to the fact that the father's failure to legitimize his child in this case was incidental; it was only relevant because the mother was killed with the child. If the mother were still alive, the father could not sue under §105-1307 regardless of his child's birth status.

Justice White directly challenged the Court's assertion that the classification in question did not discriminate on the basis of gender because it did not "make overly broad generalizations based on sex which are entirely unrelated to any differences between men and women" (*Parham*, p.354). In his dissent, he countered with the observation that "[t]he plain facts of the matter are that the statute conferring the right to recovery for the wrongful death of a child discriminates between unmarried mothers and unmarried fathers, and that this discrimination is but one degree greater than the statutory discrimination between married mothers and married fathers" (*Parham*, p.362). Similar to the Louisiana statute in *Glona*, which excluded every unwed mother from bringing a wrongful death action, the statute in *Parham* excluded every father, regardless of his marital status, from suing for the wrongful death of his child if the child's mother was still alive.

Having conclusively established, in his opinion, the existence of a gender-based discrimination, Justice White proceeded to dismantle the state's argument that the legislated discrimination promoted its interests. With regard to the state's first interest (the problem of proving paternity), Justice White saw §105–1307 as serving a dual purpose: ensuring the accuracy of the paternity claim and serving as a prerequisite to recovery for a child's wrongful death. Yet individuals who could prove their paternity were nevertheless forbidden to sue for damages under this statute—an outcome that Justice White did not accept as justifying the statute's discriminatory classification. Justice White argued that the *possibility* of multiple recoveries in a tort case did not warrant precluding individuals who could establish their paternity beyond a reasonable doubt from participating in litigation related to a non-marital child's wrongful death. Less burdensome alternatives were available to the state, which would have been more attuned to its interests. Hence, Justice White found §105–1307 unjustified.

The state's second and third interests (promoting a legitimate family relationship and setting a moral standard) fared no better in Justice White's dissent. In his eyes, legitimation did not guarantee the formation of a traditional family unit. Quoting from *Glona*, Justice White linked the situation of the unmarried mother in that case to the situation of the unmarried father in *Parham*: "We see no possible rational basis . . . for assuming that if the natural mother is allowed recovery for the wrongful death of her illegitimate child, the cause of illegitimacy will be served. It would indeed be farfetched to assume that women have illegitimate children so that they can be compensated in damages for their death" (*Parham*, p.363, quoting *Glona*, p.75). Using this analysis, Justice White concluded that the relationship between the state's asserted interests and the classification in §105-1307 was simply too weak to be validated. For Justice White, the exhibition of judicial deference toward the state legislature under these circumstances was erroneous. Despite his assertion, however, the Court deferred to the political branches of the government in *Parham*.

If the Court had applied the reasoning in *Glona* to the facts in *Parham*, or if it had applied the same level of scrutiny in *Parham* that it had used in *Levy* and *Glona*, the Georgia Wrongful Death Statute could not have been upheld. In the two previous cases (*Levy* and *Glona*), the Court had held that birth status classifications that discriminated against either non-marital children or their parent would not be allowed (*Levy*, pp.71–72; *Glona*, pp.75-76). Yet in *Parham* the Court altered its position, maintaining that since Georgia's statutory classification distinguished between parents, not between marital and non-marital children, it did not discriminate on the basis of birth status (*Parham*, p.352). By applying the term "classifications based on illegitimacy" exclusively to non-marital children, the Court implied that unmarried parents deserve less judicial protection than their non-marital children (*Parham*, pp.352–353).

It is true that non-marital children have no control over their births. It is also true that (at least some) parents may alter their children's birth status through a legal procedure. But the Court's suggestion that classifications which disadvantage unmarried parents who do not legitimate their children are *not* classifications based on the birth status of their children seems specious. Penalties imposed on non-marital parents do not deter non-marital births ("Current Population Reports." Series P-20, No. 433); they do not eliminate the socially condemned "irresponsible liaisons beyond the bounds of marriage" (*Parham*, p.353); and they do not remove "the stigma of bastardy" from children whose parents are disadvantaged solely on the basis of the children's birth status. Such penalties do, however, reinforce "ancient prejudice formed by religious and moral taboos" (Krause, 1971, p.7).

In the seven years from *Levy* and *Glona* in 1972 to *Parham* in 1979, the Supreme Court both condoned and disavowed the idea that non-marital parents can be disadvantaged by wrongful death statutes that differentiate between "the 'legal' rather than the biological relationship" (*Glona*, p.75). One of the determining factors is the degree of risk regarding fraudulent claims—a risk that was deemed greatest, at least in the recent past, with paternity claims. The Court accepted as a matter of fact that the children in *Levy* and the mother in *Glona* were biologically connected to the deceased mother and children in the respective cases. In the Court's opinion, if the claimant is "plainly" a mother's child or a child's mother, then "the State denies equal protection of the laws to withold relief merely because the child . . . was born to her out of wedlock" (*Glona*, p.76). In *Parham*, however, while the Court stated as fact that "the appellant was the biological father" of the deceased minor child (*Parham*, p.349), it emphasized the dissimilarity between mothers and fathers vis-à-vis their non-marital children: "Unlike the mother of an illegitimate child whose identity will rarely be in doubt, the identity of the father will frequently be unknown" (*Parham*, p.355). Therefore, the Court maintained that Georgia's statutory classification constituted a rational means for dealing with the problem of proving paternity: "If paternity has not been established before the commencement of a wrongul-death action, a defendant may be faced with the possibility of multiple lawsuits by individuals all claiming to be the father of the deceased child" (*Parham*, p.357).

But the Court failed to adequately address Justice White's contention that §105–1307 constituted sex discrimination insofar as it barred all fathers, regardless of marital status, from suing for the wrongful death of their children if the children's mothers were alive; and it barred all unwed fathers who, despite their failure to legitimate their non-marital children, could establish their paternity beyond a reasonable doubt. A less restrictive alternative to the total exclusion of unwed fathers was available to the legislature. The law could have provided unwed fathers the right to sue if the following conditions were met: (1) the father could prove his paternity beyond a reasonable doubt; (2) the father had clearly supported his child; and (3) the father had physical custody of his child (if the mother was still alive). Since the non-marital father in *Parham* satisfied the first two conditions and since the child visited him on a regular basis (p.349), the Court should have found in favor of the appellant.

FATHERS' RIGHTS

The distinction articulated by the Court regarding parental identity serves as a foundation for cases focusing on paternal rights in matters of adoption, custody, and the termination of parental rights. But other important elements include the type of parent-child relationship in existence, the steps taken by the father to acknowledge his child, and the degree of parental responsibility and duty the father has assumed for his child's well-being.

Stanley v. Illinois (1972) was the first case to challenge the state's termination of a father's parental or custodial rights to his non-marital children. At issue in *Stanley* was an Illinois statute that automatically made the children of unwed fathers wards of the state on the death of their mothers; unwed mothers, however, could not be deprived of their children unless they were shown to be unfit parents. In its decision, the Court emphasized that the state has the power to implement legitimate interests in family matters. Among the interests so recognized were those codified in the Juvenile Court Act "to protect the moral, emotional, and physical welfare of the minor and the best interests of the community and to strengthen the minor's family ties whenever possible, removing him from the custody of his parents only when his welfare or safety or the protection of the public cannot be adequately safeguarded without removal" [Ill. Rev. Stat., c. 37, 701–20] (*Stanley*, p.652). The Court maintained that a contradiction existed between the aims of this act and the non-inclusion of single fathers in the act's definition of a parent.[27] Stanley, an unwed father, had his children declared wards of the state upon the death of their mother without benefit of a hearing or any proof regarding his fitness as a father. Yet all other parents (married and divorced mothers and fathers, as well as unwed mothers) were entitled to such hearings or proof before their children were removed from their custody. This procedural discrepancy thus constituted a denial of due process and equal protection of the law.

The Court did not identify which standard of review it applied to the equal protection challenge raised in *Stanley*. The closest the Court came to specifying which standard served as their guide was Justice White's comment that "we are not asked to evaluate the legitimacy of the state ends, rather, to determine whether the means used to achieve these ends are constitutionally defensible" (*Stanley*, p.652). It seemed obvious to the Court that the means were not defensible, for they presupposed that (a) all unwed fathers are by definition unfit parents, or (b) the administrative cost of holding fitness hearings in terms of money, speed, efficiency, and inconvenience to the state are extremely high, in contrast to the minuscule number of unwed fathers who would be deemed fit parents. These presumptions were viewed by the state as justification for their refusal to hold regular inquiries to evaluate an unwed father's fitness as a parent. But while the Court acknowledged that "[t]he establishment of prompt efficacious procedures to achieve legitimate state ends is a proper state interest worthy of cognizance in constitutional adjudication" (*Stanley*, p.656), the Court also observed that the Bill of Rights and the Due Process Clause were intended to protect citizens from the government's concern for speed and efficiency. According to the Court, "[p]rocedure by presumption is always cheaper and easier than individual determination. But when, as here, the procedure forecloses the determinative issues of competence and care, when it explicitly disdains present realities in deference to past formalities it needlessly risks running roughshod over the important interests of both parent and child. It therefore cannot stand" (*Stanley*, pp.656–657).

Justices Burger and Blackmun, in their dissent, expressed dismay at the Court's conclusion that if the state failed to deny hearings or proof regarding their parental fitness to all parents before making their children wards of the state, the state could not deny some parents of them without violating the Equal Protection Clause. They considered this tantamount to using "the Equal Protection Clause as a shorthand condensation of the entire Constitution" (*Stanley*, p.660). Yet the Court merely appeared to be continuing the course established in *Levy* and *Glona*—remaining ambiguous regarding the exact standard used to reach its decision. In *Stanley* the Court rejected the means chosen by the state to achieve its ends because the means did not constitute a weighty enough (compelling) interest to override a father's fundamental right to the care and custody of the children he had sired and raised.

The gender discrimination issue raised in *Stanley* mirrored to some degree the issues raised in *Glona* and *Parham*. All three of these cases focused on a burden imposed by the state that was related to individual responsibility or "wrongdoing"—the mother in *Glona* bore children outside wedlock, contrary to the state's condemnation of such action (*Glona*, p.75); the fathers in *Parham* and *Stanley* sired and raised children with whom they had established no legal relationship despite the state's negative statutory presumptions (*Stanley*, p.650).

In its *Stanley* decision the Court slightly modified the state's power to govern the family by demanding that the means utilized by the state not circumvent its own objectives. In *Stanley* the state-articulated interest regarding the integrity of the family (*Stanley*, p.652) led the Court to observe that "the law [has not] refused to recognize those family relationships unlegitimated by a marriage ceremony" (*Stanley*, p.651). While not providing an absolute protection to non-marital family relationships, the Court protected a de facto family unit that already existed (*Stanley*, p.650 fn.4a)—it limited its protection to those "unwed fathers who desire and claim competence to care for their children" (*Stanley*, p.657 fn.9); and to those instances "when the issue at stake is the dismemberment of his family" (*Stanley*, p.658).

The disputation of domestic law impinging on the rights of fathers resurfaced six years after *Stanley* in *Quilloin v. Walcott* (1978), wherein the Court rendered its first unanimous birth status decision. A non-marital father sought to block the adoption of his child by the mother's new husband. The applicable state law required the permission of both biological parents for a marital child to be adopted, but only the mother's permission for the adoption of a non-marital child. Under the auspices of Justice Marshall, the Court ruled that while the parent-child relationship is constitutionally protected, the state may under some circumstances apply a "best interests of the child" standard (*Quilloin*, p.254) without violating the Equal Protection Clause. This standard was applicable in the case of the unwed father who had "never been a *de facto* member of the child's family unit" (*Quilloin*, p.253) and who had "never exercised either actual or legal custody over his child" (*Quilloin*, p.256).

Although the Court once again neglected to specify the appropriate standard for review applicable in this case, it seemed to be using intermediate scrutiny[28] to determine the constitutionality of §§74–203 and 74–403(3) of the Georgia Code.[29] Relying upon *Stanley*, the Court balanced the unwed "father's interest in the 'companionship, care, custody, and management' of his children" (*Quilloin*, p.248, quoting *Stanley*, p.651) against "the strong state policy of rearing children in a family setting" (*Quilloin*, p.252). The Court distinguished the facts of *Stanley* from the specific circumstances in *Quilloin*: over an eleven-year period the natural father supported his child only irregularly; he never attempted to legitimate or gain custody of his child; his visits to his child were viewed as disruptive and unhealthy to the child by the child's mother; and the child himself stated his desire to be adopted and to change his last name. The Court also viewed the state's claim in *Quilloin* to be more substantial than the unwed father's. Prior to the adoption proceedings instituted by the child's mother, the unwed father had had ample opportunity to formalize his relationship with his child. However, according to the Court, he had "never shouldered any significant responsibility with respect to the daily supervision, education, protection, or care of the child. [Nor did he] complain of his exemption from these responsibilities, . . . [nor] . . . seek custody of his child" (*Quilloin*, p.256). The state, on the other hand, merely intended to grant an already-existing family unit the recognition that was opposed only by the natural father, who neither had nor wanted custody or actual responsibility for his child (*Quilloin*, p.255). The Court maintained that "whatever may be required in other situations, we cannot say that the State was required in this situation to find anything more than that the adoption, and denial of legitimation, were in the 'best interests of the child.' [For] under any standard of review, the State was not foreclosed from recognizing [the] difference in the extent of commitment to the welfare of the child" (*Quilloin*, pp.255–256).

Unlike *Stanley*, wherein the state sought to dismember an already existing family unit, in *Quilloin* the state sought to prevent the breakup of a natural family. The Court indicated in its holding that in order for a non-marital father to successfully challenge an adoption statute that distinguished between a non-marital and a separated or divorced father, he must demonstrate that he has "shouldered . . . significant responsibility with respect to the daily supervision, education, protection, or care of the child" (*Quilloin*, p.256). For these reasons the *Quilloin* Court affirmed with a single voice the constitutionality of §§74–203 and 74–403(3) of the Georgia Code.

The appellant "maintained [before the Georgia Supreme Court] that he was entitled to the same power to veto an adoption as that granted in Georgia law to married or divorced parents and to unwed mothers" (*Quilloin*, p.252). Yet he narrowed his focus to "the disparate statutory treatment of his case and that of a married father" (*Quilloin*, p.253) when he appealed his case to the U.S. Supreme Court. Consequently, the Court confined its attention in *Quilloin* to the distinction between unmarried and separated or divorced fathers; a sex-based equal protection challenge to a state's adoption policy was not heard by the Court until the following year in *Caban v. Mohammed* (1979).

The statute challenged in *Caban* was §111 of the New York Domestic Relations Law, which provided that "consent to adoption shall be required as follows: . . . (2) Of the parents or surviving parent, whether adult or infant, of a child born in wedlock; (3) Of the mother, whether adult or infant, of a child born out of wedlock."[30] If parental consent was not denied a parent under §111(II), by withholding consent, *only* an unwed mother could block her child's adoption per §111(I)(3). The effect of this statute, according to Justice Powell, was that "an unwed mother has the authority under New York Law to block the adoption of her child simply by withholding consent. The unwed father has no similar control over the fate of his child, even when his parental relationship is substantial" (*Caban*, pp.386–387). To prevent an unwed mother from adopting his children, an unwed father was required to demonstrate that the mother's action was contrary to the child's best interests. Thus, the statute granted the unwed mother virtually total authority over her child's adoptive fate, while simultaneously denying the unwed father similar control over his child's adoptive fate—regardless of how substantial his parental relationship with his child may have been (*Caban*, pp.386–387).[31]

Since §111(I)(3) unquestionably treated unmarried parents differently, Justice Powell applied the gender-discrimination test of *Craig v. Boren* (1976): in order to withstand judicial scrutiny under the Equal Protection Clause the distinctions "must serve important governmental objectives and must be substantially related to achievement of those objectives."[32]

The state characterized its interests as recognizing the fundamental differences between maternal and paternal relations and promoting the adoption of non-marital children. Both of these interests were important in the eyes of the Court—within limits. The Court noted that as children develop, the generalization that unwed mothers are closer than unwed fathers to their children becomes too broad. If the natural father accepted responsibility for his children as they grew older, or if he had been at some point part of the family unit, the relationship between an unwed father and his children might rival that which existed between an unwed mother and her children.

In response to the state's second objective, promoting adoption, the Court quoted *Reed v. Reed* (1971), wherein it ruled that a statutory classification "must be reasonable, not arbitrary, and must rest upon the ground of difference having a fair and substantial relation to the object of the legislation, so that all persons similarly circumstanced shall be treated alike" (*Caban*, p.391, quoting *Reed*, p.76, quoting *Royster Guano Co. v. Virginia*, p.415). Justice Powell pointed out that §111 failed to meet this requirement. No evidence was offered by the state to prove either that unwed fathers were more likely than unwed mothers to raise objections to the adoption of their children, or that unwed fathers as a class would be more likely to do so. Without such evidence, according to Justice Powell, the state failed to demonstrate that the gender distinction in §111 bore a substantial relation to its interest in providing adoptive homes for children born out of wedlock (*Caban*, p.391). In Justice Powell's opinion, even if legislative distinctions could be justified between unwed parents of newborns, the state's interest in promoting adoptions for older children could have been advanced through alternative methods more attuned to its interests. He noted, however, that "[i]n reviewing the constitutionality of statutory classification, 'it is not the function of a court to hypothesize independently on the desirability of feasibility of any possible alternatives" to the statutory scheme formulated by the State' " (*Caban*, 393 fn.13, citing *Lalli*, p.279, quoting *Mathews*, p.515).

The Court considered the classification in §111(I)(3), which presumed "unwed fathers [to be] invariably less qualified and less entitled than mothers to exercise a concerned judgment as to the fate of their children" (*Caban*, p.394), to be an overbroad generalization that violated the Fourteenth Amendment. This classification prevented some "loving fathers" from participating in the adoption decision of their children and (simultaneously) enabled some "alienated mothers" to arbitrarily sever a father's paternal rights. Thus, the Court remained unconvinced that the gender distinctions drawn in §111(I)(3) bore a substantial relationship to the state's asserted interests.

Justice Stewart disagreed. In his opinion, "[p]arental rights do not spring full-blown from the biological connection between parent and child. They require relationships more enduring. The mother carries and bears the child, and in this sense her parental relationship is clear. The validity of the father's paternal claims must be gauged by other measures" (*Caban*, p.397). A father's rights are traditionally created by marriage. Without marriage, Justice Stewart argued, an unwed father's actual relationship to his child, regardless of how substantial that relationship might be, is insufficient to outweigh the goal of §111(I)(3), which is to facilitate prompt adoptions of non-marital children. Moreover, Justice Stewart argued that unwed parents were not always similarly situated:

these common and statutory rules of law reflect the physical reality that only the mother carries and gives birth to the child, as well as the undeniable social reality that the unwed mother is always an identifiable parent and the custodian of the child—until or unless the State intervenes. The biological father, unless he has established a familial tie with the child by marrying the mother, is often a total stranger from the State's point of view. (*Caban*, p.399)

For these reasons, Justice Stewart contended, a gender-based distinction such as the one contained in §111(I)(3) does not violate the Equal Protection Clause.

Justice Stewart agreed with the dissenting opinion of Justice Stevens with regard to those instances in which the unwed father had established a paternal relationship with his children and was thus similarly situated with the mother. Further, Justice Stevens was joined by Justices Burger and Rehnquist when he maintained that §111(I)(3) neither invidiously discriminated against unwed fathers nor denied unwed fathers equal protection of the law. In Justice Stevens's view, the number of cases in which unwed parents were similarly situated was so small as to be an insignificant exception to the gender-based distinction codified in §111(I)(3). Hence, he asserted that there did not exist a sufficient reason for invalidating the statute and subverting the interests of the state. At the center of Justice Stevens's reasoning was the best interests of the children involved and the facilitation of their adoption. He stressed that granting an unwed father the right to veto an adoption would not only frustrate the state's interests but would also "provide a very fertile field for extortion, . . . revenge, or an opportunity to recoup their 'losses' " (*Caban*, p.411 fn.20).

Although the dissenters never referred to the equal protection standard they were using, it seems plausible that they were applying intermediate scrutiny, even though they analyzed the New York statute for invidious gender discrimination. In the balance of interests between the state (and by extension the unwed mother and the non-marital children) and the unwed father, the dissenters perceived the state's interest to be more substantial and §111(I)(3) as furthering those interests without being "unduly burdensome."

Although the *Caban* decision was fair, the majority of the Court justices failed to consider the full impact of their decisions. By placing unwed fathers on equal footing with unwed mothers in adoption cases—except when the unwed mother was dead or when the unwed father has custody of his children or has established and maintained a substantial relationship with his children—they were perpetuating the patriarchal oppression of women. Although many state laws mandate that an unwed father support his offspring, such laws are difficult to enforce. According to Cynthia Harrison, in a report issued by Sara Rix for the Women's Research and Education Institute:

The continuing refusal of some men to support their children means that the newly formed female-headed families often have trouble supporting themselves. As of 1985, only 61 percent of divorced, separated, or never married women raising children under the age of 21 had been awarded child support. Of those entitled to such payments, more than half (52 percent) failed to receive the full amount. More than a quarter who should have received payments got nothing. (Harrison, p.74)

Not only do mothers bear a disproportionate share of the economic costs associated with raising children, they are customarily relegated to the role of primary caretaker, irrespective of their marital status.

As may be seen in the different connotations attached to the terms "working father" and "working mother," equalized child-rearing responsibilities between the sexes is neither encouraged nor practiced to any considerable extent in the United States. As a general rule, from the moment they become aware of their pregnancy through childbirth itself, unwed mothers necessarily make decisions regarding the care and upbringing of their children—decisions that unwed fathers may not participate in for a variety of reasons. As Justice Stevens observed in his dissent: "as a matter of equal protection analysis, it is perfectly obvious that at the time and immediately after a child is born out of wedlock, differences between men and women justify some differential treatment of the mother and father in the adoption process" (*Caban*, pp.404, 406–407). Because of the significant difference between the economic and child-rearing responsibilities of men and women, it seems only just that—unless or until either the single mother agrees to a formalization of the existing state of affairs (via some form of parental contract), or the unwed father either has custody (sole or joint) of his children or has established and maintained a substantial relationship with his children—she alone should have final authority over her off-spring's fate.

Even assuming that the unwed father voluntarily undertakes, for a segment of time, the responsibilities and duties associated with full-time parenting nothing prevents him from discontinuing the arrangement at will.[33] The fact that he does not exercise his option does not alter his power or potential to so choose. Although a support order issued by the courts portends a continued economic arrangement between the unwed father and his children, the courts cannot force any father (marital or non-marital) to create or sustain a substantial relationship with his offspring.

Nor does a non-marital father's decision not to exercise his parental responsibilities and duties negate the social reality of institutionalized sexual discrimination that bestows upon males—solely because they are male—more rights and authority than upon females. The patriarchal infra-structure places the state's *puissance* at the disposal of the unwed father should he ever decide to undermine the single mother's illusion of self-de-termination/self-control. An unwed mother's decisions have force only when the unwed father chooses to forgo his male prerogative in familial affairs.

The Court once again addressed the constitutionality of §§111 and 111a of the New York Domestic Relations Law in *Lehr v. Robinson* (1983). This statute delineated seven possible classes of unwed fathers who were enti-tled to receive notice of any adoption proceeding involving their child;[34] in addition, any person whose name appeared on the putative father registry was entitled to such notice.[35] Lehr, the putative father, did not fit any of the designated categories (*Lehr*, pp.251–252),[36] and as a consequence was not advised of the adoption proceedings initiated by the mother of his alleged daughter.[37]

Of central concern to Justice Stevens, who delivered the majority opinion, was "whether the New York statutes [were] unconstitutional because they inadequately protect[ed] the natural relationship between parent and child or because they [drew] an impermissible distinction between the rights of the mother and the rights of the father" (*Lehr*, p.255 fn.10). In the Court's opinion, since Lehr had not established a custodial, personal, or financial relationship with his non-marital child,[38] his equal protection rights were not violated. Lehr was in a position similar to that of the putative father in *Quilloin*—he had no substantial relationship with his daughter. The inchoate relationship existing between Lehr and his daughter convinced Justice Stevens that in fact this relationship constituted little more than a biological link. None of Lehr's actions prior to or during the adoption proceedings (*Lehr*, pp.267) indicated to the Court that Lehr's relationship with his daughter warranted the protection extended to the putative fathers in *Stanley* and *Caban*. Justice Stevens reiterated the Court's observations in *Caban* that parental rights require enduring relationships beyond a biological connection between parent and child and that "the relationship between a father and his natural child is entitled to protection against arbitrary state action" when an enduring relationship is established (*Lehr*, p.260, quoting *Caban*, pp.397, 414). If, however, the unwed father fails to "come forward to participate in the rearing of his child, nothing in the Equal Protection Clause preclud[es] the State from withholding from him the privilege of vetoing the adoption of that child" (*Lehr*, p.267, quoting *Caban*, p.392).

Because of the substantive difference in the type of relationship each parent had established with their daughter, the Court concluded that the state was justified in according different legal rights to the respective parents (*Lehr*, p.268). The disparate treatment[39] of the putative father and the single mother by the state was deemed by the Court not to be an invidious, gender-based distinction. The state's utilization of gender differences would have been suspect *if* the mother and the father were similarly situated with regard to their relationship with their daughter. But they were not. The mother had a continuous custodial relationship with her child; the father, for whatever reason, had never established such a relationship. Thus, the Equal Protection Clause was not violated by §§111 and 111a of the New York statute.

It should be noted that the facts the Court relied upon to reach its decision were not uncontested. According to these facts, the appellant "has never had any significant custodial, personal, or financial relationship with Jessica, and he did not seek to establish a legal tie until after she was two years old" (*Lehr*, p.262). Justice White, however, accepted Lehr's, rather than the non-marital mother's, version of the facts (*Lehr*, pp.268–269). In his dissent he concluded that "but for the actions of the child's mother there would have been the kind of significant relationship that the majority concedes is entitled to the full panoply of procedural due process protections" (*Lehr*, p.271).

If one assumes, for the sake of argument, the accuracy of Lehr's rendition of the facts, Justice White's dissenting argument cannot be dismissed out of hand. While it is true that Lehr could have protected his parental interest by simply mailing a postcard to the putative father registry, it is also true, according to Lehr's facts, that both the adoption court and his daughter's mother were aware of his identity, interest, and location. In light of these circumstances, Justice White raises a valid criticism when he asserts that the State's position "represents a grudging and crabbed approach to due process . . . [and] it is the sheerest formalism to deny [Lehr] a hearing because he informed the State in the wrong manner" (*Lehr*, p.275).

Although neither the state nor the Supreme Court was generous in its interpretation of the challenged statute, nonetheless, Lehr had a legal forum available to him that provided a means for him to develop a relationship with his daughter. His failure to utilize the available legal process does not negate its existence. Lehr did not directly challenge the notice provision in the New York statute. What he objected to was the Family Court's strict compliance "with the notice provisions of the statute" (*Lehr*, p.265)—that is, with the fact that the court had not sent him a special notice prior to his daughter's adoption, even though "the court and the mother knew that he had filed an affiliation proceeding in another court" (*Lehr*, p.265).

The initial action Lehr needed to take in order to assert his paternal interest was dependent upon neither the unwed mother's nor the Family Court's cooperation. All that was required was for Lehr take the initiative. Even granting that the unwed mother did not facilitate Lehr's establishment of a substantial relationship with his daughter—indeed through her actions she deliberately may have thwarted it—she was not legally capable of prohibiting such a relationship from occurring if Lehr had complied with the legal process established by the New York legislature. Nothing prevented him from filing his claim through the putative father registry. The ultimate responsibility for failing to protect his right to develop a relationship with his daughter, and for losing the opportunity to do so, was his. The procedure provided by the state would have adequately protected Lehr's due process and equal protection interest if he had availed himself of it.

It is conceded that the Supreme Court's decision is "crabbed" in its interpretation of the statute. But in this instance the attitude was also warranted. When a conflict exists between parental interests and prerogatives regarding the fate of their offspring, the father's rights must not be expanded at the expense of the mother's—especially if she is the sole custodian and primary caretaker of the child. A man who has little or no involvement during or after the pregnancy should not be allowed to interfere with the mother's decision regarding the fate of her child.[40] Only if the unwed father has fulfilled his parental duties and responsibilities—if in addition to an economic tie there exists an emotional bond, or if the father is the sole custodian or primary caretaker of his child—then and only then should the pendulum swing in favor of the father. Under such circumstances, the unwed father in *Lehr* could not legally have been denied a hearing per the Supreme Court's decision in *Stanley*. Nor could he have been denied a say in the adoption of his child per the Court's *Caban* decision.

But given the facts in *Lehr*—regardless of whose version is given greater credence—the discrimination based on gender or between categories of unwed fathers was justifiable. As a general rule, uwed fathers and mothers are not similarly situated vis-à-vis their non-marital children, especially when the children are very young. In the United States the accepted norm calls for mothers, not fathers, to be primarily responsible for childcare—regardless of their marital status. As the Court rightly observed, "the rights of the parents are a counterpart of the responsibilities they have assumed" (*Lehr*, p.257). More than biology makes an individual a parent. According to the Court, "[t]he action of judges neither create nor sever genetic bonds. '[T]he importance of the familial relationship . . . stems from the emotional attachments that derive from the intimacy of daily association, and from the role it plays in 'promot[ing] a way of life' through the instruction of children . . . as well as from the fact of blood relationship' " (*Lehr*, p.261, quoting *Smith*, p.844, quoting *Yoder*, pp.231–233).

While the biological link alone is not sufficient to secure an unwed father's paternal rights, it is a pre-condition if he wishes to develop a relationship with a child he claims as his. It is true that if "unwed mothers are under [no] affirmative duty to inform putative fathers of the existence of the children, they can withhold the information indefinitely, thereby depriving putative fathers of the opportunity to develop a relationship with their children" (Hill, p.956 n.146). It should be noted, however, that a state is constitutionally required to provide, at a minimum, an unwed father with the means, independent of an unwed mother's or a custodial agent's cooperation, by which he can establish his paternity and have available to him an opportunity to develop a relationship with his children.

A problem in the Supreme Court's decision in *Lehr* is its emphasis on marriage. The Court stresses that Lehr "never offered to marry the appellant" (*Lehr*, p.252), that "state laws almost universally express an appropriate preference for the formal family" (*Lehr*, p.257), and that "[t]he most effective protection of the putative father's opportunity to develop a relationship with his child is provided by the laws that authorize formal marriage and govern its consequence" (*Lehr*, p.263). Through this emphasis, the Court reiterates its bias in favor of the states' control of family law and its own partiality toward the legal nuclear family. Even though "the form of the family is not the basic determinant for what happens in the family" (Robertson, pp.418–419 n.36, quoting Satir, p.195), the Court continues to prefer the nuclear family over other familial types. But traditional marriage is not the only healthy environment, nor is it necessarily the best environment, for raising children. The substantiality of the parent-child relationship, not the marital status of the parents, ought to be of paramount importance. A secondary consideration, as observed by Justice Stewart in his *Caban* dissent, should be a determination of "the rights the unwed father may have when [he has not established a paternal relationship with his children and] his wishes and those of the mother are in conflict" (*Caban*, p.397). Under such circumstances, the wishes of the mother should prevail.

FINANCIAL ASSISTANCE—STATE BENEFITS

While the Supreme Court has accepted as legitimate some statutory classifications that disadvantage non-marital parents—specifically unwed fathers—it rejected in *Levy* statutes that punish or deter adults from becoming non-marital parents by discriminating against their children. The test utilized by the Court to reach such decisions, however, has been neither consistent nor clear. The Court mixes the language of the equal protection standards within its reasoning of a single case, as well as in its decisions in different birth status cases. Indeed, the Court has alluded or referred to both the strict standard (by referring to "fundamental personal rights" and the "invidiousness of the classification") and the rational basis standard (by referring to its inability to characterize the state's conclusion as "arbitrary"), without articulating precisely which standard governs individual decisions.

This pattern appeared, superficially, to have been altered slightly in *Weber v. Aetna Casualty & Surety Co.* (1972), where the Court ruled on the constitutionality of denying to non-marital children benefits that marital children were granted. In fact, the pattern of uncertainty regarding the applicable standard of review continued. The Court's attempt to eschew the dichotomous relationship between strict and minimum scrutiny in *Weber* merely perpetuated the existing ambiguity regarding the applicable standard of review in birth status cases.

Justice Powell, speaking for the Court in *Weber*, attempted to balance the respective interests of the state and the individual affected by the legislative classifications. At issue were classifications that restricted the definition of children—under Louisiana laws governing Workman's Compensation[41]— to "only legitimate children, step-children, posthumous children,[42] adopted children, and illegitimate children acknowledged under the provisions of Civil Code Articles 203, 204, and 205."[43] Due to the inferior status accorded unacknowledged, non-marital children in the statute, such children could not recover benefits for the death of their natural father on an equal footing with the children specified in the above law. Consequently, the Court struck down the challenged statute.

Justice Powell, elaborating on the method he used when evaluating the soundness of a discriminatory law in *Weber*, stated that "[h]aving determined that *Levy* is the applicable precedent, we briefly reaffirm here the reasoning which produced that result. . . . The essential inquiry in all the foregoing cases is, however, inevitably a dual one: What legitimate state interest does the classification promote? What fundamental personal rights might the classification endanger?" (*Weber*, pp.172–173).

In addressing the first question, the Court examined the interests or objectives proclaimed by the state—in this case, to promote legitimate family relationships and to compensate dependents for the wage earner's death. Unable to find a rational relationship between the statute and the state interests—the standard of review required by the first question—the Court ended its inquiry without reaching the second question. That inquiry would have required the use of the strict scrutiny standard, since the question would ascertain whether a fundamental right was involved. By ending its inquiry after the first question, and in light of its reliance on the *Levy* precedent, the Court intimated in the *Weber* opinion that it might be on the verge of enlarging its application of strict scrutiny to definitively include the rights of non-marital children.[44] On the other hand, by juxtaposing the state's interests in an irreconcilable manner,[45] the Court implied that in birth status cases "the true basis of [its] decisions" (*Rodriquez*, p.10) would be obfuscated.

Justice Rehnquist stood diametrically opposed to the Court's interpretation of the Fourteenth Amendment in *Weber*. In his opinion, the Fourteenth Amendment's Equal Protection Clause was only applicable in cases that addressed questions of racial classifications. Moreover, as he pointed out, the Equal Protection Clause "requires neither that state enactments be 'logical' nor . . . that they be 'just' in the common meaning of those terms. It requires only that there be some conceivable set of facts that may justify the classification involved" (*Weber*, p.183). For Justice Rehnquist, this condition was amply satisfied by Louisiana's Workman's Compensation Statute. Therefore, he maintained that if the Court was intent on applying the Equal Protection Clause to the *Weber* case, it should have at least adhered to the *Dandridge v. Williams* (1970)[46] ruling—a conclusion the majority explicitly rejected. In *Dandridge*, the Court clearly relied upon the rational basis test, affirming that classifications in the areas of economic and social welfare did not violate the Equal Protection Clause so long as such classifications had some reasonable justification (*Weber*, pp.180–181, quoting *Dandridge*, p.485). Indeed, Justice Rehnquist stated that the Court could have followed the *Labine v. Vincent* (1971) decision[47] and thereby upheld the challenged statute.

The Court, however, was resolute in distinguishing *Weber* from *Labine*. Unlike *Labine*, *Weber* did not address "the substantial state interest in providing for 'the stability of . . . land titles and in the prompt and definitive determination of the valid ownership of property left by decedents' " (*Weber*, p.170). The Court was not required to address the institutionalized social dominance of males perpetuated through the legal concepts of "legitimacy" and the nuclear family,[48] since these issues were not formally expressed or raised in *Weber*. The disposition of Workmen's Compensation benefits does not threaten a man's wealth or estate; these benefits are paid by the government. In addition, contrary to *Labine*, *Weber* did not allow the decedent to acknowledge the non-marital child. Under the law being challenged in *Weber*, the non-marital father "could not have acknowledged his illegitimate children even had he desired to do so" (*Weber*, p.171),[49] since the statute "prohibits acknowledgment of children whose parents were incapable of contracting marriage at the time of conception" (*Weber*, p.171 n.9).

The Court was equally forceful in establishing the similarities between *Weber* and *Levy*. Both cases involved "state-created compensation schemes, designed to provide close relatives and dependents of a deceased a means of recovery for his often abrupt and accidental death. Both wrongful-death statutes and workman's compensation codes represent outgrowths and modifications of our basic tort law" (*Weber*, p.171). The Court protected the socially venerated, patriarchal family unit, even while it simultaneously enabled non-marital children to receive limited economic relief in both *Levy* and *Weber*. Thus, the standards propounded by the Court in *Levy*—strict scrutiny—and *Labine*—rational basis—continued to stand, with only slight modifications after *Weber*, as the two-pronged inquiry devised by Justice Powell incorporated the essence of both standards.

The government once more found itself on the wrong side of the juridical scale in *New Jersey Welfare Rights Organization v. Cahill* (1973). On the basis of *Levy*, *Weber*, and *Gomez v. Perez* (1973),[50] the Court, in a *per curiam* decision,[51] voided the New Jersey Assistance to Families of the Working Poor program. This program limited benefits to "traditional" families that consist of "a household composed of two adults of the opposite sex ceremonially married to each other who have at least one minor child . . . of both, the natural child of one and adopted by the other, or a child adopted by both" (N.J. Stat. Ann. §44:13–3(a), as cited in *Cahill*, p.619). In essence, the statute recognized only marital and adopted children, thereby excluding non-marital children from receiving financial assistance and other services provided under this program. However, the Court believed that a child bore no responsibility for its social/legal status at birth and that penalizing the non-marital child by discouraging persons from having children outside wedlock or encouraging them to marry "is an ineffectual—as well as unjust—way of deterring the parent" (*Cahill*, p.620, citing *Weber*, p.171). The Court thus equated the biological family unit with the traditional family supported by the legislative statute.

Justice Rehnquist stood alone as he questioned the Court's reliance upon *Weber* in *Cahill*: "There a disability was visited solely on an illegitimate child. Here the statute distinguishes among types of families" (*Cahill*, p.622

fn.37). He argued that because the classification was based on a particular type of family unit, and because the ceremonial marriage required could "quite reasonably be found to be an essential ingredient of the family unit that the New Jersey Legislature is trying to protect from dissolution due to the economic vicissitudes of modern life" (*Cahill*, p.622 fn.37), there existed a rational basis for the legislative classification. Hence, in Justice Rehnquist's view, *Dandridge*, not *Weber*, should have governed.

The Court disagreed. While it noted the state's claim that the statute promoted the traditional family, it did not, as in previous cases, offer commentary regarding the validity of the state's interest. Nor did the Court actually judge the adequacy of the means relied upon by the state to achieve its objective "to preserve and strengthen family life" (*Cahill*, p.620) or evaluate how well the New Jersey statute served the state's interest. Instead, the Court concentrated on the "practical effects" of the New Jersey plan—its discrimination against children born outside wedlock. The Court reiterated its observation from *Weber* that "imposing disabilities on the illegitimate child is contrary to the basic concept of our system that legal burden should bear some relationship to individual responsibility or wrongdoing" (*Cahill*, p.620). It also stated that "there can be no doubt that the benefits extended under the challenged program are as indispensable to the health and well-being of illegitimate children as to those who are legitimate" (*Cahill*, p.621).

Although the Court's decision invalidated discrimination against a family unit, it emphasized individual responsibility (or more accurately, the lack thereof) as the determining element in its conclusion.[52] By evaluating New Jersey's statutory classifications on the basis of individual responsibility and the need of the recipients, rather than on whether the means chosen by the state to achieve its objective were rational or served a compelling governmental interest, the Court appears to have done three things. First, it measured the statute by a standard of review that demanded less than strict scrutiny, but more than a merely plausible configuration of the facts. Second, it relied upon *Weber* as precedent without actually utilizing the balancing test Justice Powell had articulated in that case. Finally, it remained silent regarding the appropriate standard of review to be employed when evaluating discrimination against non-marital children and their families. As a result, the Court left unresolved the circumstances under which the state's interest in promoting the traditional nuclear family would prove more compelling than the discrimination inflicted upon single mothers. While the Court invoked *Levy*, *Weber*, and *Gomez* to justify its decision, it declined the opportunity to declare birth status a suspect classification or to declare that non-marital children have a fundamental right to equality. However, because these three precedents demanded a standard more stringent than mere rationality, the Court was unable to ground its *Cahill* opinion on *Dandridge*.

FINANCIAL ASSISTANCE—FEDERAL BENEFITS

While the Court rejected birth status as a basis for classification in both cases concerned with the receipt of state benefits designed to assist a needy class of individuals, this condition has not been completely eliminated as a legitimate factor in determining the eligibility of persons seeking federal social insurance benefits. Initially, in *Richardson v. Davis* (1972) and *Richardson v. Griffin, et al.* (1972), the Supreme Court summarily affirmed the decisions of two lower courts that had relied upon *Weber* as the controlling precedent. Both *Davis* and *Griffin* disputed the constitutionality of §203(a) of the Social Security Act, as it affected §216(h)(3) of the same Act. They argued that the statute discriminated against certain non-marital children[53]—that is, those who were qualified to receive benefits under §216(h)(3), but who were denied benefits because of the existence of individuals who could claim benefits other than by §216(h)(3). A "child who attains the right to benefits through section 216(h)–(3) . . . may receive only the residual, if any, of the maximum family grant remaining when other individuals entitled to benefits have taken their maximum grants" (*Davis*, p.590). If the children in these respective cases had been "legitimate," their monthly benefits would have decreased proportionately with the shares of all other dependents, rather than being reduced first.

Using a method similar to the one proposed by Justice Powell in *Weber*, the lower courts engaged in a balancing process in *Davis* and *Griffin*. On one side of the scale were the arguments of the government in favor of §203(a); on the other side was the position of the non-marital children affected by the contested statutory provision. Relying upon *Levy* and *Weber* for precedent,[54] the lower courts deduced that the government's position in these two cases had no rational basis, was not free from invidious discrimination, was not justified by a compelling state interest, and did not significantly promote the avowed interest of the state. Thus, the scale tipped in favor of the non-marital children, and the lower courts deemed their claim weightier or more substantial than the government's.

Two years after *Davis* and *Griffin*, the Supreme Court was again asked to judge whether provisions of the Social Security Act,[55] which irrationally discriminated among classes of non-marital children, violated the Equal Protection Clause. At issue in *Jimenez v. Weinberger* (1974) was a provision that absolutely barred certain non-marital children from receiving insurance benefits through their disabled father. Excluded from statutory recovery were non-marital children whose fathers' paternity could neither be proven through acknowledgment by the father nor affirmed by evidence of domicile and support by the father prior to the onset of his disability (*Jimenez*, p.631 fn.2).

Chief Justice Burger, delivering the Court's opinion in *Jimenez*, declined the appellant's urging that the Court deem the contested provision to be "based on the so-called 'suspect classification' of illegitimacy" (*Jimenez*, p.631). In his opinion, it was sufficient for the Court merely to note that "the Equal Protection Clause . . . enable[s it] to strike down discriminatory laws relating to status of birth where . . . the classification is justified by no legitimate state interest, compelling or otherwise" (*Jimenez*, p.632, citing *Weber*, pp.175–176). The Court also rejected the government's urging that the Court rely on the "rational basis" test in *Dandridge* to reach its verdict in *Jimenez*. According to Chief Justice Burger, "there is no evidence support-ing the contention that to allow illegitimates in the classification of appel-lant to receive benefits would significantly impair the federal Social Security trust fund and necessitate a reduction in the scope of persons benefited by the Act" (*Jimenez*, p.633). However, the Court utilized the language of the rational basis test when it accepted the legitimacy of the state's interest in preventing spurious claims, yet challenged the reason-ableness of the state's implementation policy to achieve the purpose of the statutory scheme: "to provide support for dependents of a wage earner who has lost his earning power . . . [and to] ensure that only those actually entitled to benefits receive payments" (*Jimenez*, pp.633–634).

The Court's reluctance to declare birth status a "suspect classification" would not have precluded it from using the strict scrutiny standard to evaluate the challenged classification in *Jimenez*. But its explicit refusal to apply the rational basis test of *Dandridge* suggested that a rational justifica-tion for the statutory classification would not be sufficient, by itself, to validate the legislative distinction. Rather than relying solely on either of these standards, the Court collapsed the strict scrutiny and reasonable basis standards, asserting that the challenged statutory classification was both overinclusive and underinclusive. It presumed the dependency of all mari-tal children and those non-marital children covered by 42 U.S.C. §§416(h)(2)(A)&(B) of the Social Security Act regardless of their actual dependency. It also postulated the non-dependency of non-marital children who were unable to inherit from the wage-earner parent; who were unable to establish that their birth status resulted soley from formal, non-obvious defects in their parents' ceremonial marriage; who had not been legitimated by law; or who were born after the wage earner became disabled—despite their potential ability to prove both paternity and dependency. Since the Court could find no justification for the distinction between the two sub-classes of non-marital children, it judged the classification to be violative of "the equal protection of the laws guaranteed by the due process provi-sion of the Fifth Amendment" (*Jimenez*, p.633).

Once again Justice Rehnquist dissented, on the grounds that "whatever may be the rationale for giving some form of stricter scrutiny to classifica-tions between legitimates and illegitimates, that rationale simply vanishes when the alleged discrimination is between classes of illegitimates. Such classifications should instead be evaluated according to the traditional principle set forth in *Dandridge*" (*Jimenez*, p.639). Insofar as the government's classifications were an attempt to prevent spurious claims, Justice Rehnquist maintained, a rational basis existed to justify the classifications. He further argued that the underinclusiveness that plagued these classifications could not be resolved within a judicial forum, given the fact that the judiciary was not empowered to conduct legislative hearings. Hence, in Justice Rehnquist's view, the Court should have deferred to Congress rather than disguise the due process argument of irrebuttable presumptions in equal protection concepts (*Jimenez*, p.639). But Justice Rehnquist was unable to persuade the Court to follow his line of reasoning in *Jimenez*. He fared no better in *Weinberger v. Beaty* (1973). Although Justice Rehnquist would have noted probable jurisdiction and set the case for oral argument, the Court merely affirmed a lower court's judgment in *Beaty*, which had followed the reasoning of Chief Justice Burger in *Jimenez*.

Beaty addressed the same question and possessed almost the identical circumstances as *Jimenez*, which had declared §416(h)(3)(B)(ii) of the Social Security Act to be unconstitutional. Under this section, all non-marital children who were governed by its provisions were required to prove actual support prior to the onset of the insured parent's disability. No other children, as defined by 42 U.S.C.§§416(h)(2)(A) or (B) or §§416(h)(3)(i) or (ii),[56] were required to demonstrate dependency, as defined by 42 U.S.C. §402(d)(3).[57]

In fact, children who were eligible under §§416(h)(2)(A) or (B) or §416(h)(3)(i) could receive insurance payments regardless of whether they were being supported by the disabled parent. Children who did not satisfy the criteria established by these sections, and who therefore had their claims evaluated under §416(h)(3)(ii), were systematically denied the insurance benefits even if they could substantiate their claim regarding both their receipt of support and their parentage. The lower court ruled that there was disparate treatment of marital and non-marital children, as well as classes of non-marital children, that was prohibited by the Equal Protection Clause via the Fifth Amendment's Due Process Clause.

In 1976 the Court brushed aside almost all of its previous opinions[58] and allowed a statute that discriminated against non-marital children to withstand an equal protection challenge in *Mathews v. Lucas* (1976). The statute in question provided Social Security benefits to children of a deceased parent but required certain non-marital children to prove that the parent had been supporting them at the time of the parent's death. The Court, through Justice Blackmun, upheld the statute, downplaying the history of discrimination against children born out of wedlock: "[D]iscrimination against illegitimates has never approached the severity and pervasiveness of the historic legal and political discrimination against women and Negroes" (*Mathews*, pp.505–506). Unlike gender and race, birth status is not visually obvious, and thus the Court was unwilling to apply the same level of scrutiny to discrimination against non-marital children as it applied to gender and racial discrimination. The Court explicitly rejected the idea that birth status was a suspect classification (*Mathews*, pp.505–510). As a consequence, the Court refused to subject the statutory classification to strict scrutiny; it merely demanded that any distinctions made between children on the basis of birth status be rationally justified.

In *Mathews* the justification offered by the government was quite simple: it was highly probable that marital children and non-marital children who satisfied the eligibility criteria dictated by 42 U.S.C. §§416(h)(2)(A) or (B) or §§416(h)(3)(C)(i) or (ii) most likely had been financially supported by the insured wage earner. Consequently, the financial support these children received should be unchanged when the wage earner died. This probability, agreed to by a three-judge court in *Norton v. Weinberger* (1973), became the basis of the government's argument. In terms of administrative convenience, it was deemed both rational and reasonable for the government to presume dependency for some children—those who were legitimate and those who were able to inherit from the insured parent's estate; those whose parents were married in a ceremony that, but for a non-obvious legal defect, would have been legal; and non-marital children who had been acknowledged in writing, had been decreed to be the father's child by the courts, were being supported by their father by court order, or were living with an insured father who was contributing to their support at the time of his death—while denying that presumption to other children—those not covered by the statute. The government grounded its argument in the legislative history of 42 U.S.C. §402(d)(1),[59] which indicated that "the applicant child's classification as legitimate, or acknowledged, etc., is ultimately relevant only to the determination of dependency [;] . . . the statute was not a general welfare provision for legitimate or otherwise 'approved' children of deceased insureds, but was intended just 'to replace the support lost by a child when his father . . . dies.' " (S.Rep. No. 404, 89th Cong., 1st Sess., 110 (1965), as quoted in *Mathews*, p.507).

Deferring to Congress,[60] the Court concluded that the statute did not "impermissibly discriminate" against non-marital children to whom the presumption of dependency was not extended. It also concluded that the challenged classifications were justified as reasonable legislative judgments designed to link entitlement of survivor's benefits to dependency at the time of the parent's death.

Justice Stevens began his Supreme Court tenure by having Justices Brennan and Marshall join him in a dissenting opinion (*Mathews*, pp.517–518). He perceived no significant difference between *Jimenez* and *Mathews* and therefore was perplexed by the Court's reasoning. Justice Stevens neglected to consider, however, the Court's passing comment regarding inheritance. Yet this remark provides the Court with a logical connection between *Labine* and *Mathews*. The Court, which had explicitly stated its position on intestacy laws in *Labine*, extended its arguments in *Mathews*:

inheritance eligibility portended dependency. Consistent with its *Labine* decision, the Court asserted that

> where state intestacy law provides that a child may take personal property from a father's estate, it may reasonably be thought that the child will more likely be dependent during the parent's life and at his death. For in its embodiment of the popular view within the jurisdiction of how a parent would have his property devolve among his children in the event of death, without specific directions, such legislation also reflects to some degree the popular conception within the jurisdiction of the felt parental obligation to such an "illegitimate" child in other circumstances, and thus something of the likelihood of actual parental support during, as well as after, life. (*Mathews*, pp.514–515)

Rather than addressing the Court-drawn link between inheritance and dependency, Justice Stevens argued instead that if the statute in *Jimenez* was declared unconstitutional because it was both underinclusive and overinclusive, then the statute in *Mathews* should have been invalidated for the same reasons. Children, regardless of their birth status, were sometimes abandoned prior to their father's death, yet only those children covered by the statute were still presumed to be dependents. Children who were not favored by the statute found themselves without support when their father died even if they had been financially dependent upon their father at some point in the past (*Mathews*, pp.514–515).

In Justice Stevens's view, the Court drew a fallacious conclusion from its original premises. Although it acknowledged that, legally, birth status was like race and national origin, and that imposing disabilities on non-marital children was "illogical and unjust," the Court permitted children born outside marriage to be discriminated against in the interest of administrative convenience: "[B]y presuming dependency on the basis of relatively readily documented facts, such as legitimate birth, or existence of a support order or paternity decree, which could be relied on to indicate the likelihood of continued actual dependency, Congress was able to avoid the burden and expense of specific case-by-case determination in the large number of cases where dependency is objectively probable" (*Mathews*, p.509). The Court's acceptance of administrative convenience as a valid justification for discrimination against non-marital children in *Mathews*—a justification it had rejected in *Jimenez*—was unpalatable to Justice Stevens. He pointed out that since non-marital children were traditionally disfavored by society, classifications of these children could easily be a product of habit, inertia, or stereotypes. In his view, the Court should have been sensitive to the plight of these children and should not have accepted "administrative convenience" as a valid primary justification for such discrimination. The Court supported its conclusion by noting that "such presumptions in aid of administrative functions . . . are permissible . . . so long as that lack of precise equivalence [does] not exceed the bounds of substantiality tolerated by the applicable level of scrutiny" (*Mathews*, p.503).

To the consternation of Justice Stevens, the Court never explicitly identified the "applicable level of scrutiny" in *Mathews*. While the Court rejected the standard of strict scrutiny,[61] it did not revert to the minimal scrutiny of the rational basis test. It seemed to be searching for a compromise between these two extreme standards—one which was neither extremely strict nor entirely "toothless"—similar to the dual inquiry approach it had established in *Weber*.

In addition to the Court searching for a non-ambiguous, workable standard of scrutiny against which to evaluate challenged statutes, the result in *Mathews* was inconsistent with the results reached by the Court in *Levy*, *Weber*, and *Jimenez*. These cases might be reconcilable, perhaps, if it were assumed that the essential factor in *Mathews* for determining whether benefits would be provided to non-marital children was dependency, while in *Levy*, *Weber*,[62] and *Jimenez* it was birth status. Such reconciliation seems more a matter of form than substance, however, especially for *Jimenez* and *Mathews*, since the Court attributed different purposes to essentially the same statutory provision.[63]

By shifting the emphasis from "a claim to support" to "actual support," the Court created a technical difference between its *Jimenez* reading of 42 U.S.C. §§416(h)(2)(A)&(B) and its *Mathews* reading of 42 U.S.C. §§416(h)(2)(A) or (B) and §§416(h)(3)(C)(i) or (ii) in order to support its acceptance of administrative convenience as a valid justification for the discrimination. Yet this reading does not alter the underlying issue in both cases: the conclusive denial of benefits, based solely on factors that could not be altered by the disadvantaged individual (birth status and the actions of their parents), regardless of the individual's dependency on the wage earner.[64] By interpreting the support requirement as actual, instead of potential, the Court attached "greater weight to support at a particular moment in time than to support of several years' duration" (*Mathews*, p.518).[65] But such a characterization allows non-marital children to be penalized for conduct and status over which they have no control for the mere sake of administrative convenience.

The Court's deferential interpretation of statutory classifications continued in *Califano v. Boles* (1979), as did its willingness to redraw the history and structure of a statutory purpose (i.e., *Boles* pp.294 n.12, 298). At issue in *Boles* was the constitutionality of §202(g)(1) of the Social Security Act.[66] This act denied insurance benefits to the mother of a non-marital child because the mother had never married the wage earner who fathered the children.

Justice Rehnquist deemed the relationship in *Boles* between the government's interest in easing the economic privation brought on by a wage earner's death and the classification of mothers covered by §202(g)(1) to be reasonable. In his view, it seemed highly unlikely that a woman who had never married the deceased wage earner would be economically dependent on him at the time of his death. Because the couple in *Boles* was never married and the wage earner was not legally required to support the mother of his children, Justice Rehnquist argued that Congress could have logically deduced that the wage earner was not an important source of income to the woman, and she probably did not suffer economic dislocation when he died. The rationale of *Weinberger v. Salfi* (1975)[67] was reaffirmed by Justice Rehnquist: "the only relevant constitutional argument was whether 'the test [appellees could not] meet [was] not so rationally related to a legitimate legislative objective that it [could] be used to deprive them of benefits available to those who [did] satisfy that test' " (*Boles*, pp.290–291, quoting *Salfi*, pp.781–782).

Two questions formed the crux of *Boles*: who were the intended beneficiaries of §202(g)(1) of the Social Security Act, and does the denial of benefits to an unwed parent constitute discrimination against a non-marital child? The Court, through Justice Rehnquist—who analyzed §202(g)(1) against the background of *Salfi*—answered these questions by asserting that since the economic needs of non-marital children were met directly through the "child's insurance benefits," which were distinct from "mother's benefits," the actual beneficiaries of "mother's benefits" were mothers who had been married to the wage earner, not children born outside wedlock. Since non-marital children were only indirectly affected by the denial of "mother's benefits" to their mother, the interest of non-marital children in their mothers' receipt of "mother's benefits" was at best "incidental" (*Boles*, p.296). The denial of benefits was held to have only a "speculative impact" on non-marital children as a class (*Boles*, p.296). Thus, discrimination against unwed mothers, through the denial of mother's benefits, was not viewed by the Court as equivalent to discrimination against non-marital children. According to Justice Rehnquist, it was simply the outcome of a congressionally rational choice. Congress chose to concentrate the available finite resources where they judged the greatest need to exist—with "those who actually suffer economic dislocation upon the death of a wage earner and are likely to be confronted at that juncture with the choice between employment or the assumption of full-time child-care responsibilities" (*Boles*, pp.290–291).

Justice Rehnquist felt compelled to acknowledge that this interpretation of §202(g)(1) was significantly different from the one he had authored three years earlier in *Weinberger v. Wiesenfeld* (1975) (*Boles*, p.292, n.12). In his separately written concurring opinion in *Wiesenfeld*, Justice Rehnquist had asserted that §202(g) "convincingly demonstrates that [its] only purpose . . . [was] to make it possible for children of deceased contributing workers to have the personal care and attention of a surviving parent" (*Boles*, p.298, quoting *Salfi*, p.655). Even if one accepts his admission that his prior interpretation of §202(g) had "proven untenable" (*Boles*, p.294 n.12) and that his new interpretation was "a better considered position" (*Boles*, p.294 n.12), the statute's eligibility requirements for mother's benefits, as he construed them, discriminate on the basis of birth status. Non-marital children are absolutely foreclosed from enjoying the same opportunity available to marital children, regardless of whether their mother suffers economic dislocation as a result of her partner's death. Mothers of non-marital children are systematically denied the option to "elect not to work and to devote themselves to [child]care" (*Boles*, p.288). A distribution system that summarily excludes unwed mothers from the class of eligible recipients of mother's benefits discriminates against non-marital children in a manner that is, in the words of Justice Marshall, "unjust, and, under [the] Court's settled precedents, unconstitutional" (*Boles*, p.304).

Justice Rehnquist's interpretation of §202(g) additionally condoned discrimination between types of families. Through his attribution to Congress of a logical connection between marital status and dependency, Justice Rehnquist was able to summarily dismiss alternative realities. For example, §202(g)(1) prohibited payment of mother's benefits to single mothers solely because they lacked a marriage license (*Boles*, p.289). Whether they could prove actual economic dependency on the wage earner under the terms of the statute is irrelevant. Hence the primary function of §202(g)(1), contrary to Justice Rehnquist's position, was not to alleviate economic dislocation in general, but to offer yet another institutionalized protection only to those women whose sexual behavior conformed with the dicta of patriarchal social norms.

Justice Marshall, with Justices Blackmun, Brennan, and White, faulted the Court's decision in *Boles*. His attack on the Court's reasoning centered on two main arguments. First, Justice Marshall detected nothing in the legislative history of §202(g)(1) to support the Court's contention that the purpose of this statute was to benefit dependent spouses rather than dependent children. According to his assessment of the statute, there was no dependency requirement. Recipients of "mother's benefits" included all mothers, even those separated or divorced from the deceased wage earner who had not remarried as well as their legally recognized children, "regardless of whether [the wage earner] was living with them or supporting them at the time of his death, or even if he never lived with or supported them" (*Boles*, p.300). Justice Marshall's second argument focused on the discriminatory impact which denial of "mother's benefits" had on non-marital children. He maintained that the economic restriction in §202(g)(1)—as well as the condition in §202(d)(5), which terminated mother's benefits when a child reached eighteen or left the parent's home or custody—substantiated the conclusion that children were in fact the intended beneficiaries of §202(g)(1). As such, the denial of these benefits to unwed mothers had more than an "incidental" effect on non-marital children. For Justice Marshall, the impact was unquestionably discriminatory and should have been evaluated accordingly.

Once Justice Marshall established that the dispute in *Boles* centered on discrimination against non-marital children, he criticized the Court's violation of settled precedent as characterized by *Weber* and *Jimenez*. Citing these cases, Justice Marshall noted that in both *Weber* and *Jimenez* "the Court recognized that the marital status of parents [was] not a sufficiently accurate index of the economic needs of their children to warrant conclusively denying assistance to illegitimates" (*Boles*, p.305). Yet the marital restrictions in §202(g)(1) served to conclusively bar recovery by non-marital children, while automatically allowing recovery by marital children without regard for their state of dependency on the deceased wage earner. Justice Marshall concluded that this disparity of treatment between categories of children signaled the existence of a constitutional infirmity that bore no substantial relationship to the state's expressed statutory purpose. Consequently, in Justice Marshall's opinion, §202(g)(1) should have been declared unconstitutional.

In *United States v. Clark* (1980), the Court once more utilized a standard stricter than mere rationality. Non-marital children were the direct recipients of the survivor's annuities benefits in *Clark*, rather than indirect recipients via their mothers as they had been deemed to be in *Boles*, and thus the Court was less inclined to confine itself to the question of actual dependency. Instead, the Court addressed "the question [of] whether [non-marital] children of a federal civil service employee are entitled to survivor's benefits under the Civil Service Retirement Act when the children once lived with the employee in a familial relationship, but were not living with the employee at the time of his death" (*Clark*, p.898).

Justice Marshall offered a broad construction of the "lived with" requirement in §8341(a)(3)(A) of the Civil Service Retirement Act[68] in order to prevent it from violating the Equal Protection Clause. If survivors' annuities were available to non-marital children on the condition that they "lived with the employee . . . in a regular parent-child relationship," and if the phrase "lived with" was narrowly construed—that is, if the non-marital children must have lived with the employee at the time of his death—then, Justice Marshall argued, a serious constitutional question surfaced regarding discrimination against non-marital children. In accordance with a Court principle "not [to] pass on the constitutionality of an Act of Congress if a construction of the statute is fairly possible by which the question may be avoided" (*Clark*, p.899), Justice Marshall adopted the appellee's construction of the "lived with" phrase. He accepted the appellee's contention that this phrase was not restricted to a particular time. By accepting this interpretation of the phrase in question, Justice Marshall was able to avert a constitutional challenge to §8341(a)(3)(A).

Justice Marshall justified his acceptance of the appellee's rendition of the "lived with" phrase by appealing to the legislative history and intent of this statute. He accepted the government's declaration that the purpose of the annuities granted under §8341(a)(3)(A) was to replace the support a wage earner's dependents lost when the wage earner died. But he found "the legislative history . . . devoid of any indication whether Congress intended that annuities could be recovered by all recognized natural children who had once lived with the employee in a family relationship or only such children who were still living with the employee at the time of death" (*Clark*, p.901). Unable to discern the purpose of the "lived with" provision from the statute's legislative history, Justice Marshall directed his inquiry to the 1966 amendment of §8341(a)(3)(A)—which deleted the dependency requirement, but retained the "lived with" requirement[69]—in an unsuccessful search for a clue.

In the absence of persuasive evidence to the contrary, Justice Marshall was convinced that the appellee's reading of the statute was both fair and reasonable. To reject the appellee's construction of the "lived with" phrase in favor of the government's, which stated that this phrase actually meant "living with at the time of death," would have rendered §8341(a)(3)(A) constitutionally suspect, since only non-marital children were compelled to satisfy this requirement. As Justice Marshall pointed out, "such a classification based on illegitimacy is unconstitutional unless it bears 'an evident and substantial relation to the particular . . . interests this statute [was] designed to serve' " (*Clark*, p.899, quoting *Lalli*, p.268, with attention directed also to *Trimble*, p.767). In Justice Marshall's opinion, the government was unable to relate the classification in §8341(a)(3)(A) adequately to its stated purpose.[70] Hence, in order to save this statute from violating the Equal Protection Clause, Justice Marshall maintained that the "lived with" phrase had to be construed as the appellee suggested.

Justice Powell, who was joined by Chief Justice Burger, agreed with the Court's judgment, but argued that Justice Marshall was too lenient in his analysis of the 1966 amendment to §8341(a)(3)(A). He noted that the Court's broad construction of the "lived with" requirement did not eliminate all of the constitutional problems inherent in the phrase. For example, as Justice Powell noted in his concurrence, "the imposition of the 'lived with' requirement as a test of actual dependency may be unconstitutional in a case in which a father has always supported, but never lived with, an illegitimate child" (*Clark*, p.904, n*). Moreover, in Justice Powell's estimation, Congress's elimination of the dependency requirement in those instances where the "lived with" requirement was fulfilled should not have been viewed as a total eradication of the dependency requirement for all children born outside wedlock. Where the wage earner was not living with the non-marital children at the time of death, "Congress may require illegitimate children to demonstrate actual dependency even though legitimate children are presumed to be dependent [*Mathews*, pp.507–509], so long as the means by which illegitimates must demonstrate such dependency are substantially related to achievement of the statutory goal [*Lalli*, pp.275-276]" (*Clark*, p.905).

Justice Rehnquist, joined by Justice Stewart, dissented on the grounds that *Clark* should have been remanded to the Court of Claims for consideration of the statutory claim. Although he agreed with Justice Marshall's construction of the "lived with" phrase, Justice Rehnquist asserted that the lower court was the proper judicial level for deciding the statutory issue: "By remanding here, we would conform the disposition of this case to our customary practice which recognizes the usefulness of District and Appellate Court opinions on the questions ultimately reviewed here, as well as the need to reserve this Court's plenary consideration for questions still warranting final decision here after decision by another court" (*Clark*, p.905).

Although none of the justices mentioned individual responsibility in *Clark*, this concept serves to distinguish *Boles* from *Clark*. Children have no control over either their parents' marital status or their parents' residency decisions. In a very real sense, children are powerless over their circumstances. The Court has frequently refused to inflict punishment upon non-marital children (i.e., *Levy*, *Glona*, *Weber*, *Gomez*, *Cahill*, *Jimenez*, *Beaty*, *Mathews*, *Trimble*), emphasizing the relative blamelessness of the children even as they castigate the erring parent (i.e., *Quilloin*, *Boles*, *Parham*, *Lehr*). This is not to imply that the Court always requires similar treatment of children irrespective of their birth status—obviously they do not (i.e., *Mathews*, *Labine*, *Fiallo*, *Lalli*).

INHERITANCE

The Supreme Court continues to allow birth status distinctions to be drawn between marital and non-marital children who seek to inherit from their fathers. Its reluctance to invalidate statutes that deny, on the basis of birth status, equal intestate succession rights to children illustrates the "uneasy constitutional tension" (Kay, 1988, p.354) that exists in the Court's treatment of non-marital children's rights.

In *Labine v. Vincent* (1971), a non-marital child who had been publicly acknowledged but never officially legitimated by her father was denied a share of her father's estate when he died without a will. At issue were two articles of the Louisiana Civil Code of 1870. The first, Article 206 provided that "Illegitimate children, though duly acknowledged, cannot claim the rights of legitimate children" (*Labine*, p. 534); Article 919 provided that "Natural children are called to the inheritance of their natural father, who has duly acknowledged them, when he has left no descendants nor ascendants, nor collateral relations, nor surviving wife, and to the exclusion of the State" (Labine, p. 534). Justice Black, writing for a plurality, upheld Louisiana's intestate succession laws whereby the collateral relations of the decedent could claim his or her property to the exclusion of acknowledged, but not legitimated, children. He observed that "[t]o further strengthen and preserve family ties, Louisiana regulates the disposition of property upon the death of a family man" (Labine, p.536).

Noting that the applicant's reliance on Levy and Glona was misplaced, Justice Black declined to extend the rationale "to those cases where it does not apply" (Labine, p.535). He distinguished these two cases by observing that neither case was analogous to Labine (pp.536, 536 fn.6) and rejected the idea that "a State can never treat an illegitimate child differently from legitimate offspring" (Labine, p.536). Even though the challenged statute discriminated against non-marital children, Justice Black maintained that since it did not create an insurmountable barrier for children born outside wedlock, it did not violate the Equal Protection Clause.

Justice Black never referred by name to the test used in Labine, save for one statement in footnote six wherein the he stated that "[e]ven if we were to apply the 'rational basis' test to the Louisiana intestate succession statute, that statute clearly has a rational basis in view of Louisiana's interest in promoting family life and of directing the disposition of property left within the State" (Labine, p.536, fn.6). This statement suggests that the Court did not perceive itself as applying the rational basis test, even though the Court's reasons for upholding the statute includes deference to the state's power "of regulating the manner of terms upon which property real or personal within its domain may be transmitted by last will or testament, or by inheritance, and of prescribing who shall and who shall not be capable of taking it" (Labine, p.539 fn.16, quoting Mager v. Grima, p.493).

Justice Brennan, joined by Justices Douglas, Marshall, and White, was unable to find a rational basis for the distinction made by the Louisiana statute "between an acknowledged illegitimate child and a legitimate one" (Labine, p.558). In his view, the plurality's affirmation of Louisiana's birth status discrimination could only be supported by the "untenable and discredited moral prejudice of bygone centuries which vindictively punished not only the [unwed] parents, but also the hapless, and innocent, children" (Labine, p.541). He asserted, contrary to the plurality, that "the discrimination is clearly invidious" (Labine, p.558) and implied that birth status is a suspect classification and subject to strict scrutiny since "the Court has generally treated as suspect a classification that discriminates against an individual on the basis of factors over which [one] has no control" (Labine, p.551, fn.19).[71]

Contrary to the Labine plurality, Justice Brennan found Levy and Glona to be indistinguishable from Labine (pp.550–552, 558). According to Justice Brennan, if the state of Louisiana's intestate succession statutes did not create an insurmountable barrier to non-marital children in Labine, then neither did Louisiana's Wrongful Death statute in *Levy*. Just as the father in *Labine* could have executed a will, married his child's mother, or stated his desire to legitimate his daughter when he acknowledged his paternity, thereby making his child eligible to inherit from him (*Labine*, p.539), the mother could have formally acknowledged her child, thereby making her child eligible to recover in tort for the mother's death (*Labine*, p.550).

Moreover, Article 2315 of the Louisiana Code—held unconstitutional in *Levy* and *Glona*—stated that "the right to recover damages under the provisions of this paragraph is a property right which, on the death of the survivor, is inherited by his legal, instituted, or irregular heirs" (*Levy*, p.69 fn.1). Thus, it would seem that if the Wrongful Death statutes in *Levy* and *Glona* violated the Equal Protection Clause, then the intestate succession statutes in *Labine* also violated it—the right to recovery in both *Levy* and *Glona* was contingent on the claimant's eligibility to inherit from the deceased. If, on the other hand, the intestate succession statutes in *Labine* do not violate the Equal Protection Clause, then the Wrongful Death statute cannot violate it. It is inconsistent, however, for the Court to hold that the Wrongful Death statute challenged in *Levy* and *Glona* violated the Equal Protection Clause, but the intestate succession statutes at issue in *Labine* did not—since the question of who is an eligible inheritor underlies all three cases.

By utilizing more than one standard to analyze birth status classifications under the Equal Protection Clause—(a) close examination of the state statute, as employed in *Levy* and *Glona*; (b) broad deference to the state regulatory power, as enunciated in *Labine*—without offering appropriate guidelines for distinguishing when either standard would prevail, the Court left unresolved the ways in which subsequent cases should be judged. One could argue that the Court was merely differentiating between legal distinctions that might influence behavior (such as the intestate succession statutes in *Labine*, which ensure that a father's non-marital children can inherit from him, provided the father complies with the statutory requirements; or the Wrongful Death statute in *Glona*, which allows an unwed mother to recover for the wrongful death of her children provided she has acknowledged them) and legal discrimination that cannot affect behavior (such as the Wrongful Death statute in *Levy*, since it is outside the power of non-marital children to legitimate themselves, despite their desire not to have their mother wrongfully killed). While superficially a valid argument, it does not account for the fact that the non-marital daughter in *Labine* could no more write herself into her father's will than the non-marital children in *Levy* could legitimate themselves in order to comply with the respective statutory eligibility requirements. Nor does it account for the fact that the unwed mother in *Glona* was allowed to recover for the wrongful death of her non-marital child—despite her own failure to comply with the legal formalities articulated in the statute, but the non-marital child in *Labine* was denied her inheritance right because of her father's failure to comply with the statutory requirements.

By departing from its position in *Levy* and *Glona*, the Court voiced in *Labine* "the prejudice of bygone centuries" against non-marital children and their mothers. According to Justice Black, "[t]he social difference between a wife and a concubine is analogous to the difference between a legitimate and an illegitimate child. One set of relationships is socially sanctioned, legally recognized and gives rise to various rights and duties. The other set of relationships is illicit and beyond the recognition of the law" (*Labine*, p.538). The Court thus upheld a statutory provision in *Labine* which punished non-marital children for the behavior and decisions of their fathers.

Six years after *Labine*, the Supreme Court examined once more the constitutionality of a state intestate succession law in *Trimble v. Gordon* (1977). Justice Powell, writing for the Court, began the analysis of *Trimble* by identifying the principal equal protection standards the Court had employed in past cases: the minimum rationality standard, which "require[d] at a minimum that a statutory classification bear a rational relationship to a legitimate state purpose" (p.766, citing *Weber*, p.172); the "most exacting" or strict scrutiny standard that applied when the "statutory classifications approach[ed] sensitive and fundamental personal rights" (p.767, citing *Weber*, p.172) or when a "suspect class [was] involved" (p.767, citing *Mathews*, p.506). He then pronounced that the appropriate level of scrutiny in *Trimble* was intermediate scrutiny—a middle ground that is "less than strictest scrutiny," but "not a toothless one" (p.767, citing *Mathews*, pp.506, 510). Using this measure, the Court examined the relationship between the classification stemming from §12 of the Illinois Probate Code[72] and the state's twin interests—promoting legitimate family relationships and establishing an accurate method for the disposition of property at death. It found that the Illinois statute, which allowed non-marital children to inherit by intestate succession only from their mothers, violated the Equal Protection Clause of the Fourteenth Amendment.

In reaching this decision, Justice Powell rejected, without completely overruling, the reasoning of *Labine*:

The Illinois statute can be distinguished in several aspects from the Louisiana statute in *Labine*. The discrimination in *Labine* took a different form, suggesting different legislative objectives. . . . Despite these differences, it is apparent that we have examined the Illinois statute more critically than the Court examined the Louisiana statute in *Labine*. To the extent that our analysis in this case differs from that in *Labine* the more recent analysis controls. (*Labine*, p.766 fn.17)

In lieu of *Labine* the Court relied upon *Weber* and *Mathews*. The Court reiterated its holding in *Weber* that it was unreasonable, unjust, and ineffectual for the state to punish non-marital children in an effort to influence parental conduct. Unlike their parents, children born outside wedlock lack individual responsibility for both their parents' conduct and their own birth status (*Trimble*, pp.764–765). Consequently, §12 bore only "the most attenuated relationship to the [state's] asserted goal" of promoting legitimate family relationships (*Trimble*, p.768). The state's first argument was thus quickly dismissed by the Court on the ground that §12 failed to advance the state's interests.

The state's second argument in defense of §12 was that the provisions of the statute established a method of property disposition. Although more substantial, this argument was also dismantled by the Court. The Court conceded that the state has a legitimate interest in establishing a method of property disposition and in protecting estates against spurious claims. But the state unnecessarily excluded groups of children from paternal inheritance rights (*Trimble*, p.772). The Court maintained that §12 of the Probate Code exceeded its intended purpose by totally barring children born out of wedlock from ever inheriting their deceased father's intestate estate, even in those instances where paternity was certain, unless the father married the mother *and* acknowledged the children. Section 12 also failed to conform with the *Mathews* requirement that the challenged statute should be "carefully attuned to alternative considerations" (*Trimble*, p.772 fn.14, citing *Mathews*, p.513)[73]—since the problems associated with proving paternity under some circumstances "[do] not justify the total statutory disinheritance of [non-marital] children whose fathers die intestate" (*Trimble*, p.772). The Court thus found the statute to be constitutionally flawed.

In reaching its conclusion, the Court reaffirmed the *Mathews* rejection of birth status as a suspect classification. It reiterated its prior conclusion that birth status was not sufficiently analogous to the personal characteristics labeled judicially "suspect" to be itself so labeled. The Court then defined the applicable standard of review—less than "strict scrutiny" but more than "mere rational basis." This intermediate standard encompassed the dual approach of *Weber*[74]—it weighed the character of the legal discrimination against the legitimate state function (*Trimble*, p.769) and it considered the " 'fit' between [the statutory] 'purpose' and the statutory means adopted to achieve it" (*Trimble*, p.761). As a result, the Court examined the Illinois statute more critically than the Louisiana statute in *Labine* and dictated that *Trimble* would limit the application of *Labine* in the future. The Court also attempted to distinguish *Labine* from *Trimble*:

[P]enalizing children as a means of influencing their parents seems inconsistent with the desire of the Illinois Legislature to make the intestate succession law more just to illegitimate children. Moreover, the difference in rights of illegitimate children in the estates of their mothers and their fathers appears to be unrelated to the purpose of promoting family relationships. In this respect the Louisiana laws at issue in *Labine* were quite different. Those laws differentiated on the basis of the character of the child's illegitimacy.... The Louisiana categories are consistent with a theory of social opprobrium regarding the parents' relationships and with a measured, if misguided, attempt to deter illegitimate relationships. (*Trimble*, pp.768–769 fn.13)

The dissenters, Chief Justice Burger and Justices Stewart, Blackmun, and Rehnquist, were unable to distinguish between *Labine* and *Trimble*. Indeed, these two cases contain identical facts: paternity of the non-marital children was acknowledged, the fathers could have ensured the inheritance rights of their non-marital children by leaving a will, and both Louisiana and Illinois had as a state interest "encouraging family relationships and . . . establishing an accurate and efficient method of disposing of property at death" (*Trimble*, p.766).

Justice Rehnquist added a separate dissent wherein he outlined the original intent of the Fourteenth Amendment (to bar racial discrimination) and criticized the Court's analysis of birth status cases involving the Equal Protection Clause. He charged that the Court's habit of expanding the meaning of the Fourteenth Amendment beyond classifications based on race or national origin caused confusion regarding the proper level of scrutiny to be applied to non-racial cases. According to Justice Rehnquist, "[t]he appropriate 'scrutiny,' in the eyes of the Court, appeared to involve some analysis of the relation of the 'purpose' of the legislature to the 'means' by which it chooses to carry out that purpose" (*Trimble*, p.781).

Hence, according to Justice Rehnquist, the Court was constantly required to second-guess the legislature's judgment and decide "how much 'imperfection' between means and ends [was] permissible" (*Trimble*, p.784). This was a function that Justice Rehnquist asserted was outside the commission and qualifications of the Court. In order for the Court to remain within its proper domain, Justice Rehnquist prescribed a return to the rational basis test in all equal protection cases—excluding race and national origin classifications, since he reasoned that "if race was an invalid sorting tool where blacks were concerned [since the Amendment grew out of the Civil War and the freeing of the slaves], it followed logically that it should not be valid where other races were concerned either" (*Trimble*, p.780). Using the rationality standard, the distinctions between marital and non-marital children would be neither mindless nor patently irrational. Hence, Justice Rehnquist would have sustained the constitutionality of §12 of the Probate Act.

If the Court had followed Justice Rehnquist's logic, it would not have invalidated §12. Nor would it have progressed to the point of making non-marital children its primary focus in analyzing state intestate succession laws. The Court declared in *Trimble* that the "difficulties of proving paternity in some situations do not justify the total statutory disinheritance" of children born out of wedlock (*Trimble*, p.772). While this statement does not represent an uninterrupted linear progression of the Court's Equal Protection analysis of birth status cases—insofar as Justice Powell noted in

Trimble that *"Labine* . . . is difficult to place in the pattern of [the] Court's equal protection decisions" (p.767 fn.12)—it does represent the general trend of its decisions. While the Court still sought to leave the state's interests uncompromised in *Trimble* (p.771), the dividing line between acceptable and unacceptable discrimination shifted. The Court implied that discrimination against non-marital parents might still be constitutionally permissible—as evidenced by the Court's reference to individual responsibility (*Trimble*, pp.769–770)—while it depreciated the weightiness of a child's birth status in those instances where paternity was undisputed.

Paternity was not proven to the satisfaction of all members of the Court in *Lalli v. Lalli* (1978). While the dissent maintained that all interested parties conceded that the appellant was the son of the deceased, that the father supported the appellant during appellant's youth, and that the father acknowledge the appellant as his son (*Lalli*, p.277); the plurality noted that the document relied upon by the appellant to prove his parentage was not an acknowledgment of paternity at all (*Lalli*, p.275 fn.11). But Justice Powell was able to convince only two other Justices (Burger and Stewart) to uphold a New York statute[75]—that allowed a non-marital child to inherit from an intestate father only if, during the father's lifetime, a judicial declaration of paternity was obtained—by distinguishing *Trimble*.[76] While Justices Blackmun and Rehnquist joined these three justices to form a plurality in upholding the statute, they argued that *Trimble* should have been overruled. The dissenters (Justices Brennan, Marshall, Stevens, and White) disagreed both with the Court's conclusion and its rationale. They voted to invalidate the statute on the strength of *Trimble*, since they saw no significant difference between *Trimble* and *Lalli*.

In essence, the plurality in *Lalli* withdrew from the intermediate standard utilized in *Trimble* but failed to clearly articulate the precise standard it used in considering the constitutionality of §4–1.2 of New York's Estates, Powers, and Trusts Law. Justice Powell, writing for the plurality of the Court, initially used the balancing approach established in *Trimble*—weighing the relationship between the state's interest and the means adopted to achieve its interest (*Lalli*, p.271). He asserted that "the primary goal underlying the challenged aspects of §4–1.2 [was] to provide for the just and orderly disposition of property at death" (*Lalli*, p.268). The requirement that a filiation order declaring paternity be issued during the father's lifetime, according to Justice Powell, facilitated the state's interest in avoiding fraudulent claims and alleviating administrative problems associated with notification of non-marital children whose existence was unknown.

Having established that §4–1.2 was related to the state's interest, Justice Powell next had to determine whether "the state statute [was] carefully tailored to eliminate imprecise and unduly burdensome methods for establishing paternity" (*Lalli*, p.275 fn.11, quoting *Trimble*, p.72 fn.14). The statute barred all "known" non-marital children who could convincingly substantiate their paternity even though they lacked the official order of filiation. Since these children would not be disruptive to the orderly disposition of their fathers' estates, §4–1.2 lacked precision and, consequently, was unfair insofar as it extended beyond the state's asserted purpose. If Justice Powell had relied upon the *Trimble* precedent, he could not have upheld the constitutionality of §4–1.2 of the New York law. Instead, he analyzed the challenged statute in terms of whether it had a "rational basis": "our inquiry under the Equal Protection Clause does not focus on the abstract 'fairness' of a state law, but on whether the statute's relation to the state interests it is intended to promote is so tenuous that it lacks the rationality contemplated by the Fourteenth Amendment" (*Lalli*, p.273).

In refuting the arguments put forth in Justice Brennan's dissenting opinion, Justice Powell asserted that

even if, as Justice Brennan believes, §4–1.2 could have been written somewhat more equitably, it is not the function of a court "to hypothesize independently on the desirability or feasibility of any possible alternative[s]" to the statutory scheme formulated by New York. [*Mathews* . . . at 515]. "These matters of practical judgement and empirical calculation are for the [State]. . . . In the end, the precise accuracy of [the State's] calculations is not a matter of specialized judicial competence; and we have no basis to question their detail beyond the evident consistency and substantiality" [*Id.* at 515-516]. (*Lalli*, p.274)

With these words the Court signaled a step backward to the deferential attitude toward the legislature exhibited in *Labine*. The approval of both Justices Blackmun and Rehnquist for this retreat can be gleaned from their respective concurring opinions. Justice Blackmun was gratified that the Court was reverting to the *Labine* principles. His main point of disagreement with the Court was its reluctance to overrule *Trimble*, since "the corresponding statutes of other States will be of questionable validity (if *Trimble* is not derelict) until this Court passes on them, one by one, as being on the *Trimble* side of the line or the *Labine-Lalli* side" (*Lalli*, p.277). Justice Rehnquist would also have adopted the *Labine* rationale. His dissent in *Trimble* served as his concurrence in *Lalli*, where he advocated a return to the rational basis test and criticized the *Trimble* Court for balancing means against ends—a censure that could also have been levied against the *Lalli* Court.

The dissenters could not accept the application of *Labine* to *Lalli*. In their opinion, the governing precedents were *Mathews* and *Trimble*. Justice Brennan succinctly stated the main arguments of the dissenting justices: (1) fathers who acknowledged or voluntarily supported their non-marital children were unlikely to have paternity suits filed against them. Consequently, since non-marital children in this category would virtually never possess a judicial filiation order declaring paternity, they would always be excluded from inheriting their intestate father's estate under the New York statute; (2) acknowledged non-marital children were unnecessarily prohibited from claiming their father's intestate estate even though they could prove their paternity without compromising the state's interests. Because the state could devise "less drastic means" for preventing spurious paternity claims and for solving the problem of notifying unknown non-marital children, Justice Brennan concluded that §4–1.2 "discriminates against illegitimates through means not substantially related to the legitimate interests that the statute purports to promote" (*Lalli*, p.279). To be affirmed by the dissenters, the statute would have had to establish a closer relationship between the state's interests and the burden carried by those individuals affected by the statute—that is, it would have had to satisfy the level of scrutiny applied in *Mathews* and *Trimble* rather than *Labine*.

The Bennett Commission was created by the New York Legislature in 1961 in order to recommend needed changes in state law pertaining to "the descent and distribution, and the practices and procedure relating thereto" (*Lalli*, p.269 fn.7). The legislative recommendation in the Commission's report became §4–1.2, which sought "to protect innocent adults and those rightfully interested in their estates from fraudulent claims of heirship and harassing litigation by those seeking to establish themselves as illegitimate heirs" (*Lalli*, p.271). By upholding the constitutionality of §4–1.2, the Court validated the medieval prejudices stemming from a desire to protect property from all but legally designated heirs.[77] The indisputable consequence of §4–1.2, which codified the Bennett Commission Report, was that non-marital children who had been formally acknowledged and voluntarily supported by their fathers were forestalled from ever inheriting intestate since "the Bennett Commission considered it necessary to impose the strictures of §4–1.2 in order to mitigate serious difficulties in the administration of the estates of both testate and intestate decedents" (*Lalli*, pp.271–272). Thus, unless an order of filiation was tendered by a "court of competent jurisdiction" during the father's lifetime (*Lalli*, p.267), non-marital children were prohibited from being distributees of the paternal estate.

In the Court's opinion, which echoed the Bennett Commission Report, the restriction inherent in §4–1.2 served a dual function. First, it ensured accuracy in the disposition of paternity claims, since the putative father could assist in the fact-finding process and defend his reputation (*Lalli*, p.271). Second, it mitigated serious difficulties in the settlement of intestate estates with regard to fraudulent claims and finality of decree, since "entitlement of an illegitimate child to notice and participation [would be] a matter of judicial record before the administration commences" (*Lalli*, p.271).

Intrinsic in the purpose and implementation of §4–1.2 is the importance of protecting the economic assets of the traditional family. Only one form of proof is accepted to authenticate a child's paternity and thereby eliminate the statutory obstacles to their inheritance right. If a filiation order is not entered on behalf of the non-marital children prior to their father's death, they are forever denied their paternal inheritance. No decree, no inheritance. As long as a man supports his child while he is alive, §4–1.2 secures his estate for his legal family, since "social welfare agencies . . . are unlikely to bring paternity proceedings against fathers who support their children" (*Lalli*, p.278) and "similarly, children who are acknowledged and supported by their fathers are unlikely to bring paternity proceedings against them" (*Lalli*, p.278). Thus, the legally recognized family benefits in *Lalli*, as it did in *Labine*, since "the New York statute makes it virtually impossible for acknowledged and freely supported non-marital children to inherit intestate" (*Lalli*, p.278).

Five years after its *Lalli* decision, the Supreme Court once more heard arguments on the question of the inheritance rights of non-marital children to their intestate father's estate. In *Reed v. Campbell* (1986), a unanimous Court declared that §42 of the Texas Probate Code[78] was invalid under the Fourteenth Amendment as a result of its decision in *Trimble*.

The U.S. Supreme Court challenged the Texas Supreme Court's application of *Trimble* (*Reed*, p.853). According to Justice Stevens, who delivered the Court's decision, *after* the distribution of an estate had been finished, the state's interest in the orderly disposition of a decedent's estate and its interest in finality "may provide [a] . . . valid justification for barring the belated assertion of claims, even though they may be meritorious and even though mistakes of law or fact may have occurred during the probate process" (*Reed*, pp.855–856). Since the administration of the estate, though in progress, was not yet completed when the deceased's non-marital daughter notified the administratrix and the Probate Court of her claim (*Reed*, p.854), the state's rejection of her claim was unjustified; her claim neither jeopardized nor compromised the state's interests.

Although the question presented in *Reed* focused on the issue of the "retroactivity" of the *Trimble* decision, the Court avoided using "retroactivity" as the basis for its decision. Since *Trimble* had been decided before the appellant filed her claim, the Court maintained that the Texas Supreme Court should have assented to the governing law as defined by *Trimble* (*Reed*, p.856). Having dismissed the question of "retroactivity," the Court grounded its *Reed* decision upon the "rather clear distinction that [had] emerged from cases considering the constitutionality of statutory provisions that impose special burdens on [non-marital] children" (*Reed*, p.854). Relying on its previous decisions, the Court ruled that barring the existence of an evident and substantial state interest, the equal protection rights of children born outside wedlock should control inheritance disputes between the state and non-marital children.

By upholding the applicability of *Trimble* in *Reed*, the Court concentrated on the issue of paternity. Although the non-marital child's paternity was not considered to be in dispute for the Supreme Court (*Reed*, p.854; *Trimble*, p.764), the children in both cases were barred by statute from inheriting the paternal estate (*Reed*, p.853; *Trimble*, p.772). The Court's decisions in *Reed* and *Trimble* imply that marital status is less important than paternity. If the latter can be established, then a *legal* relationship exists between non-marital children and their fathers—one aspect of which encompasses inheritance claims.

The Court, however, failed to eliminate all legal discrimination against non-marital children. It noted in *Reed* that "there is a permissible basis for some 'distinctions made in part on the basis of legitimacy'; specifically, . . . statutory provisions that have an evident and substantial relation to the State's interest in providing for the orderly and just distribution of a decedent's property at death" (*Reed*, p.855, quoting *Mathews*, p.505 and *Lalli*, p.259).

PATERNITY AND SUPPORT ACTIONS

Statutory limitations curtailing non-marital children's right to inherit from their fathers' estates seem less tolerable to the Court when they interfere with non-marital children's right to be supported by their fathers. Although the Court remains sensitive to the problems of proving paternity, it also recognizes that the likelihood of fraudulent claims has been significantly reduced by scientific advances in blood and genetic testing.

In *Gomez v. Perez* (1973), the first case to raise the issue of a non-marital child's right to paternal support, the Court's *per curiam* decision,[79] struck down §4.02 of the Texas Family Code and Articles 602 and 602–A of the Texas Penal Code. These statutes granted to marital children an enforceable right to receive support from their natural fathers while denying the same right to non-marital children. Although the Court did not offer a protracted explanation, it stated that on the basis of *Levy* and *Weber*, "a State may not invidiously discriminate against illegitimate children by denying them substantial benefits accorded children generally" (*Gomez*, p.538). While the Court recognized the problems associated with proving paternity, it asserted that those problems could not "be made into an impenetrable barrier that works to shield otherwise invidious discrimination" (*Gomez*, p.538). According to the Court, a state must provide non-marital children with a means for securing their most basic needs. The Court justified its decision on the grounds that "once a state posits a judicially enforceable right on behalf of children to needed support from their natural fathers there is no constitutionally sufficient justification for denying such an essential right to a child simply because its natural father has not married its mother" (*Gomez*, p.538).

But the Court failed to provide an explicit statement regarding the applicable level of scrutiny to statutory restrictions on a non-marital child's right to paternal support. It utilized the language of both the rational basis test and strict scrutiny in *Gomez*, asserting that state action which deprives children of their father's support solely on the basis of their birth status is "illogical and unjust" and that such deprivation constitutes "an invidious discrimination" which fails to promote a legitimate state interest. By combining the language of both the traditional rational basis and the strict scrutiny standard of review, the Court left uncertain which standard governs discrimination against the right of non-marital children to paternal support. If, in fact, the right to "needed support" is equivalent to an "essential right" as implied by the Court, then statutory obstacles created by the state may be subject to strict scrutiny. But the Court's cursory reference to *Weber* also suggests that it might prefer the dual inquiry analysis articulated in *Weber* to the standard of review used in *Levy*, subjecting the discrimination to an intermediate, as opposed to strict, scrutiny.

The standard of review remains imprecise, but the Court has firmly established that a non-marital child's right to paternal support cannot be temporally limited by the state. In *Mills v. Habluetzel* (1982), Justice Rehnquist, as spokesperson for a unanimous Court, declared Chapter 13 Title 2 §13.01 of the Texas Code[80] a violation of the Fourteenth Amendment's Equal Protection Clause. According to Justice Rehnquist, the one-year time limit imposed by the challenged statute for establishing the paternity of a non-marital child failed to meet the dual equal protection requirements the Court focused on: "First, the period for obtaining support granted by Texas to [non-marital] children must be sufficiently long in duration to present a reasonable opportunity for those with an interest in such children to assert claims on their behalf. Second, any time limitation placed on that opportunity must be substantially related to the State's interest in avoiding the litigation of stale or fraudulent claims" (*Mills*, pp.99–100). Justice Rehnquist argued that any statutory limitation that impinged on a non-marital child's right to support must be "sufficiently long to present a real threat of loss or diminution of evidence, or an increased vulnerability to fraudulent claims" (*Mills*, p.99).[81] He recognized that because of the contentiousness of the non-marital child's paternity, the opportunity provided a child born out of wedlock to obtain support need not be identical with that provided a child born in wedlock (*Mills*, p.97).

The difference in acceptable treatment accorded these two groups of children arose because (1) "traditional blood tests do not prove paternity," (2) "the proper evidentiary weight given to these techniques are still a matter of academic dispute," and (3) "more conventional types of evidence are of paramount importance" in deciding paternity cases (*Mills*, pp.98–99 fn.4).[82] Hence, Justice Rehnquist contended that the state may justifiably limit the time period within which non-marital children must press their claim for paternal support. He noted, however, that the time limitation in §13.01 denied non-marital children a reasonable opportunity to assert claims regarding paternity and obtain paternal support. Although infants are dependent upon their mothers to file the requisite claim, numerous obstacles may prohibit unwed mothers from complying with the specified time limit (*Mills*, p.100).[83] Yet despite the mother's reason for not filing the claim within the required twelve months, the consequence for her non-marital children was the same—they were "forever barred from the right to sue their natural father for child support" (*Mills*, p.100).

Justice Rehnquist stressed that while "a bona fide opportunity to obtain paternal support [did] not mean . . . that [a state] must adopt procedures for illegitimate children that [were] coterminous with those accorded legitimate children" (*Mills*, p.97), the opportunity provided must be more than illusory. In his view, the truncated time limit specified in §13.01 perpetuated an illusion—one which was not substantially related to the state's interest in avoiding the prosecution of stale or fraudulent claims. Because the Court could "conceive of no evidence essential to paternity suits which invariably [would] be lost in only one year, nor [was] it evident that the passage of [twelve] months [would] appreciably increase the likelihood of fraudulent claims" (*Mills*, p.101), the Court ruled that the one-year statute of limitation effectively weakened the non-marital child's equal protection right to paternal support—established in *Gomez* (pp.537–538).

In her concurring opinion, Justice Sandra Day O'Connor, who replaced Justice Stewart on the Court, agreed with the Court's conclusion that §13.01 of the Annotated Texas Family Code violated the Fourteenth Amendment's Equal Protection Clause. The reasons she offered, however, extended beyond the Court's. Justice O'Connor juxtaposed the state's declared interest (to prevent prosecution of stale or fraudulent claims) with the state's countervailing interest (to ensure the satisfaction of genuine child support claims) and found the latter to be weightier and more substantial. By enforcing the one-year statute of limitation, the state increased its welfare responsibilities and thereby assumed a financial burden that was contrary to its economic self-interest.

The state's designated time limit, furthermore, deprived non-marital children of their right to establish paternity or to obtain paternal financial support throughout their minority. Yet Justice O'Connor indicated that "the risk that the child will find himself without financial support from his father seems as likely throughout his minority as during the first year of his life" (*Mills*, p.106). This being the case, she questioned why paternity suits were singled out by Texas as a cause of action not tolled during a non-marital child's minority (*Mills*, p.104). She noted that the state's concern about stale or fraudulent claims was substantially alleviated because of the development in blood tests which "could provide over a 90% probability of negating a finding of paternity for erroneously accused men" (*Mills*, p.104 fn.2). Justice O'Connor observed that practical obstacles could exist that would dissuade a mother or her non-marital child from filing a paternity suit

within the legally prescribed time (*Mills*, p.105 fn.4). Finally, Justice O'Connor contended that "[a] review of the factors used in deciding that the
one-year statute of limitation cannot withstand an equal protection challenge indicates that longer periods of limitation for paternity suits also may
be unconstitutional" (*Mills*, p.106).

In *Pickett v. Brown* (1983), Justice Brennan delivered a unanimous Court
decision that substantiated Justice O'Connor's contention. This case challenged the constitutionality of a Tennessee law that mandated that the
father of an non-marital child was responsible for child support if a paternity and support action was filed within two years of the child's birth or if
the child is or was likely to become a public charge. After citing at length
Justice O'Connor's concurring opinion in *Mills*, Justice Brennan asserted
that "[m]uch of what was said in the opinion in *Mills* is relevant here, and
the principles discussed in *Mills* require us to invalidate [the] limitation
period on equal protection grounds" (*Pickett*, p.11). Thus, the Court denied
the constitutionality of §36–244(2) of the Tennessee Annotated Family
Code,[84] which imposed a two-year limitation for "the filing of petitions
which [could] lead to both the establishment of paternity and to enforcement of the father's duty of support" (*Pickett*, p.4).

The questions raised and addressed in *Pickett* were identical to those of
Mills. Using intermediate scrutiny, as it had in *Mills*, the *Pickett* Court once
again engaged in a two-pronged inquiry: was the designated time limit
sufficiently long to provide a *real* opportunity for compliance? And was the
statutory limitation substantially related to the state's interest in preventing
the prosecution of stale or fraudulent claims? In both instances, the Court
replied negatively.

Problems that might be encountered by a single mother during the first
year following her child's birth, and which might prevent her from filing a
paternity suit within the regulated time period, could well persist through
the second year (*Pickett*, pp.12–13). For this reason, the Court concluded in
Pickett that the two-year limitations period failed to grant non-marital
children an adequate opportunity to establish paternity and obtain paternal
support. Indeed, the Court suggested that any statute imposing a limitations period that expired prior to a child's eighteenth birthday might
deprive "certain [non-marital] children the equal protection of the laws
guaranteed by the Fourteenth Amendment" (*Pickett*, p.18).

In response to the second inquiry, the Court ruled that the wording of
the statutory limitation, rather than promoting the state's interest in avoiding the litigation of stale or fraudulent claims, served to undermine the
state's argument. According to the Court, the problems regarding proof of
paternity raised by the state of Tennessee were of insufficient substance to
justify a "restriction [which] effectively extinguish[ed] the support right of
[non-marital] children" (*Pickett*, p.13). As the Court noted in *Mills*, the
essential evidence in paternity suits would not be automatically lost after

a longer period; nor would the likelihood of fraudulent claims drastically increase because of the passage of time (*Mills*, p.101; *Pickett*, pp.13–14). Indeed, the state indirectly conceded this point through the exception clause contained in §36–244(2), which stated that "the department of human services or any person shall be empowered to bring a suit in behalf of any child under the age of eighteen . . . who is, or is liable to become, a public charge" (*Pickett*, p.3, fn.1). By incorporating this exception into the statute, the state differentiated among non-marital children, thereby creating two classes—those who were, or were likely to become, public charges; and those who were not, or were unlikely to become, public charges. If a child belonged to the first group, the state was willing to litigate paternity claims throughout the child's minority. If, however, a child belonged to the second group, the state was willing to litigate only those paternity claims that were commenced within two years of the child's birth.

The state neglected to explain why the evidence essential to establishing a child's paternity would be less stale or fraudulent because of the child's economic status at the time of the claim's filing. It offered no explanation to account for the seeming change in the nature of the evidence regarding paternity. Thus, the following scenario becomes theoretically possible: a non-marital child who does not receive public assistance is barred from establishing their paternity or obtaining a support order at the age of five because the state wishes to prevent the litigation of a stale or fraudulent claim. The claim loses its suspect nature, however, if the non-marital child becomes a welfare recipient several years later. Suddenly the claim would be considered less stale or vulnerable to fraud by the state. Indeed, the Court commented on the state's faulty logic, observing that "[t]here is no apparent reason why claims filed on behalf of illegitimate children who are receiving public assistance when they are more than two years old would not be just as stale, or as vulnerable to fraud, as claims filed on behalf of illegitimate children who are not public charges at the same age" (*Pickett*, p.15).

The Court concluded that the state's interest in preventing stale or potentially fraudulent paternity claims was undermined by the two-year limitation period imposed on only some non-marital children. Either all claims must be stale or vulnerable to fraud after the requisite time limit or all must be tolled during minority. For the state to hinge the justiciability of a claim seeking to establish paternity and obtain paternal support on the mother's or the child's economic status is unreasonable, unjustifiable, and unfair. Such state action, in effect, absolves the putative father of his duty to support his child and places total responsibility on the single mother to provide for her child, whether she desires to be the sole caretaker or not. A single mother who desires economic assistance from the putative father to raise their child is thus penalized because she somehow manages to support her child without the assistance of a surrogate father (i.e., the state).

In light of the technological developments in blood and genetic testing, neither women nor non-marital children should be deprived of the opportunity to establish paternity or to obtain paternal support. Justice Brennan noted that "blood tests currently can achieve a 'mean probability of exclusion [of] at least . . . 90 percent' " (*Pickett*, p.17). To substantiate his contention that scientific advances have alleviated the problems of proof surrounding paternity he relied upon the research of Michael Stroud, Teril Bundrant, and D. Leo Galindo, who stated that "[r]ecent advances in scientific techniques now enable the properly equipped laboratory to routinely provide attorneys and their clients with a 95–98 percent probability of excluding a man falsely accused of paternity" (*Pickett*, p.17. fn.16).

The Court noted its rejection in *Mills* of the argument that these scientific advances negated the state's interest regarding the litigation of stale or fraudulent claims. But, it asserted that

[i]t is not inconsistent with this view, however, to suggest that advances in blood testing render more attenuated the relationship between a statute of limitations and the State's interest in preventing the prosecution of stale or fraudulent paternity claims. This is an appropriate consideration in determining whether a period of limitations governing paternity actions brought on behalf of illegitimate children is substantially related to a legitimate state interest. (*Pickett*, pp.17–18)

While the Court never specified the length of a permissible statutory time limit, it did indicate that two years was unacceptable. Such a short time period denied non-marital children an adequate opportunity to assert their claim and was not substantially related to the voiced state interest. Consequently, the Court ruled that the two-year limitation period contained in §36–224(2) violated the Equal Protection Clause of the Fourteenth Amendment.

After *Mills* and *Pickett*, a question remained: what, if any, statute of limitations for paternity actions would survive an equal protection challenge? In the opinion of the Court, neither one nor two years was sufficiently long to overcome the problems that, as identified in both *Mills* (p.105 fn.4) and *Pickett* (pp.12–13), might prevent an unwed mother from pursuing a paternity action during the specified time limit. While the Court suggested that the optimum period might be eighteen years, it never asserted that paternity actions must be tolled during a child's minority in order to be constitutional. In *Clark v. Jeter* (1988), the Court was asked once more to determine whether a statute of limitations on paternity actions was valid. The two main issues presented to the Court were whether Congress's 1984 Child Support Enforcement Amendments were retroactive and whether a six-year statute of limitations violated the Equal Protection and Due Process clauses of the Fourteenth Amendment. According to the facts of *Jeter*, one year prior to the passage of the Child Support Enforcement Amendments of 1984—which "require all States participating in the federal child support program to have procedures to establish the paternity of any child who is less than 18 years old" (98 Stat. 1307, 42 U.S.C. §666(a)(5) (1982 ed., Supp. IV), as quoted in *Jeter*, p.459)—Cherlyn Clark filed a complaint to obtain support for her ten-year-old non-marital daughter. At the time of her initial filing, Pennsylvania had a six–year statute of limitations for paternity actions,[85] and on this basis the putative father moved to dismiss the complaint. When the trial court ruled in favor of the putative father, the unwed mother appealed to the Superior Court of Pennsylvania that the statute of limitations violated both the Due Process and the Equal Protection clauses of the Fourteenth Amendment. Before a decision was rendered on her appeal, the Pennsylvania Legislature enacted an eighteen-year statute of limitations for actions to establish paternity, thereby bringing Pennsylvania's law into compliance with the congressional statute on child support enforcement. Despite the new state law, the Superior Court "concluded . . . that Pennsylvania's new 18–year statute of limitations did not apply retroactively, and that . . . the 6–year statute of limitations was constitutional" (*Jeter*, p.459).

The U.S. Supreme Court dismissed the retroactivity issue. It stated that because the petitioner "did not adequately present a federal pre-emption argument to the lower court[,] . . . [i]t is our practice, when reviewing decisions by state courts, not to decide federal claims that were not 'pressed or passed upon' below" (*Jeter*, pp.459–460). It thus let stand the Superior Court's interpretation of the relationship between the laws in question: the federal child support act and the new Pennsylvania law were not retroactive and thus did not override the challenged Pennsylvania law which contained a six-year statute of limitations in paternity actions.

Once the Court had dispensed with the retroactivity question, it directed its attention to the equal protection issue raised in *Jeter*. Justice O'Connor, writing for a unanimous court, reiterated the principles articulated in *Mills* and *Pickett* and concluded that "it is questionable whether a State acts reasonably when it requires most paternity and support actions to be brought within six years of a [non-marital] child's birth" (*Jeter*, p.464). Although Justice O'Connor remained sensitive to the state's concerns regarding problems of establishing paternity, she observed that the state itself permitted exceptions to the six-year statute of limitations and that these exceptions "cast doubt on the State's purported interest in avoiding the litigation of stale or fraudulent claims" (*Jeter*, p.464). Moreover, the Pennsylvania Legislature's passage of a law bringing its policy into compliance with the federal Child Support Enforcement Amendments represented a tacit concession that proof problems were neither insurmountable nor overwhelming (*Jeter*, p.465).

The Court acknowledged in *Jeter* that the appropriate standard of review when evaluating the statutes of limitations applying to paternity and support actions is intermediate scrutiny, as embodied in the *Mills* framework: "any time limitation placed on the opporunity [for obtaining support] must be substantially related to the State's interest in avoiding stale or fraudulent claims" (*Jeter*, p.462, citing *Mills*, pp.99–100). The general rule thus seems to be that the only statutes that will pass constitutional muster under the Equal Protection Clause of the Fourteenth Amendment will be those which permit paternity and support actions to be initiated any time prior to a child's reaching the age of eighteen. This rule, however, is not absolute. The blanket protection offered to non-marital children was qualified by the Court, insofar as it allowed that "it is not entirely evident that [a statute of limitations that tolled before eighteen years] would necessarily be an unreasonable limitations period for child support actions involving [non-marital] children" (*Jeter*, p.464). Consequently, while the Court offers the promise that non-marital children will not suffer discrimination on the basis of birth status, at least in the area of paternity and support actions, it refuses to "carve that promise into stone" and uncompromisingly state that birth status discrimination is intolerable.

IMMIGRATION

The Court's refusal to eliminate all legal discrimination based on birth status surfaced once more in *Fiallo v. Bell* (1977). At issue was §§101(b)(1)(D) and 101(b)(2) of the Immigration and Nationality Act of 1952,[86] which excluded the relationship between non-marital children and their natural fathers—as opposed to their natural mothers—from the special preference immigration status accorded by the Act to the "child" or "parent" of a U.S. citizen or lawful permanent resident. The special preference immigration status permitted the "parents" or "children" of U.S. citizens (independent of the numerical quota, or the labor certificate requirement) and U.S. permanent residents (subject to the numerical quota, but not the labor certificate) entry into the United States. In *Fiallo*, several unwed fathers and their non-marital children challenged the constitutionality of their exclusion from the special preference status due to the children's birth status.

Justice Powell, writing for the majority, stressed that matters involving the admission of aliens into the United States were policy questions that fell outside the domain of the judiciary. Such questions were governed almost exclusively by Congress. The Court emphasized:

We are dealing here with an exercise of the Nation's sovereign power to admit or exclude foreigners in accordance with perceived national interests. . . . [L]imits and classifications as to who shall be admitted are traditional and necessary elements of legislation in this area. . . . Congress has accorded a special "preference status" to certain aliens who share relationships with citizens or permanent resident aliens. But there are widely varying relationships and degrees of kinship, and it is appropriate for Congress to consider not only the nature of these relationships but also problems of identification, administration, and the potential for fraud. . . . [I]n the inevitable process of "line drawing," Congress has determined that certain classes of aliens are more likely than others to satisfy national objectives without undue cost, and it has granted preferential status only to those classes. (*Fiallo*, p.795 fn.1)

The Court was thus extremely reluctant to subject §§101(b)(1)(D) and 101(b)(2) of the Immigration and Nationality Act of 1952 to any but the most limited judicial review.

Because the Court focused on the fact that aliens were involved in this case, it abandoned its previous rulings on birth status discrimination and readily deferred to Congress. As a result, the Court sanctioned the discrimination suffered by U.S. citizens from this statute, especially with regard to §101(b)(1)(D)—a point which Justice Marshall, joined by Justices Brennan and White in dissent, did not overlook. Justice Marshall summarized the effect of §§101(b)(1)(D) and 101(b)(2):

The definitions cover virtually all parent-child relationships except that of a biological father-illegitimate child. Thus while all American citizens are entitled to bring in their alien children without regard to either the numerical quota or the labor certification requirement, fathers are denied this privilege with respect to their [non-marital] children. Similarly, all citizens are allowed to have their parents enter without regard to the labor certification requirement, and if the citizen is over 21, also without regard to the quota. [Non-marital] children, however, are denied such preferences for their fathers. (*Fiallo*, p.803)

Justice Marshall rebuked the Court for abdicating its function to Congress—that is, for granting Congress immunity from judicial review on immigration policies when citizens' rights were involved. He declared that

it is irrelevant that aliens have no constitutional right to immigrate and that Americans have no constitutional right to compel the admission of their families. The essential fact here is that Congress did choose to extend such privileges to American citizens but then denied them to a small class of citizens. When Congress draws such lines among citizens, the Constitution requires that the decision comport with Fifth Amendment principles of equal protection and due process. The simple fact that the discrimination is set in immigration legislation cannot insulate from scrutiny the invidious abridgement of citizens' fundamental interests. (*Fiallo*, p.807)

In Justice Marshall's view, since the rights of citizens, not aliens, were infringed by §§101(b)(1) and 101(b)(2), the statute became constitutionally vulnerable. He alleged that, on the basis of most of the Court's previous opinions, the classifications found in the statute may have owed more to habit and stereotypical notions regarding the relationship of non-marital children to their respective parents than to actual analysis or reflection. Indeed, in light of the legislative history of §§101(b)(1) and 101(b)(2), this statute failed to satisfy any of the standards formerly established by the

Court. Moreover, the statute was flawed insofar as it was both overinclusive (some parent-child relationships that were granted special privileges under §§101(b)(1) and 101(b)(2) were not close) and underinclusive (some parent-child relationships not accorded preferential treatment were very close). Justice Marshall concluded that on the basis of these facts, §§101(b)(1) and 101(b)(2) should have been declared unconstitutional. He based his conclusion on the grounds that "when Congress grants a fundamental right to all but an invidiously selected class of citizens, and it is abundantly clear that such discrimination would be intolerable in any context but immigration, it is our duty to strike the legislation down" (*Fiallo*, p.816). Contrary to the Court's stance, Justice Marshall viewed immigration laws as being within the sphere of judicial scrutiny, within the scope of equal protection standards, and subject to prior Court rulings.

Immigration law ought to be constructed by the Court along the lines proposed by Justice Marshall. Even if the Court actually believed that "the power over aliens is of a political character" (*Fiallo*, p.792), the belief does not justify the denial of judicial relief from legislative abuse. The same government officials who enact domestic policy legislate international policy. The selfsame beliefs, habits, stereotypes, presumptions, and/or biases exist in the congressional membership regardless of the geographic parameters of a statute. These officials do not "disrobe their psyche" before they initiate, debate, or vote on pieces of legislation—as is apparent from the legislative history of any bill (*Fiallo*, p.811). While the Court generally refuses to uphold governmental prejudices or conjectures that ultimately discriminate against non-marital children in domestic statutes, it blinds itself to such congressional predilections contained within international statutes.

The Court's unequivocal abnegation of its responsibility to U.S. citizens and permanent resident aliens in *Fiallo* exacerbated the plight of non-marital children and their parents. By blanketing immigration law in a shroud of protective congressional exclusivity, the Court vitiated the constitutional protection of individual rights espoused in the cases analyzed above. In the single instance when the Court referred to *Trimble*, it did so in order to differentiate between international and domestic legislative distinctions regarding marital and non-marital children.[87] In effect, with this decision, the Court erected "an impenetrable barrier that works to shield otherwise invidious discrimination" (*Fiallo*, p.813) by deliberately conceding "that Congress has license to deny fundamental rights to citizens according to the most disfavored criteria simply because the Immigration and Nationality Act is involved" (*Fiallo*, p.800).

CONCLUSION

The Court has refused, steadfastly, to declare birth status a suspect classification. Moreover, its decisions regarding birth status fail to provide a precise, unambiguous standard for reviewing discriminatory legislation—indeed, the level of scrutiny applied by the Court since 1968 has been inconsistent.

While the legal status of non-marital children has improved in the past quarter century, since many legal barriers have been deemed violative of the Equal Protection Clause of the Fourteenth Amendment, the Supreme Court has never declared all birth status distinctions to be illegal. Nor has it been willing to eliminate all legal obstacles encountered by children born outside wedlock. Instead, it has ruled that legislation which denies benefits to non-marital children *solely* on the basis of birth status is unconstitutional (*Levy, Weber, Jimenez, Clark*). If, however, birth status classifications do not result in the erection of an insurmountable barrier, they can be used in conjunction with other facts for determining benefit eligibility (*Mathews, Lalli, Fiallo*).

The Court has not extended to the parents or family units of non-marital children the same level of judicial protection as it has to children born outside wedlock. According to the Court, classifications that disadvantage unwed parents or alternative family units are not necessarily classifications based on birth status (*Boles, Paraham,* and *Cahill*). Moreover, unlike children, who are frequently portrayed as individuals who are powerless to change their situation, the Court does not view parents as blameless for their own circumstances. Consequently, while the Court has expanded the constitutional protection available to non-marital children per se, it has not asserted that the government must accord equal protection under all circumstances to marital and non-marital children or their parents.

In the area of wrongful death statutes, the Court has held that while unwed mothers cannot be denied recovery for the wrongful death of their non-marital children, even if their maternity has not been established prior to their children's death, the same is not true for unwed fathers. A single father, who has failed to establish his paternity prior to the commencement of a wrongful death claim, can be prohibited by the government from recovering due to the state's interest in minimizing the risk of fraudulent claims. Since non-marital children are not the direct subjects of such legislation, the Court has refused to heighten the level of scrutiny it employs beyond mere rationality.

The same is true with regard to parental rights. The Court is willing to legitimate statutory disadvantaging of parents (*Boles, Parham*), statutory discrimination against "deviant" family units—that is, those households that lack two opposite sexed adults ceremonially married to each other (*Cahill*)—and disparate treatment of parents based on gender (*Lehr, Caban, Quilloin, Parham, Glona*). It should be noted, however, that the Court has been least restrictive of a non-marital father's rights in those instances where he has sole custody, is the primary caretaker, or has established a substantial relationship with his non-marital children. In those instances where a conflict exists between the desires of the two single parents, the Court has vacillated (*Caban, Quilloin, Lehr*).

Although the Court has asserted, for the most part, that statutes of limitations not tolled during a child's minority for paternity and support actions are violative of the Equal Protection Clause, this position is not absolute. As the Court noted in *Jeter*, it might not deem as unreasonable all statutes of limitations tolled prior to a non-marital child's eighteenth birthday. The conditions under which shorter time periods might qualify for constitutional protection has, as yet, been unspecified by the Court.

Perhaps the greatest judicial latitude for discriminatory statutes based on birth status has been granted in the area of immigration. Indeed, the Court has been extremely deferential to birth status classifications regulated by immigration law. In conceding that Congress's "power over aliens is of a political character and therefore subject only to narrow judicial review" (*Fiallo*, p. 792), the Court has validated classifications which, if enacted in the domestic realm, would clearly violate the Fourteenth Amendment's Equal Protection Clause.

The Court is also much more tolerant of statutory classifications that limit the inheritance rights of non-marital children—unless the statutory classification interferes unduly with their right to paternal support. A child who is capable of proving their paternity is considered to have proven the existence of a legal relationship between themselves and their father. However, the Court has noted that discriminatory provisions based on birth status might be deemed legitimate in those instances where the government is able to establish a substantial and evident relation between the challenged birth status provisions and its interest in providing for an orderly and just distribution of a decedent's property. The Court would also allow to stand birth status discrimination in those instances when a child's paternity is in doubt.

Overall, the Court's birth status decisions have reinforced the importance of the marital status of a child's biological parents at the time of the child's birth, the legal action taken by a child's father to acknowledge or recognize his child's paternity, the designation of non-marital family units as inferior, and the state's right to define the parameters within which women are permitted to make reproductive decisions. Through its refusal to elevate birth status to a suspect class, or to eliminate all legal discrimination based on birth status, the Court finds itself more and more entangled by the very equal protection tests it has devised to evaluate these statutory classifications. The only position consistently taken by the Court is its repeated refusal to "carve into stone" the promise it frequently extends to non-marital children and their families that legal birth status discrimination will cease.

NOTES

1. *Levy v. Louisiana* (1968); *Glona v. American Guarantee & Liability Co.* (1968); *Labine v. Vincent* (1971); *Stanley v. Illinois* (1972); *Weber v. Aetna Casualty & Surety Co.* (1972); *Richardson v. Davis* (1972); *Richardson v. Griffin* (1972); *New Jersey Welfare*

Rights Organization v. Cahill (1973); *Gomez v. Perez* (1973); *Jimenez v. Weinberger* (1974); *Beaty v. Weinberger* (1974); *Norton v. Mathews* (1975); *Mathews v. Lucas* (1976); *Fiallo v. Bell* (1977); *Quilloin v. Walcott* (1978); *Lalli v. Lalli* (1978); *Parham v. Hughes* (1979); *Caban v. Mohammed* (1979); *Califano v. Boles* (1979); *United States v. Clark* (1980); *Mills v. Habluetzel* (1982); *Pickett v. Brown* (1983); *Lehr v. Robertson* (1983); *Reed v. Campbell* (1986); *Bowen v. Gilliard* (1987); *Clark v. Jeter* (1988).

2. See Chapter 1 *supra*.

3. See Chapter 1 *supra*.

4. Although there is no explicit constitutional provision requiring that the federal government provide equal protection of the law, the Supreme Court suggested that the Fourteenth Amendment's Equal Protection Clause applied to federal action via the Fifth Amendment's Due Process Clause in *Korematsu v. United States*. This position was reiterated by the Supreme Court in *Bolling v. Sharpe* (p.499), wherein Chief Justice Earl Warren stated: "The Fifth Amendment [does] not contain an equal protection clause. [However], the concepts of equal protection and due process, both stemming from our American ideal of fairness, are not mutually exclusive. The 'equal protection of the laws' is a more explicit safeguard of prohibited unfairness than 'due process of law,' and, therefore, we do not imply that the two are always interchangeable phrases. . . . In view of our decision that the Constitution prohibits the states from maintaining racially segregated public schools, it would be unthinkable that the same Constitution would impose a lesser duty on the Federal Government."

5. *Davis; Griffin; Jimenez; Beaty; Norton; Mathews; Fiallo; Boles; Clark; Bowen.*

6. *Levy; Glona; Labine; Stanley; Weber; Gomez; Cahill; Trimble; Quilloin; Lalli; Parham; Caban; Mills; Pickett; Lehr; Campbell; Jeter.*

7. *Levy; Glona; Parham.*

8. *Stanley; Quilloin; Parham; Caban; Lehr.*

9. *Weber; Clark.*

10. *Davis; Griffin; Jimenez; Beaty; Mathews; Boles; Clark.*

11. *Labine; Trimble; Lalli; Campbell.*

12. *Gomez; Cahill; Norton; Mills; Pickett; Bowen; Jeter.*

13. *Fiallo.*

14. La. Civ. Code Ann. Article 2315 (Supp. 1967) states:

Every act whatever of man that causes damage to another obliges him by whose fault it happened to be to repair it. . . . The right to recover damages to property caused by an offense or quasi offense is a property right which, on the death of the obligee, is inherited by his legal, instituted, or irregular heirs, subject to the community rights of the surviving spouse. The right to recover all other damages caused by an offense or quasi offense, if the injured person dies, shall survive for a period of one year from the death of the deceased in favor of (1) the surviving spouse and child or children of the deceased, or either such spouse or child or children; (2) the surviving father and mother of the deceased, or either of them, if he left no spouse or child surviving; and (3) the surviving brothers or sisters of the deceased, or any of them, if he left no spouse, child, or parent surviving. The survivor in whose favor this right of action survives may also recover the damages they sustained through the wrongful death of the deceased. A right to recover damages under the provisions of this paragraph is a property right which, on the death of the survivor in whose favor the right of action survived, is inherited by his legal, instituted, or irregular heirs, whether suit has been instituted thereon by the survivors or not. . . . As used in this article, the words "child," "brother," "sister," "father," and "mother" include a child, brother, sister, father, and mother by adoption, respectively.

15. Justice Douglas notes that "the Court of Appeals affirmed, holding that 'child' in Article 2315 means 'legitimate child,' the denial to illegitimate children of 'the right of recovery' being 'based on moral and general welfare because it discourages bringing children into the world out of wedlock' " (*Levy* p.70); "Louisiana has chosen . . . to define these classes of proper plaintiffs in terms of their legal rather than their biological relation to the deceased" (*Glona*, p.79); "Children referred to in this law (the wrongful death statute) include only those who are the issue of lawful wedlock and who, being illegitimate, have been acknowledged or legitimated pursuant to methods expressly established by law" (*Glona*, p.79 fn.7, quoting *Thompson v. Vestal Lumber & Mfg. Co.*).

16. Under strict scrutiny approach, the state has the burden of establishing that the statutory classification serves a "compelling interest" which justifies a statutory classification which is drawn along lines deemed "suspect" by the Court [race or national origin] or which touches upon a fundamental right—i.e., a right that is "explicitly or implicitly guaranteed by the Constitution." See: *Loving v. Virginia* (prohibition on miscegenation); *Korematsu v. U.S.* (restrictions on Japanese-Americans' movements); *Skinner v. Oklahoma* (sterilization of criminals).

17. Under rational basis approach, the state is required to show that the statutory classification is rationally related to a conceivably "legitimate state interest." (See: *Vance v. Bradley*.)

18. The Court began its analysis in *Levy* by announcing: "Though the [equal protection] test has been variously stated, the end result is whether the line drawn is a rational one. . . . In applying the Equal Protection Clause to social and economic legislation, we give great latitude to the legislature in making classification" (*Levy*, p.71). The Court proceeded to raise the possibility that this case involves a fundamental right or suspect classification: "[W]e have been extremely sensitive when it comes to basic civil rights . . . and have not hesitated to strike down an invidious classification even though it had history and tradition on its side. . . . The rights asserted here involve the intimate, familial relationship between a child and his own mother. . . . [I]t is invidious to discriminate against them when no action, conduct, or demeanor of theirs is possibly relevant to the harm that was done the mother" (*Levy*, pp.71–72).

19. "[T]he State must base its arbitrary definition of the plaintiff class on biological rather than legal relationships. Exactly how this makes the Louisiana scheme even marginally more 'rational' is not clear" (*Glona*, p.79, Justice Harlan's dissenting opinion in *Glona* also applies to *Levy*.)

20. *Parham* Court versus *Levy/Glona* Court: Earl Warren = Warren Burger; Abe Fortas = Harry Blackmun; Hugo Black = William Rehnquist; John Harlan = Lewis Powell; William O. Douglas = John Paul Stevens.

21. Section 105–1307 (1978) of the Georgia Code provides (as quoted in *Parham*, p.348 fn.1) states: "A mother, or, if no mother, a father, may recover for the homicide of a child, minor or sui juris, unless said child shall leave a wife, husband, or child. The mother or father shall be entitled to recover the full value of the life of such child. In suits by the mother the illegitimacy of the child shall be no bar to a recovery."

22. Section 74–103 of the Georgia Code (1978) (as quoted in *Parham*, p.349 fn.2) states:

A father of an illegitimate child may render the same legitimate by petitioning the superior court of the county of his residence, setting forth name, age, and sex of such child, and also the name of the mother; and if he desires the name changed, stating the new name, and praying the legitimation of such child. Of this application the mother, if alive, shall have notice. Upon such application, presented and filed, the court may pass an order declaring said child to be legitimate, and capable of inheriting from the father in the same manner as if born in lawful wedlock, and the name by which he or she shall be known.

23. Justice Powell explicitly makes this point in *Lalli*:

That the child is the child of a particular woman is rarely difficult to prove. Proof of paternity, by contrast, is frequently difficult when the father is not part of a formal family unit. The putative father often goes his way unconscious of the birth of a child. Even if conscious, he is very often totally unconcerned because of the absence of any ties to the mother. Indeed, the mother may not know who is responsible for her pregnancy. (*Parham*, p.355 fn.7, quoting *Lalli*, pp.268–269)

24. At this point the Court attempted to distinguish this case from *Caban* by noting the difference between the two: The unwed father in *Caban* "could change neither his children's status nor his own for purposes of the New York adoption statute"; the unwed father in *Parham* could change both his and his child's status for purposes of the Georgia wrongful death statute (*Parham*, p.356 fn.9).

25. The Court ignored the question of whether §105–1307 was rationally related to the other two state interests—promoting the traditional family and setting a standard of morality—without explanation. However, it can be assumed that since the Court had discovered a rational connection between the statutory classification and at least one of the state's interests, the Court believed that the statute must be upheld.

26. Justice White argued that the sex discrimination in the wrongful death statute, which *required* unwed fathers to pursue the legitimization procedure, was not alleviated by resorting to the fact that under Georgian law only fathers *may* legitimate their non-marital children: "The plurality not only fails to examine whether required resort by fathers to the legitimation procedure bears more than a rational relationship to any state interest, but also fails to even address the constitutionality of the sex discrimination in allowing fathers but not mothers to legitimate their children. It is anomalous, at least, to assert that sex discrimination in one statute is constitutionally invisible because it is tied to sex discrimination in another statute, without subjecting *either* of these classifications on the basis of sex to an appropriate level of scrutiny" (*Parham*, pp.361–362 fn.2).

27. "Parents . . . means the father and mother of a legitimate child, or the survivor of them, or the natural mother of an illegitimate child, and includes any adoptive parents" (*Parham*, p.650, quoting the Ill. Rev. Stat., c. 37, §701–14).

28. Although an argument can be made that the Court used the rational basis test, it seems more probable that the intermediate scrutiny standard was employed in this case, given the composition of the Court and the Court's previous rulings. However, perhaps the ruling is unanimous because either standard would have produced the same result, and the Court was more concerned with the result than the method.

29. In order to gain the full import of §§74–203 and 74–403(3), it is necessary to include §§74–103, 74–403(1), and 74–403(2). These sections of the Georgia Code (as quoted in *Quilloin*, pp.248–249 fn.2–5) are as follows:

Section 74–403(1) sets forth the general rule that "no adoption shall be permitted except with the written consent of the living parents of a child." Section 74–403(2) provides that consent is not required from a parent who (1) has surrendered rights in the child to a child-placing agency or to the adoption court; (2) is found by the adoption court to have abandoned the child, or to have willfully failed for a year or longer to comply with a court-imposed support order with respect to the child; (3) has had his or her parental right terminated by court order, see Ga. Code 24A-3201; (4) is insane or otherwise incapacitated from giving consent; or (5) cannot be found after a diligent search has been made.

Section 74–403(3), which operates as an exception to the rule stated in 74–403(1) provides: Illegitimate children.—If the child be illegitimate, the consent of the mother alone shall suffice. Such consent, however, shall not be required if the mother has surrendered all of her rights to said child to a licensed child-placing agency, or to the State Department of Family and Children Services.

Sections of Ga. Code (1975) will hereinafter be referred to merely by their numbers.

Section 74–103 provides in full: A father of an illegitimate child may render the same legitimate by petitioning the superior court of the county of his residence, setting forth the name, age, and sex of such child, and also the name of the mother; and if he desires the name changed, stating the new name, and praying the legitimation of such child. Of this application the mother, if alive, shall have notice. Upon such application, presented and filed, the court may pass an order declaring said child to be legitimate, and capable of inheriting from the father in the same manner as if born in lawful wedlock, and the name by which he or she shall be known.

Section 74–203 states: The mother of an illegitimate child shall be entitled to the possession of the child, unless the father shall legitimate him as before provided. Being the only recognized parent, she may exercise all the paternal power.

In its opinion in this case, the Georgia Supreme Court indicated that the word "paternal" in the second sentence of this provision was the result of a misprint and was instead intended to read "parental."

See *Quilloin*, p.249 n.5. Ga. Code §74–403 (1933) has been recodified since the decision in *Quilloin* and replaced by Ga. Code §19–8–3 (1982)—Editors of 3(1) *Antioch Law Journal* Spring 1985.

Thus §§74–203 and 74–403(3) treated the children of an unwed father differently than the children of a married father (i.e., a father who is legally married to the children's mother) insofar as the adoption of an unwed father's children never required the father's consent, but the same was not true for a married father's who had not voluntarily surrendered his right to his children, or who had not been judged an unfit parent by the courts. In addition, though an unwed father was automatically presumed unfit by law, a married father was not.

30. At the time of the proceedings, before the Surrogate, §111, as amended by 1975 NY Laws, ch. 246 and 704 (and quoted in *Caban*, pp.385–386 fn.4) provided:

I. Subject to the limitations hereinafter set forth consent to adoption shall be required as follows:
1. Of the adoptive child, if over fourteen years of age, unless the judge or surrogate in his discretion dispenses with such consent;
2. Of the mother, whether adult or infant, of a child born out of wedlock;
4. Of any person or authorized agency having lawful custody of the adoptive child.
II. The consent shall not be required of a parent who has abandoned the child or who has surrendered the child to an authorized agency for the purpose of adoption under the provisions of the social services law or of a parent for whose child a guardian has been appointed under the provisions of section three hundred eighty-four of the social services law or who has been deprived of civil rights or who is insane or who has been judicially

declared incompetent or who is mentally retarded as defined by the mental hygiene law or who has been adjudged to be an habitual drunkard or who has been judicially deprived of the custody of the child on account of cruelty or neglect, or pursuant to a judicial finding that the child is a permanently neglected child as defined in section six hundred eleven of the family court act of the state of New York; except that notice of proposed adoption shall be given in such manner as the judge or surrogate may direct and an opportunity to be heard thereon may be afforded to a parent who has been deprived of civil rights and to a parent if the judge or surrogate so orders. Notwithstanding any other provision of law, neither the notice of a proposed adoption nor any process in such proceeding shall be required to contain the name of the person or persons seeking to adopt the child. For the purposes of this section, evidence of insubstantial and infrequent contacts by a parent with his or her child shall not, of itself, be sufficient as a matter of law to preclude a finding that such parent has abandoned such a child.

31. The provisions of §111(I)(3) encode the same traditional thinking embodied in many laws in our society. By locating in unwed mothers the authority to decide whether her child can be adopted, the New York law encoded the stereotypical attitudes regarding the proper sexual domain of individuals—men are assigned the realm of production; women, reproduction. Since a non-marital child is not valued by the dominant society, their fate remains attached to another whose value is questioned—their unwed mother.

32. This test was a form of the intermediate scrutiny standard found in *Trimble*, p.771—i.e., the Court balances the interests of the state against the interests of the individuals affected by the classification.

33. While a father may legally be required to support his child, the inadequacy of child support enforcement makes it possible for a father to in fact not pay.

34. At the time the child's adoption order was entered, N.Y. Dom. Rel. Law §§111–a(2) and (3) (McKinney, 1977 and Supp. 1982–1983, as quoted in *Lehr* pp.251–252 fn.5) provided:

2. Persons entitled to notice, pursuant to subdivision one of this section, shall include:
   (a) any person adjudicated by a court in this state to be the father of the child;
   (b) any person adjudicated by a court of another state or territory of the United States to be the father, of the child, when a certified copy of the court order has been filed with the putative father registry, pursuant to section three hundred seventy-two-c of the social services law;
   (c) any person who has timely filed an unrevoked notice of intent to claim paternity of the child, pursuant to section three hundred seventy-two of the social services law;
   (d) any person who is recorded on the child's birth certificate as the child's father;
   (e) any person who is openly living with the child and the child's mother at the time the proceeding is initiated and who is holding himself out to be the child's father;
   (f) any person who has been identified as the child's father by the mother in written, sworn statement; and
   (g) any person who has married to the child's mother within six months subsequent to the birth of the child and prior to the execution of a surrender instrument or the initiation of a proceeding pursuant to section three hundred eighty-four-b of the social services law.
3. The sole purpose of notice under this section shall be to enable the person served pursuant to subdivision two to present evidence to the court relevant to the best interests of the child.

35. At the time the child's adoption order was entered, N.Y. Soc. Serv. Law §372–c (McKinney Supp. 1982–83, as quoted in *Lehr*, pp.250–251 fn.4) provided:

1. The department shall establish a putative father registry which will record the names and addresses of . . . any person who has filed with the registry before or after the birth of a child out-of-wedlock, a notice of intent to claim paternity of the child. . . .
2. A person filing a notice of intent to claim paternity of a child . . . shall include therein his current address and shall notify the registry of any change of address pursuant to procedures prescribed by regulations of the department.
3. A person who has filed a notice of intent to claim paternity may at any time revoke a notice of intent to claim paternity previously filed therewith and, upon receipt of such notification by the registry, the revoked notice of intent to claim paternity shall be deemed a nullity nunc pro tunc.
4. An unrevoked notice of intent to claim paternity of a child may be introduced in evidence by any party, other than the person who filed such notice, in any proceeding in which such fact may be relevant.
5. The department shall, upon request, provide the names and addresses of persons listed with the registry to any court or authorized agency, and such information shall not be divulged to any other person, except upon order of a court for good cause shown.

36. Justice White stated in his dissenting opinion that

§111–a defines six categories of unwed fathers to whom notice must be given even though they have not placed their names on file pursuant to the section. Those six categories, however, do not include fathers such as Lehr who have initiated filiation proceedings, even though their identity and interest are as clearly and easily ascertainable as those fathers in the six categories. (*Lehr*, p.274)

37. The Court noted that "[a]ppellee never conceded that appellant is Jessica's biological father, but for purposes of analysis in this opinion, it is assumed that he is" (*Lehr*, p.250 fn.3).

38. Justice White, in his dissenting opinion, points out that

Lehr's version of the "facts" paints a far different picture than that portrayed by the majority. The majority's recitation that "[a]ppellant has never had any significant custodial, personal, or financial relationship with Jessica, and he did not seek to establish a legal tie until after she was two years old," . . . obviously does not tell the whole story. Appellant has never been afforded an opportunity to present his case. . . . We cannot fairly make a judgment based on the quality or substance of a relationship without a complete and developed factual record. This case requires us to assume that Lehr's allegations are true—that but for the actions of the child's mother there would have been the kind of significant relationship that the majority concedes is entitled to the full panoply of procedural due process protections. (*Lehr*, pp.270–271)

39. Justice Stevens, speaking for the Court, observed that "the legislation guarantees to certain people the right to veto an adoption and the right to prior notice of any adoption proceeding. The mother of an illegitimate child is always within that favored class, but only certain putative fathers are included" (*Lehr*, p.266).

40. See Justice Stewart's dissent in *Caban*, p.399; and Justice Steven's dissent in *Caban*, pp.404–406, wherein they explicitly discuss the biological differences between unwed mothers and fathers of newborns.

41. La. Rev. Stat. Ann. §23:1021(3) (West 1964).

42. The Court noted that the statute failed to treat posthumously born non-marital children the same as posthumously born marital children (*Weber*, p.169 fn.7).

43. The relevant provisions for acknowledgment of a child born outside wedlock (as quoted in *Weber*, p.167 fn.3) are as follows:

La. Civ. Code, Art. 202 (1967): "Illegitimate children who have been acknow-ledged by their father, are called natural children; those who have not been acknowledged by their father, or whose father and mother were incapable of contracting marriage at the time of conception, or whose father is unknown, are contradistinguished by the appellation of bastards."

La. Civ. Code, Art. 203 (1967): "The acknowledgment of an illegitimate child shall be made by a declaration executed before a notary public, in presence of two witnesses, by the father and mother of either of them, whenever it shall not have been made in the registering of the birth or baptism of such child."

La. Civ. Code, Art. 204 (1967): "Such acknowledgment shall not be made in favor of children whose parents were incapable of contracting marriage at the time of conception; however, such acknowledgment may be made if the parents should contract a legal marriage with each other."

44. Justice Powell noted that

[t]he status of illegitimacy has expressed through the ages society's condemnation of irrespon-sible liaisons beyond the bonds of marriage. But visiting this condemnation on the head of an infant is illogical and unjust. Moreover, imposing disabilities on the illegitimate child is contrary to the basic concepts of our system that legal burdens should bear some relationship to individual responsibility or wrongdoing. Obviously, no child is responsible for his birth and penalizing the illegitimate child is an ineffectual—as well as unjust—way of deterring the parent. Courts are powerless to prevent the social opprobrium suffered by these hapless children, but the Equal Protection Clause does enable us to strike down discriminatory law relating to status of birth where—as in this case—the classification is justified by no legitimate state interest, compelling or otherwise" (*Weber*, pp.175–176).

45. The Court asserts: "Nor can it be thought here that persons will shun illicit relations because the offspring may not one day reap the benefits of workmen's compensation" (*Weber*, p.173). It then concludes that "the inferior classification of dependent unacknowledged illegitimates bears, in this instance, no significant relationship to those recognized purposes of recovery which workmen's compen-sation statutes commendably serve" (*Weber*, p.174).

46. At issue in *Dandridge* was a provision of Maryland's Aid to Families with Dependent Children program that granted most families their computed "standard of need" but imposed a maximum monthly grant of $250 per family, regardless of size or computed need. While Justice Stewart, speaking for the majority, maintained that "[a] state regulation in the social and economic field, not affecting freedoms guaranteed by the Bill of Rights" (*Dandridge*, p.484) need only have a "rational basis" for its classifica-tion; Justice Marshall, in his dissenting opinion, argued that the "Court has already recognized [in *Shapiro v. Thompson* (1969) and *Goldberg v. Kelly* (1970), for example, that] when a benefit [is] necessary to sustain life, stricter constitutional standards, both procedural and substantive, are applied to the deprivation of that benefit" (Dandridge, p.522). None of the Justices discussed whether or not welfare was a fundamental right, although the question was raised in the case.

47. Discussed in the section on inheritance.

48. See Chapter 1.

49. Note: Justice Blackmun, in his concurring opinion, asserts that the fatal flaw in Los Angeles's Workmen's Compensation Statute was the acknowledgement barrier established in Art. 204. If the absolute bar were not part of the statutory structure and if workmen's compensation benefits were merely denied to those

non-marital children whose "father had the power to acknowledge his illegitimates but refrains from doing so" (*Weber*, p.177), Justice Blackmun would not have
found the statutory structure violative of the Equal Protection Clause.

50. Discussed in the section on financial assistance—federal benefits section.

51. The Chief Justice concurred in the results.

52. For example: *Levy, Glona, Parham, Stanley, Lehr, Caban*, and *Quilloin*.

53. §203(a) of the Social Security Act provides, in part (as quoted in *Griffin*, 346
F. Supp., p.1229), that

[w]henever a reduction is made under this subsection in the total of monthly benefits to which
individuals are entitled for any month on the basis of the wages and self-employment income
of an insured individual, each such benefit other than the old-age or disability insurance
benefit shall be proportionately decreased; except that if such total or benefits for such month
includes any benefit or benefits under section 402(d) of this title which are payable solely by
reason of section 416(h)(3) of this title, the reduction shall be first applied to reduce (proportionately where there is more than one benefit so payable) the benefits so payable (but not
below zero).

The requirements of §216(h)(3)(c) of the Social Security Act (as quoted in *Griffin*,
346 F. Supp., p.1228 n.2.) provide that:

[A]n applicant who is the son or daughter of a fully or currently insured individual, but who
is not (and is not deemed to be) the child of such insured individual under paragraph (2) of
this subsection, shall nevertheless be deemed to be the child of such insured individual if:

Subsections 216(h)(3)(A) and (B) applying to old age and disability benefits, respectively,
have provisions identical to those in subsection 216(h)(3)(C) except, of course, that the basis
of receipt of benefits is different.

(C) in the case of a deceased individual:
    (i) such insured individual: (I) had acknowledged in writing that the applicant is his son
    or daughter. (II) had been decreed by a court to contribute to the support of the applicant
    because the applicant was his son or daughter, and such acknowledgment, court decree,
    or court order was made before the death of such insured individual, or
    (ii) such insured individual is shown by evidence satisfactory to the Secretary to have been
    the father of the applicant, and such insured individual was living with or contributing
    to the support of the applicant at the time such insured individual died.

54. The lower court stated that "[i]n light of the Supreme Court's recent decision in *Weber v. Aetna Casualty and Surety* . . . we do not regard as controlling earlier
decisions relying on *Labine v. Vincent* . . . to hold the provision constitutional"
(*Davis*, p.593 fn.4).

55. As quoted in *Jimenez*, p.631 n.2:

The contested Social Security scheme provided, in essence, that legitimate or legitimated
children (42 U.S.C. §402(d) (3)), illegitimate children who can inherit their parent's personal
property under intestacy laws of the State of the insured's domicile (42 U.S.C. §416(h)(2)(A)),
and those children who cannot inherit only because their parents' ceremonial marriage was
invalid for nonobvious defects (42 U.S.C. §416(h)(2)(B)), are entitled to receive benefits without
any further showing of parental support. However, illegitimate children . . . who were not
living with or being supported by the applicant at the time the claimant's period of disability
began, and who do not fall into one of the foregoing categories, are not entitled to receive any
benefits (42 U.S.C. §416(h)(3)).

56. §416(h)(2)(A) (as cited in *Beaty v. Weinberger*, 478 F.2d, p.304 fn.4):

In determining whether an applicant is the child or parent of a fully or currently insured
individual for purposes of this subchapter, the Secretary shall apply such law as would be

applied in determining the devolution of intestate personal property by the courts of the State in which such insured individual is domiciled at the time such applicant files application, or, if such insured individual is dead, by the courts of the State in which he was domiciled at the time of his death, or, if such insured individual is or was not so domiciled in any State, by the courts of the District of Columbia. Applicants who according to such law would have the same status relative to taking intestate personal property as a child or parent shall be deemed such.

(B):If an applicant is a son or daughter of a fully or currently insured individual but is not (and is not deemed to be) the child of such insured individual under subparagraph (A), such applicant shall nevertheless be deemed to be the child of such insured individual and the mother or father, as the case may be, of such applicant went through a marriage ceremony resulting in a purported marriage between them which, but for a legal impediment described in the last sentence of paragraph (1)(B), would have been a valid marriage.

(3):An applicant who is the son or daughter of a fully or currently insured individual but who is not (and is not deemed to be) the child of such insured individual under paragraph (2) of this subsection, shall nevertheless be deemed to be the child of such insured individual under paragraph (2) of this subsection, shall nevertheless be deemed to be the child of such insured individual if: (C) in the case of an insured individual entitled to disability insurance benefits, or who was entitled to such benefits in the month preceding the first month for which he was entitled to old-age insurance benefits—

(i) such insured individual—

(I)   has acknowledged in writing that the applicant is his son or daughter,
(II) has been decreed by a court to be the father of the applicant, or
(III) has been ordered by a court to contribute to the support of the applicant because the applicant is his son or daughter, and such acknowledgment, court decree, or court order was made before such insured individual's most recent period of disability began; or

(ii) such insured individual is shown by evidence satisfactory to the Secretary to be the father of the applicant and was living with or contributing to the support of that applicant at the time such period of disability began.

57. §402(d)(3) (as cited in *Beaty v. Weinberger*, 478 F. 2d, p.306 fn.8) provides:

A child shall be deemed dependent upon his father or adopting father or his mother or adopting mother at the time specified in paragraph (1)(C) of this subsection unless, at such time, such individual was not living with or contributing to the support of such child and—

(A)such child is neither the legitimate nor adopted child of such individual, or
(B) such child has been adopted by some other individual.

For purposes of this paragraph, a child deemed to be a child of a fully or currently insured individual pursuant to section 416(h)(2)(B) or section 416(h)(3) of this title shall be deemed to be the legitimate child of such individual.

58. For example: *Levy, Weber, Davis, Griffin, Cahill,* and *Jimenez.*

59. This section (as quoted in *Mathews,* p.498 fn.1) defines who may apply for and be entitled to survivor's benefits:

Section 202(d)(1) of the Act, as set forth in 42 U.S.C. §402(d)(1), provides in pertinent part: Every child (as defined in section 416(e) of this title) . . . of an individual who dies a fully or currently insured individual, if such

(A)has filed application for child's insurance benefits,
(B) at the time such application was filed was unmarried and
(i) either had not attained the age of 18 or was a full-time student and had not attained the age of 22 . . . and
(C)was dependent upon such individual

(ii) if such individual has died, at the time of such death, . . .
      shall be entitled to a child's insurance benefit for each month, beginning with the first
      month after August 1950 in which such child becomes so entitled to such insurance
      benefits . . .

Section 216(e), 42 U.S.C. §416(e), includes, under the definition of child, *inter alia*, "the natural child . . . of an individual," certain legally adopted children, certain stepchildren, and certain grandchildren and stepgrandchildren.

In addition, 42 U.S.C. §§416(h)(2)(A) and (B) and §§416(h)(3)(i) and (ii) further defines a "child." For the text of these statutes, see *Mathews*, p.498 fn.1.

   60. Justice Blackmun states:

The constitutional question is not whether such a presumption is required, but whether it is permitted. Nor, in ratifying these statutory classifications, is our role to hypothesize independently on the desirability or feasibility of any possible alternative basis for presumption. These matters of practical judgement and empirical calculations are for Congress. . . . Our role is simply to determine whether Congress' assumptions are so inconsistent or insubstantial as not to be reasonably supportive of its conclusions that individualized factual inquiry in order to isolate each nondependent child in a given class of cases is unwarranted as an administrative exercise. In the end, the precise accuracy of Congress' calculations is not a matter of specialized judicial competence; and we have no basis to question them beyond the evident consistency and substantiality." (*Mathews*, pp. 515–516, Stevens, J. dissenting)

   61. This is evidenced by the Court's statement that "the Act's discrimination between individuals on the basis of their legitimacy does not 'command extraordinary protection from the majoritarian political process,' [*Rodriguez*, p.28], which our most exacting scrutiny would entail" (*Mathews*, p.506). Further elaboration on this point comes when the Court explains that: "in cases of strictest scrutiny, such approximations must be supported at least by a showing that the Government's dollar 'lost' to overincluded benefit recipients is returned by a dollar 'saved' in administrative expense avoided. . . . Under the standard of review appropriate here, however, . . . Congress is [not] required in this realm of less than strictest scrutiny to weigh the burdens of administrative inquiry solely in terms of dollars ultimately 'spent,' ignoring the relative amounts devoted to administrative rather than welfare uses" (*Mathews*, pp.509–510).

   62. Similar to *Mathews*, the issue in *Weber* involved the receipt of benefits by a wage earner's dependents. While in *Weber* the state's presumption that non-marital children are less likely to be dependent on their father than marital children was rejected by the Court, in *Mathews* it was upheld.

   63. The Court held in *Jimenez* that the statutory purpose was: "to provide support for dependents of a disabled wage earner, and . . . to prevent spurious claims" (p.634); while it held in *Mathews* that the statutory purpose was: to provide support for "children of deceased insureds who can demonstrate their 'need' in a given class of cases is unwarranted as an administrative exercise. In the end, the precise accuracy of Congress' calculations is not a matter of specialized judicial competence; and we have no basis to question them beyond the evident consistency and substantiality" (*Mathews*, pp. 515–516, Stevens, J. dissenting).

   64. The individuals denied in *Jimenez* were non-marital children born after the occurrence of a disability—in *Mathews*, non-marital children who were neither living with nor receiving support from the wage earner at the time of the insured's death. In both cases, the precluded individuals had been dependent on the insured

wage earner for support, even if they had not received it in a manner that satisfied the eligibility criteria of the challenged statute.

65. Such a distinction could exacerbate the plight of non-marital children who, due to parental poverty, receive only sporadic or insubstantial economic support from the insured wage earner.

66. Section 202(g)(1), as set forth in 42 U.S.C. §402(g)(1) (and quoted in *Boles*, p. 286 fn.5), provided:

(1) The widow and every surviving divorced mother (as defined in section 416(d) of this title) of an individual who died a fully or currently insured individual, if such widow or surviving divorced mother:

(A) is not married,

(B) is not entitled to a widow's insurance benefit,

(C) is not entitled to old-age insurance benefits, or is entitled to old-age insurance benefits each of which is less than three-fourths of the primary insurance amount of such individual,

(D) has filed application for mother's insurance benefits, or was entitled to wife's insurance benefits on the basis of the wages and self-employment income of such individual for the month preceding the month in which he died,

(E) at the time of filing such application has in her care a child or such individual entitled to a child's insurance benefits, and

(F) in the case of a surviving divorced mother—

 (i) the child referred to in subparagraph (E) is her son, daughter, or legally adopted child, and

 (ii) the benefits referred to in such subparagraph are payable on the basis of such individual's wages and self-employment income, shall (subject to subsection(s) of this section) be entitled to a mother's insurance benefit for each month, beginning with the first month after August 1950 in which she becomes so entitled to such insurance benefits and ending with the month preceding the first month in which any of the following occurs: no child of such deceased individual is entitled to a child's insurance benefit, such widow or surviving divorced mother becomes entitled to an old-age insurance benefit equal to or exceeding three-fourths of the primary insurance amount of such deceased individual, she remarries, or she dies. Entitlement of such benefits shall also end, in the case of a surviving divorced mother, with the month immediately preceding the first month in which no son, daughter, or legally adopted child of such surviving divorced mother is entitled to a child's insurance benefit on the basis of the wages and self-employment income of such deceased individual.

Section 216(d)(3), as set forth in 42 U.S.C. 416(g)(3) defined the term "surviving divorced mother":

(3) The term 'surviving divorced mother' means a woman divorced from an individual who had died, but only if (A) she is the mother of his son or daughter, (B) she legally adopted his son or daughter while she was married to him and while such son or daughter was under the age of 18, (C) he legally adopted her son or daughter while she was married to him and while such son or daughter was under the age of 18, or (D) she was married to him at the time both of them legally adopted a child under the age of 18.

67. The "9–month duration-of-relationship eligibility requirement" of the Social Security Act, which maintained that in order for a spouse of a wage earner to receive benefits, the spouse must have been married to the wage earner for at least nine months prior to the wage earner's death was challenged in *Weinberger v. Salfi*. The purpose of this requirement according to the government was to "prevent sham marriages to secure Social Security payments" (*Boles*, p.290).

68. 5 U.S.C. §8341(a)(3)(A) of the Civil Service Retirement Act (as quoted in *Clark*, p.898) provides: "All legitimate and adopted children under 18 years of age qualify for [a survivor's annuity], but stepchildren or 'recognized natural' children under 18 may recover only if they . . . received more than one-half [of their] support from and 'lived with the employee . . . in a regular parent-child relationship.' "

69. H.R. Doc. No. 402, 89th Congress, 2d Session, 41 (1966) states: "Stepchildren and natural children are eligible for benefits at present only when they have been dependent on the deceased parent and living with the parent in a regular parent-child relationship. The latter requirement should be retained; but, if it is fulfilled, the benefits should be paid as for any other child, without regard to the dependency requirement" (*Clark*, p.902).

70. According to Justice Marshall: "[t]he Government's asserted justification for the classification—that it is an administratively convenient means of identifying children who actually were deprived of support by the employee's death" (*Clark*, p.899). Justice Marshall noted a second justification offered by the state for the "lived with" phrase: "Congress intended the 'lived with' requirement to serve as a means of thwarting fraudulent claims of dependency or parentage, and to promote efficient administration by facilitating the prompt identification of eligibility annuitants" (*Clark*, p.901).

71. Justice Brennan noted that since "the present discrimination cannot stand even under the 'some rational basis' standard, I need not reach the questions whether illegitimacy is a 'suspect' classification that the State could not adopt in any circumstances without showing a compelling state interest, or whether fundamental rights are involved" (*Labine*, p.551 fn.19).

72. Section 12 of the Illinois Probate Act provides that "an illegitimate child is heir of his mother and of any maternal ancestor, and of any person from whom his mother might have inherited, if living; and the lawful issue of an illegitimate person shall represent such person and take, by descent, any estate which the parent would have taken, if living. A child who was illegitimate whose parents intermarry and who is acknowledged by the father as the father's child is legitimate" (Ill. Rev. Stat. ch. 3, §12 (1973) as cited in *Trimble*, pp.764–765). In effect, this statute allows a non-marital child to inherit through intestate succession from the mother only, while a marital child is allowed to inherit through intestate succession from both the mother and the father.

73. Indeed, the Court maintained that §12 was unable to withstand judicial scrutiny given the fact that the Illinois Supreme Court "failed to consider the possibility of a middle ground between the extremes of complete exclusion and case by case determination of paternity. For at least some significant categories of [non-marital] children of intestate men, inheritance rights can be recognized without jeopardizing the orderly settlement of estates or the dependability of titles or property passing under intestacy laws" (*Trimble*, p.771).

74. A comparison of the intermediate standard with the stricter scrutiny as characterized by the dual questions posed in *Weber* (p.107), suggests that the difference between these two approaches is one of degree. Both standards focus on a means-ends inquiry, that is, both ask whether the classification in question achieves the government's purported interest. However, the intermediate standard seems to go a step farther by investigating the means imposed by the statutory

scheme. Hence, the government must convince the Court not only of the fact that the means employed are necessary but also that the desired end cannot be realized by any other means.

75. N.Y. Est. Powers & Trusts Law §4–1.2 [McKinney 1967]. This section (as quoted in *Lalli v. Lalli* 439 U.S. at 261–261 fn.2) provides:

(a) For the purposes of this article:
   (1) An illegitimate child is the legitimate child of his mother so that he and his issue inherit from his mother and from his maternal kindred.
   (2) An illegitimate child is the legitimate child of his father so that he and his issue inherit from his father if a court of competent jurisdiction has, during the lifetime of the father, made an order of filiation declaring paternity in a proceeding instituted during the pregnancy of the mother or within two years from the birth of the child.
   (3) The existence of an agreement obligating the father to support the illegitimate child does not qualify such child or his issue to inherit from the father in the absence of an order of filiation made as prescribed by subparagraph (2).
   (4) A motion for relief from an order of filiation may be made only by the father, and such motion must be made within one year from the entry of such order.

(b) If an illegitimate child dies, his surviving spouse, issue, mother, maternal kindred and father inherit and are entitled to letters of administrations as if the decedent were legitimate, provided that the father may inherit or obtain such letters only if an order of filiation has been made in accordance with the provisions of subparagraph (2).

76. *Trimble* was distinguished from *Lalli* on two grounds: In *Trimble* the Illinois statute required both the father's acknowledgment of paternity and the intermarriage of the parents in order to permit inheritance by the child, whereas in *Lalli* the New York statute required only that the father's paternity be judicially declared prior to his death. The second difference between *Trimble* and *Lalli* was that the Illinois statute possessed a dual purpose—to encourage legitimate family relationships and to ensure the orderly distribution of intestate estates, whereas the New York statute sought only to insure an orderly disposition of property at death (See *Lalli*, pp.266–268).

77. See Chapter 1.

78. "§38 of the Texas Probate Code provided that a decedent's estate should descend to 'his children and their descendants,' but §42 prohibited an illegitimate child from inheriting from her father unless her parents have subsequently married" (*Reed*, p.52). Texas Probate Code Annotated §42 (Vernon [1956]): "For the purpose of inheritance to, through, and from an illegitimate child, such child shall be treated the same as if he were the legitimate child of his mother, so that he and his issue shall inherit from his mother and from his maternal kindred, both descendants, ascendants, and collaterals in all degrees, and they may inherit from him" (*Reed*, p.852 n.2).

79. Justices Stewart and Rehnquist dissented on the grounds that neither of the challenged statutes had been litigated in the Texas courts.

80. Chapter 13 Title 2 §13.01 states: "A suit to establish the parent-child relationship between a child who is not the legitimate child of a man and the child's natural father by proof of paternity must be brought before the child is one year old, or the suit is barred" (as quoted in *Mills*, p.94).

81. See also: *Gomez*, p.538; *Lalli*, p.269; *Parham*, pp.357, 361.

82. The Court explained in detail that it had

previously recognized that blood tests are highly probative in proving paternity, *Little v. Streater*, 452 U.S. 1, 6–8 (1981), but disagree[d] with appellant's contention that their existence negates the State's interest in avoiding the prosecution of stale or fraudulent claims. Traditional blood tests do not prove paternity. They prove nonpaternity, excluding from the class of possible fathers a high percentage of the general male population. . . . Thus, the fact that a certain male is not excluded by these tests does not prove that he is the child's natural father, only that he is a member of the limited class of possible fathers. More recent developments in the field of blood testing have sought not only to "prove nonpaternity" but also to predict paternity with a high degree of probability. . . . The proper evidentiary weight to be given to these techniques is still a matter of academic dispute. . . . Whatever evidentiary rules the courts of a particular State choose to follow, if the blood test evidence does not exclude a certain male, he must thereafter turn to more conventional forms of proof—evidence of lack of access to the mother, his own testimony, the testimony of others—to prove that, although not excluded by the blood test, he is not in fact the child's father. As to this latter form of proof, the State clearly has an interest in litigating claims while the evidence is relatively fresh.

This interest is particularly real under Texas procedures. Texas law requires that putative fathers submit to blood tests. . . . Refusal to submit to the tests may result in a citation of contempt . . . and may be introduced to the jury as evidence that the putative father has not been biologically excluded from the class of possible fathers. . . . The results of the blood tests are introduced at a pretrial conference held for the purpose of dismissing the complaint if the father has been excluded by the tests from the class of possible fathers. . . . Thus, the only paternity cases which actually go to trial in Texas are those in which the putative father has refused to submit to blood tests or has not been excluded by the results, cases in which conventional types of evidence are of paramount importance. (*Mills*, pp.99–100 fn.4)

83. As Justice O'Connor pointed out,

[t]he unwillingness of the mother to file a paternity action on behalf of her child, which could stem from her relationship with the natural father, or . . . from the emotional strain of having an illegitimate child, or even from the desire to avoid community and family disapproval, may continue years after the child is born. The problem may be exacerbated if, as often happens, the mother herself is a minor. The possibility of this unwillingness to file suit underscores that the mother's and child's interests are not congruent, and illustrates the unreasonableness of the Texas statute of limitation (*Mills*, p.105 fn.4).

84. Tennessee Code Ann. §36–224(2) (1977) reads as follows:

(2) Proceedings to establish the paternity of the child and to compel the father to furnish support and education for the child may be instituted during the pregnancy of the mother or after the birth of the child, but shall not be brought after the lapse of two (2) years from the birth of the child, unless paternity has been acknowledged by the father in writing or by the furnishing of support. Provided, however, that the department of human services or any person shall be empowered to bring a suit in behalf of any child under the age of eighteen (18) who is, or is liable to become a public charge. (*Pickett*, p.3 fn.1)

85. "Although Jeter's motion referred to §6704(e), that section had been altered slightly and relabeled §6704(b) at the time of the litigation below. See Act of Dec. 20, 1982, Bo. 326, Art. II, §201, 1982 Pa. Laws 1409. As amended, the section provided: "All actions or proceedings to establish the paternity of a child born out of wedlock brought under this section must be commenced within six years of the birth of a child, except where the reputed father shall have voluntarily contributed to the support of the child or shall have acknowledged in writing his paternity, in which case an action or proceeding may be commenced at any time within two years of any such contribution or acknowledgement by the reputed father." [42 Pa. Cons. Stat. §6704(e) (1984) (repealed 1985)] (*Clark*, p.458 n*).

86. Title 8 U.S.C. §1101(b)(1) provides:

(1) The term 'child' means an unmarried person under twenty-one years of age who is—

(A) a legitimate child; or

(B) a step-child, whether or not born out of wedlock, provided the child has not reached the age of eighteen years at the time the marriage creating the status of step-child occurred; or

(C) a child legitimated under the law of the child's residence or domicile, or under the law of the father's residence or such domicile, whether in or outside of the United States, if such legitimation takes place before the child reaches the age of eighteen years and the child is in the legal custody of the legitimating parent or parents at the time of such legitimation.

(D) an illegitimate child, by, through whom, or on whose behalf a status, privilege, or benefit is sought by virtue of the child to its natural mother;

(E) a child adopted while under the age of fourteen years if the child has thereafter been in the legal custody of, and has resided with, the adopting parent or parents for at least two years: Provided, that no natural parent of any such adopted child shall thereafter, by virtue of parentage, be accorded any right, privilege, or status under this charter.

(F) a child, under the age of fourteen at the time a petition is filed in his behalf to accord a classification as an immediate relative under section 1151(b) of this title, who is an orphan because of the death or disappearance of, abandonment or desertion by, or separation or loss from, both parents, or for whom the sole or surviving parent is incapable of providing the proper care which will be provided the child if admitted to the United States and who has in writing irrevocably released the child for emigration and adoption; who has been adopted abroad by a United States citizen and his spouse who personally saw and observed the child prior to or during the adoption proceedings; or who is coming to the United States with the preadoption requirements, if any, of the child's proposed residence: Provided, that no natural parent or prior adoptive parent of any such child shall thereafter, by virtue of such parentage, be accorded any right, privilege, or status under this chapter.

Title 8 U.S.C. §1101(b)(2) provides: "The term 'parent,' 'father,' or 'mother' means a parent, father, or mother only where the relationship exists by reason of any of the circumstances set forth in subdivision (1) of this subsection" [§§1101(b)(1) and 1101(b)(2) of the Immigration and Nationality Act of 1952 (Act), 66 Stat. 182, as amended, 8 U.S.C. §§1101(b)(1) and 1101(b)(2) as quoted in *Fiallo*, pp.802–803 fn.2–3).

87. Justice Powell observed that:

This inherent difficulty of determining the paternity of an illegitimate child is compounded when it depends upon events that may have occurred in foreign countries many years earlier. Congress may well have given substantial weight, in adopting the classification here challenged, to these problems of proof and the potential for fraudulent visa applications that would have resulted from a more generous drawing of the line. Moreover, our cases clearly indicate that legislative distinctions in the immigration area need not be as "carefully tuned to alternative considerations," *Trimble v. Gordon*, ante, at 772 [quoting *Mathews v. Lucas*, 427 U.S. 495, 513 (1976)], as those in the domestic area. (*Fiallo*, p.799 fn.8)

3

Perspective Shades Perception: Equal Protection Theory

INTRODUCTION

The Equal Protection Clause,[1] in conjunction with the enforcement section,[2] of the Fourteenth Amendment explicitly prohibits discriminatory state action. It also directly empowers Congress to correct all state failures (Harris, 1960, p.43; Redenius, p.77). It does not, however, provide a definition of the term "equal protection," nor does it delineate the exact scope of non-permissible state action. While the Supreme Court is left "to expound and interpret this amendment . . . [to say what the law is],"[3] as with any explanation or translation, perspective shades perception. Interpretation is neither static nor absolute. Although the Court's explication of the key concepts (equality, equal protection, and non-permissible state action) has been derived from several sources—the literal meaning of the words (Baer, p.20; Ely, p.11), the intent of the constitutional writers (Baer, p.21),[4] and the values/views of Court members—inevitably, their own beliefs and biases have prevailed.[5] As a result, the equal protection decisions rendered by the Court are not consistent with regard to these key concepts.[6] This lack of consistency raises several questions: What constitutes equality, equal protection, and non-permissible state action? What method does the Court employ to reach its equal protection decisions? How well do the birth status cases fit into the Court's methodology? Does the Court's method provide consistent results in the birth status cases? Is the Court's method adequate? Although all of these questions are important, the first is the most significant; the answer to it shapes the answers to the rest. While all five questions will be discussed in the body of this chapter, they will be approached in the context of the first.

Inherent in the concept of equal protection is the ideal of equality. The Fourteenth Amendment is the only segment of the U.S. Constitution which explicitly encompasses the notion of equality. Essentially, equality is a "relationship of relevant identities between two or more persons or things by reference to a standard of measure" (Western, 1982a, p.1169). Since equality, by definition, cannot exist independent of a standard or unit of measure, it is a subjective concept. "In the absence of substantive criteria indicating which people are equal for particular purposes and what constitutes equal treatment, the formal principle of equality provides no guidance for how people should be treated" (Greenawalt, p.1169). Its meaning is relative to the perspective of whoever demarcates the applicable standard. The values/vision of the definer determine what aspect is focused upon to ascertain whether two things or persons are equal. Consequently, only things or persons that can be measured by the *same* unit or standard can be deemed equal; otherwise the comparison becomes unintelligible (Wolgast, pp.37–39). For example, two horses can be judged equal because of their speed, bloodline, or strength; two knives because of their balance, edge, or design. But what unit of measure would render meaningful an equality statement about an orangutan and an oscilloscope? A nadir and a human? Quite possibly no meaningful one. Unless some relevant identical attribute is possessed by members of both groups and can be specified, these items cannot be measured by the same standard.

The examples above may seem exaggerated or extreme, yet they accurately illustrate the point made by Elizabeth Wolgast that "[t]aking any pair of things at random, [there is] no guarantee that there is an answer to the question are they equal or not?" (Wolgast, p.39). The answer is contingent upon the selected criterion of relevant identities. Yet what is evident in the aforementioned examples becomes less obvious, though no less true, when the compared categories are *presumed* to be measurable by the same standard—males and females, heterosexuals, bisexuals, and homosexuals,[7] or marital and non-marital children.

Any equality statement about these groups can be approached in one of three ways. The first approach identifies the characteristic(s) deemed relevant by the prevailing social order and then judges how well each group meets the standard. The second approach asserts that the concept of equality is "empty of content" and seeks to ground the equal protection claim substantively. The third approach maintains that equality statements place groups in "binary opposition" and thereby preclude the possibility of equality between them. While the first two approaches reinforce and legitimate existing normative standards, the third approach requires a rethinking of the existing structural framework (MacKinnon, 1987; MacKinnon, 1991; Jehlen). Significantly, the Court relies almost exclusively on the first approach in its equal protection decisions.

FIRST APPROACH: IDENTIFY RELEVANT CHARACTERISTICS

The relevant characteristic in birth status cases is either the marital status of a child's biological parents at the time of parturition or the subsequent legal action taken by the father to acknowledge/recognize his child's parentage. If the parents have acted in accordance with the societal norm that these sexual relations, which result in procreation, be confined to marriage, then certain benefits, rights, and privileges are bestowed upon the couple and their offspring; if the parents do not conform to this societal norm, then benefits, rights, and privileges can be denied to the couple and their offspring. Thus not only the parents, but also their children, bear the consequences of the couple's sexual choices and behavior. If any of the parties wants to avoid these negative consequences, they are required to demonstrate that the discriminatory practices levied against them are impermissible, or that the government's conduct is legally prohibited.

The first approach implies the assumption of a defensive stance by those who would contest the discriminatory treatment of non-marital children, voice the grievances of these children, or analyze decisions of the Court regarding the statutes challenged by non-marital children or their parents. Instead of questioning the legitimacy of the classification which differentiates between individuals on the basis of birth status,[8] they attack the reasonableness of the regulation or the legitimacy of the legislative purpose. According to Joseph Tussman and Jacobs tenBroek, in their classic article "The Equal Protection of the Laws," the challengers attempt to demonstrate that the disputed statute embodies "motives of hate, prejudice, vengeance, hostility, or favoritism, and partiality. . . . [For] when and if the proscribed motives replace a concern for the public good as the 'purpose' of the law, there is a violation of the equal protection prohibition against discriminatory legislation" (Tussman & tenBroek, pp.358–359). In addition to trying to prove the existence of these motives, the challengers argue that the classification as drawn is over- or underinclusive (Tussman and tenBroek, pp.348–351; Tribe, pp.997–999),[9] that the classification does not advance the government's articulated objective,[10] or that less-restrictive alternatives are available.[11]

Decisions of the Court that reflect this approach become a pseudo-apologia. That is, the Court neither "explains how the decisions fit into a larger social or political context" (Karst, 1984, p.498) nor explicitly states the underlying assumptions or values upon which its decisions rest (Wallach and Tenoso, p.39).[12] The juridical evidence posited by the Court appears forced or contrived, insofar as the Court is unable to demonstrate conclusively that one outcome is superior to another or that one governmental action is more acceptable than another. Because the basis of the Court's arguments remain at a subtextual level, the Court reaches inconsistent conclusions, as illustrated by its decisions in *Labine-Trimble-Lalli-Reed*, *Caban-Parham-Lehr*, *Levy-Glona-Parham*, and *Mathews-Jimenez*. The Court's refusal to pronounce birth status classifications as either always valid or always invalid stems, at least in part, from the ensnarement of the Court in the very tests and standards it formulated for the adjudication of equal protection cases.

Overall the Court has established three equal protection standards (rational basis, quasi-suspect, and suspect) and three corresponding tests (minimum scrutiny, heightened or intermediate scrutiny, and strict scrutiny) (Gunther, 1980, pp.581–591; Tribe, p.1089). Under the rational basis standard, which is employed whenever economic or social welfare regulations are challenged, the Court subjects a challanged statute to minimum or deferential scrutiny. According to the Court:

The equal protection clause of the Fourteenth Amendment does not take from the State the power to classify in the adoption of police laws, but admits of a wider scope of discretion in that regard, and avoids what is done only when it is without any reasonable basis and therefore is totally arbitrary. A classification having some reasonable basis does not offend against the clause merely because it is not made with mathematical nicety or because in practice it results in some inequality. When the classification in such a law is called in question, if any state of facts reasonably can be conceived that would sustain it, the existence of the state of facts must be assumed. One who assails the classification in such a law must carry the burden of showing that it does not rest upon any reasonable basis but is essentially arbitrary (*Lindsley*, p.78).[13]

Generally, the Court accords enormous deference to the legislatures, considering only the legislative means, not the legislative ends, for a classification. Because the Court seldom challenges the state or federal government's interpretation of the Equal Protection Clause[14] in the areas of economics or social welfare, discriminatory classifications—despite their invidious effect—tend to be upheld whenever a conceivable justification, not prohibited by the Constitution, can be offered by the government for the statutory distinctions imposed.[15] Since the Court allows legislatures to proceed "one step at a time"—that is, to address one phase of a problem as opposed to the entire problem—it seldom invalidates statutes evaluated at this level of scrutiny (*Railway Express Agency*; *Williamson*; *McGowan*). Hence, for all intents and purposes, the test is "toothless" (Tribe, p.1089).

Strict scrutiny, on the other hand, usually results in the challenged statute's being declared unconstitutional, save in those rare instances when the government can successfully demonstrate a compelling interest that is furthered by the law—that is, the legislative means selected are necessary to attain a compelling state objective. Invocation of this level of scrutiny is generally "fatal" to legislative classifications that infringe fundamental or preferred rights—those legally protected against government interference or personal freedoms catalogued in the Bill of Rights (*Memorial Hospital*; *Mosley*; *Griswold*; *Shapiro*)—or which impinge on suspect classes—that is, classes that possess "the traditional indicia of suspectness" insofar as the class is "saddled with such disabilities, or subjected to such [a] history of purposeful unequal treatment, or relegated to such a position of political powerlessness as to command extraordinary protection from the majoritarian political process" (*Carolene Products*, pp.152–153 n.4; *Loving; Brown; Korematsu*).

Since the conclusion reached by the Court when it uses either minimum or strict scrutiny is fairly predictable (Tribe, p.1089; Gunther, 1972; *Mitchell*), it becomes relatively unimportant *how* the Court applies these two standards. What becomes significant is *which* standard the Court selects. Not all cases presented to the Court, however, can be characterized accurately or adequately in terms of the rigid dichotomies embodied by the Court's application of mere rationality or strict scrutiny. This point is emphasized by Justice Thurgood Marshall's dissenting opinion in *San Antonio Independent School District v. Rodriguez*: "The Court apparently seeks to establish [that] equal protection cases fall into one of two neat categories which dictate the appropriate standard of review—strict scrutiny or mere rationality. But . . . [a] principled reading of what the Court has done reveals that it has applied a spectrum of standards in reviewing discrimination allegedly violative of the Equal Protection Clause" (*Rodriquez*, p.98).[16]

Gerald Gunther, a leading constitutional scholar, maintains that while the "spectrum of standards" referred to by Justice Marshall "may describe many of the modern decisions, . . . it is a formulation that the majority [of the Court] has refused to embrace" (Gunther, 1980, p.673). But the Court's reluctance to formally recognize the existence of a middle tier of scrutiny— which it did not clearly articulate until 1976 in *Craig v. Boren*[17]—did not prevent the Court from using it. Indeed, the Court has employed a variety of intermediate level approaches—all of which are included in the middle tier of analysis and subjected to heightened scrutiny—in its equal protection decisions.[18] Three circumstances, according to constitutional scholar Lawrence Tribe, trigger the Court's use of these approaches: when an important right is affected by a statute (*Craig; Hogan; Wengler*), when a sensitive criterion of classification is employed (*Michael M.; Levy*), or when "a rule is embedded in a setting characterized by institutional rigidity to change, so that shifting social and moral norms are less likely to be reflected in modifications of the rule" (Tribe, p.1091). As a general rule, the Court requires under heightened scrutiny that the legislative classifications must serve important governmental objectives and must be substantially related to the achievement of those objectives (*Craig*, p.197).

Essentially, when the Court utilizes an intermediate scrutiny, it attempts a means-ends inquiry. The intention of this inquiry is to balance several factors: "[the] facts and circumstances behind the law, the interests which the state claims to be protecting, and the interests of those who are disadvantaged by the classification" (*Williams v. Rhodes*, p.30). The Court then gauges its inquiry against the five techniques that characterize intermediate scrutiny:[19] (a) "assessing importance"—the objectives served by the classification are important, though not compelling; (b) "close fit"—the means used by the government to achieve its objective are substantially related to the ends; (c) "current articulation"—the Court refuses to supply an imagined or inferred rationale for a challenged statute or rejects the rationale offered by the state; (d) "limiting afterthought"—the rejection of the post-hoc rationalizations; and (e) "permitting rebuttal"—the requirement that exceptions to statutory distinctions which are over- or underinclusive be allowed by the legislators.

Through intermediate scrutiny the Court attempts to "put teeth" into the rational basis standard. Intermediate scrutiny provides the Court with a degree of flexibility when it utilizes the first approach.[20] Absent this standard, the Court's ability to adjudicate complex issues that do not fit into the Court's two-tier analysis is effectively mitigated. A prime example is the Court's analysis of statutes affecting non-marital children.[21] If the Court had faithfully adhered to its traditional two-tier equal protection standards of rational basis and suspect class, it could not strictly scrutinize classifications that discriminated on the basis of birth status. The fundamental reason is that the Court has refused consistently to include birth status as a suspect class, even though many of the briefs argued that birth status met one or all of the three indicia. By default, birth status classification would necessarily have been judged in accordance with minimum scrutiny and upheld—despite the invidious effect of the challenged classification—since the legislatures were able to justify the codified birth status classifications.

Under the quasi-suspect standard, a broad continuum of possibilities lies at the Court's disposal. Differential nuances between ostensibly similar circumstances can be accommodated by the appropriate level of review. Yet despite this advantage, state and federal legislators object to intermediate scrutiny on the grounds that the Court places itself in a position of second-guessing the legislature, promotes the creation of rights not grounded in the Constitution,[22] and oversteps the bounds of judicial procedures by usurping the legislative function.[23] Although the respective legislatures perceived the enactment of the statutory birth status distinctions contained in the challenged statutes as justified—in their view a rational difference existed between marital and non-marital children—the Court rejected this contention in seventeen cases.[24] In only eight cases[25] did the Court accept the legislative justification—that the governing reason for the disputed classification was to facilitate the interests of estate, to ensure the just allocation of benefits, or to guarantee promptness and finality.[26] Where the Court invalidated the legislative classification, Justice Burger accused it of using "the equal protection clause as a shorthand condensation of the entire Constitution" (*Stanley*, p.660). The Court was perceived as turning a deaf ear to the legislatures' rational means and requesting perfection. Each time a legislature offered less than the degree of perfection desired by the Court, its arguments were dismantled and cast aside.

The justification presented by the Court for its entrance into this sphere of adjudication was initially stated in the very first birth status case analyzed within an equal protection framework—non-marital children are 'persons' under the Fourteenth Amendment's Equal Protection Clause (*Levy*, p.70). By including non-marital children within the framework of the Fourteenth Amendment, the Court established a potential constitutional bulwark against arbitrary governmental discrimination. Moreover, it laid the legal foundation necessary for its continued participation within this field.

Other justifications cited by the Court include: (a) the history of prior discrimination suffered by non-marital children; (b) the irrational and oppressive nature of the legislative distinctions; (c) the frequent lack of a legitimate governmental interest that was served by the classification; (d) the unavailability of political power to members of this group; and (e) the inherent unfairness experienced by non-marital children when they are punished for factors outside their control (Tribe, pp.997–999). These factors are almost the same as those attached to other equal protection areas, such as race, for which the legitimacy of the Court's adjudicative function is a given. Since the Court is expected to evaluate governmental action with regard to some areas of equal protection analysis where the affected group posses these indicia, the Court seems justified in extending this heightened analysis to other similarly situated groups. A final justification requires recognition of the fact that the "vague constitutional clauses . . . appeal to the concepts they employ" (Dworkin, 1977). Hence, the Court is obligated to officially "unpack" the meaning of the Equal Protection Clause as it applies to non-marital children and to enjoin the government to abide by its interpretation.[27]

Critics, worried about the waning power of the legislature, do not favorably view what they perceive as judicial policymaking. The first line of attack focuses on the Court's expanded reading of the Fourteenth Amendment,[28] which is allegedly unsupported by historical evidence. Critics charge that enlarging the meaning of the Fourteenth Amendment beyond race exhausts the original intent of this amendment[29] and causes needless confusion. Lacking explicit constitutional language to substantiate its birth status decisions, the Court should (according to Justice Rehnquist) defer to the legislature, for some of the problems plaguing birth status statutes are beyond the range of the judicial forum (*Jimenez*).

Moreover, critics continue, since the Court is not a democratic institution in the same sense as the legislature, it should not infuse its decisions with personal or partisan values.[30] It should limit itself to recognizing established constitutional rights and evaluating the rationality of legislative classifications. Going beyond these limits requires the Court to step outside the bounds of the Constitution—which is silent with regard to the definition of "fundamental interests"—and opens the possibility of judicial exegesis emanating from sources other than the Constitution. This possibility threatens to move the Court away from the Constitution, and thus away from principled decision making. As far as the critics are concerned, since the Constitution is the highest authority to which the Court can appeal, it should provide the Court's guiding principle.

The critics additionally accuse the Court of incorporating a "free-wheel-ing discretion" with regard to its equal protection analysis insofar as the Court's determination of which tests to apply to which interests is a subjective evaluation. They cite the Court's birth status rulings as evidence of its failure to formulate a uniform rule. In four sets of cases—*Levy-Glona-Parham*, *Caban-Parham-Lehr*, *Labine-Trimble-Lalli-Reed*, and *Mathews-Jime-nez*—the Court reached opposite conclusions as to the proper rule—even though there were no discernible differences between the cases in a given set. The critics deduce from this that the Court is guilty of substituting the policy preferences of the various Court members for a reasoned, neutral judgment.

The critics are incorrect when they assert that the trouble, harm, or suffering inflicted upon non-marital children and their parents through birth status classification are beyond the judicial forum. The burdens inflicted upon non-marital children and their parents have been created by legislative and judicial decisions—as evidenced by the very definition of the term "illegitimate" in both legal and popular dictionaries (Black; *Web-ster's*). It thus seems unconscionable[31] to suggest that non-marital children and their parents should be denied judicial recourse to challenge legislative actions merely because the legislature deems the classifications rational. The judiciary has a constitutional duty to protect the rights and privileges of the citizenry and the arguments offered by the Court to explicate its entrance into the arena of birth status equal protection adjudication are noteworthy.

The critics are correct, however, in maintaining that insofar as the rulings reflect the bias of its members, the Court's decisions violate the principle of neutrality.[32] They are also correct when they charge that the Court's inconsistent decisions in the sets of paired cases cited above prove the inability of the Court to provide a uniform rule in the area of birth status cases. This inconsistency mirrors the Court's ambiguity in identifying the standard employed in its birth status decisions. Although the Court pur-ports to be applying one standard, it frequently uses the terms of another standard. A reconsideration of *Levy* and *Labine* furnishes a representative illustration.[33] Both cases appeal to the rational basis test, but the Court's rationale in each contains elements of strict scrutiny. Regardless of which standard the Court purportedly relies upon in its decisions, elements of the other standards are considered. This is evidenced in *Levy* by the Court's reminder that invidious discrimination will not be tolerated, while in *Labine* the Court notes the non-existence of insurmountable barriers. Thus, by failing to articulate clear boundaries between the various equal protection standards in its birth status decisions, the Court leaves ambiguous the appropriate standard of review for evaluating birth status classifications.

Such haziness can hardly instill enormous confidence in legislators that their birth status classifications will be upheld by the Court if challenged. Although the legislators have sought to advance between one and four objectives through their statutory classifications—to legislate proper parental conduct or uphold traditional moral standards with regard to extramarital sexual behavior, to facilitate an orderly distribution of property, to prevent the litigation of stale or fraudulent claims, or to provide a just allocation of benefits from intestate estates—the validity of the challenged classifications depend upon which purpose(s) the Court considers primary. It should be noted, however, that the majority of the Court's birth status rulings have hinged on a combination of the impact of the classification and the state's interest,[34] never on a classification's impact alone. But the combination's blend remains imprecise. Thus, certainty for the legislators is reduced to three situations that describe the Court's record to date: (a) statutory distinctions between marital and non-marital children will be tolerated by the Court in those instances where paternity *cannot* be established; (b) classifications which differentiate between married and single mothers will be permitted by the Court if they have no direct impact on non-marital children; and (c) distinctions between married and single fathers will be allowed by the Court if the single father has failed to establish a substantial relationship with his non-marital child. The legislators' inability to predict, based on the Court's previous birth status decisions, which standard of review the Court will use to evaluate future birth status classifications raises the specter of uncertainty even in these three identified situations.

The legislators, therefore, must concern themselves with the judicial philosophy of the new Justices on the Court—Justices Antonin Scalia, William Kennedy, David Souter, Clarence Thomas, and Ruth Bader Ginsburg—who were appointed after the Court decided the cases included in this study. Since more than half the Justices currently sitting on the Supreme Court have not ruled on the validity of classifications that discriminate based on birth status, their predilections regarding the traditional nuclear family and the birth of children outside wedlock, will determine the level of equal protection scrutiny to which birth status statutes will be subjected and the direction of the Court in this policy area. The legislators also need to determine whether Chief Justice Rehnquist[35] is strong enough to shape the direction of the Court under his leadership, and what stance the Rehnquist Court will take on birth status classifications. It is not possible to predict accurately the stance the Rehnquist Court will take on birth status in view of the large number of new Court appointments since this study was completed.What is known about the Chief Justice, however, is that in *Mills, Pickett, Lehr, Reed,* and *Jeter,* Justice Rehnquist shifted from denying the equal protection challenge 100 percent of the time in the cases before the Court prior to *Mills*, to upholding it 80 percent of the time in these five cases.

In the previous cases, Justice Rehnquist consistently argued that the Equal Protection Clause of the Fourteenth Amendment was primarily intended to protect Blacks from legal discrimination. On the grounds of that intent, he has maintained that the rational basis standard is the only proper level of scrutiny when equal protection challenges are raised that do not involve the issue of race. In an article entitled "The Notion of a Living Constitution," Justice Rehnquist voiced his opposition to the Court's use of the quasi-suspect standard in birth status cases. He maintained that the Court's intermediate scrutiny constitutes "an endless tinkering with legislative judgments, [and] a series of conclusions unsupported by any central guiding principles" (*Trimble*, p.777). Consequently, Justice Rehnquist has afforded the maximum level of deference to the legislative objective when evaluating statutory classifications not based on race. In his opinion, the only requirement for equal protection is "that there be some conceivable set of facts that may justify the classification involved" (*Weber*, p.183).

Any time the Court reaches beyond mere rationality and uses intermediate scrutiny to invalidate a legislative statute, it engages in judicial "meddling," which creates "a school for legislators, whereby opinions of [the] Court are written to instruct them in a better understanding of how to accomplish their ordinary legislative tasks" (*Trimble*, p.784). Yet in three of the final four cases, Justice Rehnquist supported the equal protection claim of non-marital children without an explanation. It is thus possible to do little more than speculate on the reason for his seeming change. By voting to invalidate the statute of limitations for non-marital children seeking to obtain paternal support (*Mills*, *Pickett*, and *Jeter*) and to recognize the continued validity of a precedent (*Reed*), Justice Rehnquist is doing no more than upholding the rational basis standard with a "sharper focus" that he recognized in *Michael M. v. Superior Court* (*Michael M.*, p.464). By attempting to strengthen the minimum scrutiny test, Justice Rehnquist may convince those justices who accept the middle tier of scrutiny in birth status cases to abandon it and return to a two-tiered analysis of the Equal Protection Clause in the birth status cases.

SECOND APPROACH: IDENTIFY SUBSTANTIVE RIGHTS

All equal protection cases involving non-marital children rest on an equality argument that essentially maintains that if a non-marital child can establish her/his paternity, then s/he is entitled to the same rights and privileges as those enjoyed by a marital child. The emphasis is on *legal* equality, since it was conceded by the Court in 1896 that legislation alone is incapable of overcoming social prejudices (*Plessy*, p.551). But even within the domain of legal equality there exists no guideline for judging relevant differences or similarities between or among group members. This is because "the equality formula *presupposes* anterior constitutional standards for ascertaining 'likeness' and 'unlikeness' " (Western, 1982, p.560). Thus the concept of equality is recognized as being an empty construct, according to Peter Western, devoid of any substantive content (Western, 1982, pp.578–579).

Western takes the argument even further. He asserts that

[a]s a source of entitlements, equality cannot produce substantive results unattainable under other forms of analysis, because . . . equality has no substantive content of its own. As a form of analysis, equality confuses far more than it clarifies, for at least four reasons: (1) . . . equality conceals the real nature of the substantive rights it incorporates by reference; (2) . . . equality misleadingly suggests that one person's rights vis-à-vis another's are identical in all contexts; (3) . . . equality erroneously suggests that all questions of equality are to be scrutinized under a single (or sometimes, a two-tier) standard of justification; and (4) . . . equality erroneously implies that it entails uniquely flexible remedies (Western, 1982, pp.579–580).

If Western's position is taken seriously and extended to birth status cases, then any discussion of these cases must answer his challenge to identify the substantive wrong from which non-marital children have a right to be free (Western, 1982, p.567). To date, this has not been done.[36]

Western asserts that "[s]tatements of equality (or inequality) entail comparisons of two things or persons by reference to some external criterion that specifies the relevant respect in which they are the same or different" (Western, 1982, p.554). Thus, in order to determine whether birth status discrimination affecting non-marital children is "right" or "wrong," it is first necessary to define what is "due" non-marital children under the evaluated circumstances. Only after determining which children are "like" or "unlike" those covered by a birth status classification is one capable of making an equality statement.[37]

The literature either attacks Western's arguments and/or conclusions, or it ignores the equality question and focuses on the equal protection test used by the Court in its decisions. Unfortunately, the literature does *not* consider the impact or consequences, if any, that the extension of Western's ideas might have on birth status decisions rendered by the Court. Yet this is the more interesting problem, for it suggests a method of protecting the rights of non-marital children and their parents that is not possible under the Court's current method—as delineated in the discussion of the first approach.

The Court has never explicitly grounded its equal protection decisions solely upon a classification's impact or upon the underlying rights and entitlements of non-marital children. Instead, its rulings hinge on a combination of the state's interest and the impact of the classification. Thus far the Court's birth status decisions have "failed to identify the precise sort of injury that the substance of the equal protection clause is designed to prohibit" (Western, 1982, p.567). Rather, the Court surreptitiously discusses the entitlements of non-marital children and their parents instead of addressing them in a forthright manner. The closest the Court came to extending its birth status analysis regarding the impact of statutes that punish innocent persons for the conduct of someone over whom they are powerless, for example, was in *Pyler v. Doe* (1982), wherein Justice Brennan drew an analogy between non-marital children and undocumented aliens who are minors. This analogy allowed Justice Brennan to justify using intermediate review to protect alien children who, because of their parents' conduct, are punished by the state.

The Court is aware that birth status classifications impinge on the economic well-being of not only non-marital children, but also their mothers, insofar as such classifications serve as the justification for determining welfare benefits, support obligations, and inheritance entitlements. What the Court seems less cognizant of is that the institutionalized construct of birth status detrimentally affects the human rights and interests of non-marital children and their parents: the right to be treated as a person, the right not to suffer from harm inflicted by legal stigmatization and inferior status [Wallach and Tenoso, pp.23, 26–27]; the right to make independent personal choices, the right of association, the right to create and maintain a family unit and/or lifestyle, the right of privacy, the right to life and basic human needs, the right to have burdens related to individual responsibility, and the right to full citizenship.

If the Court had identified the harm from which non-marital children and their parents have a substantive right to be free, had asserted that the aforementioned rights and entitlements provided the substantive principles against which legislative policies regarding birth status would be weighed, and had maintained that these rights constituted the anterior standard for determining whether birth status classifications should be allowed to make a constitutional difference, then the Court's equal protection rationale and/or decisions in this area of law would have been different. In the seventeen cases that invalidated the legislative classification, the Court's reasoning would have been altered, but the outcome of the cases would have remained unchanged.[38] Rather than being ambiguous regarding the relevant factors for evaluating birth status statutes, the Court would have substantiated in each case the fact that the rights possessed by persons affected by birth status distinctions exist independent of the Fourteenth Amendment's Equal Protection Clause. Conversely, in the eight cases that upheld the legislative classifications on birth status, not only would the Court's arguments have been different, but it would have reached the opposite conclusion as well.[39] Such a declaration would alleviate equivocal reasoning on the part of the Court and uncertainty on the part of the legislatures.

The implications of the second approach can be illustrated by selecting three cases—one that directly affects non-marital children and two that indirectly affect them by having an impact on their parents—and speculating on how the Court's stance would have changed had it utilized this second approach. The cases to be discussed are *Trimble* and *Labine* (inheritance), *Caban* and *Lehr* (adoption), and *Clark* and *Boles* (insurance benefits).

If the second approach had been used in *Labine*, the Court would have ruled that the child in question was entitled to inherit from her father's estate, despite the fact that, although acknowledged, she had never been officially legitimated, on the grounds that "the classification involved separates persons according to legitimate/illegitimate status and not according to ability to establish factually the parent-child relation" (Wallach and Tenoso, pp.23, 26). A judicial finding in her favor could have been rendered by the Court if it had recognized at least two substantive rights of non-marital children: to not suffer from harm inflicted by a legal stigmatization and inferior status, and to have burdens related to individual responsibility. If the Court had asserted these rights, it would have had to weigh the legislative policy challenged in *Labine* against them. By focusing on the substance of the non-marital child's rights, the Court would have recognized that the statutory unequal treatment of non-marital children caused these children a harm from which they had a substantive right to be free (Western, 1982, p.591). Thus, the judicial remedy would have been to direct the legislature to "replace the harmful classification with one that eliminates the substantive harm" (Western, 1982, p.592)—that is, the birth status classification would have to be altered by the legislature to the extent necessary to protect the non-marital children's rights to be free from legal stigmatization and inferior status and from bearing burdens unrelated to individual responsibility.

If the Court had decided *Labine* as suggested, the disputed legislative classification in *Trimble*, *Lalli*, and *Reed* might not have been drawn; or it might have been invalidated by a lower court. If these cases still had reached the Court, however, the revised version of *Labine* would have been the controlling precedent—the non-marital children would have been eligible to inherit their father's estate regardless of whether their respective fathers and mothers had ever married, or whether they had ever been formally acknowledged. The Court's official recognition of non-marital children's rights would have outweighed any legislative policy that inflicted harm or infringed upon the children's rights. The sole exception might be those instances when a child's paternity could not factually be established. Under such circumstances—which to date has not occurred, since the existence of the parent-child relation was unquestioned by the

Court in all of its birth status decisions—the state's interest in preventing spurious claims might outweigh the non-marital child's inheritance claim.

In the adoption cases of *Caban* and *Lehr*, the question arises regarding how non-marital fathers are treated vis-à-vis single mothers. Conflict between the parents arises because both are entitled to be treated as persons, to make independent personal choices, and to create and maintain a family unit and/or lifestyle. Yet even if the Court had clearly recognized these rights, it would still have had to determine whose rights were weightier. It could be argued that the mother's rights are more substantial than the father's in instances in which the child is an infant or in which the child is older and the father has failed to establish a (significant) relationship with his child. Otherwise, an unwed mother's right to be treated as a person would be seriously compromised, if not completely negated, since her decisions and choices regarding her child would amount to naught against male prerogative.[40] If, however, both parents are similarly situated with respect to their non-marital child, the weight attached to their rights would be in balance. In this situation, their position in relation to their non-marital child's adoption would be ostensibly similar to that of divorced parents— consent would have to be given by both, as articulated by the Court in *Caban*.

By using the second approach, the *Boles* Court would have acknowledged that non-marital children and their mothers are entitled to all of the rights heretofore discussed, as well as the right to life and to basic human needs. Recognition of these rights by the Court would have prohibited legislative discrimination between types of families and/or invalidated statutes that threaten, even indirectly, a non-marital child's economic well-being and/or their ability to have their basic needs met. Such a decision in *Boles* would have rendered moot the issue in *Clark*. If *Clark* were to have reached the Court despite the revised *Boles* rationale, the Court's opinion would have conformed with *Boles*.

In all of these cases, the Court would have established that non-marital children and their parents possessed substantive rights that could not be transgressed by legislative policy. This judicial position would allow non-marital children to enjoy at least the same level of protection currently offered by the Court under the first approach, without making its rationale subject to the degree of criticism levied under that approach. Through the second approach, the Court would not need to second-guess legislative judgments, and the legislatures would be clear as to the validity of birth status classifications that affected either non-marital children or their parents.

Affirmation by the Court that non-marital children and their parents possess substantive rights superseding any legislative justifications for birth status classifications may not be sufficient in and of itself. The Court might also need to avouch normative legal standards, in addition to the Fourteenth Amendment's Equal Protection Clause, corroborating the rights of non-marital children and their parents. Instruments that would provide the necessary external foundation for strengthening the Court's protection of the substantive rights of non-marital children and their parents might include the Declaration of Independence, the Ninth Amendment, and the Privileges or Immunities Clause of the Fourteenth Amendment of the U.S. Constitution, and the international law of human rights as represented by the International Bill of Rights,[41] the Charter of the United Nations,[42] the European Convention of Human Rights,[43] the American Convention on Human Rights,[44] the Helsinki Accord,[45] the Convention on the Elimination of All Forms of Discrimination Against Women,[46] the European Convention of Legal Status of Children Born Out of Wedlock, and the Study of Discrimination Against Persons Born Out of Wedlock: General Principles on Equality and Non-Discrimination in Respect of Persons Born Out of Wedlock.

Through the use of these instruments, the Court would be able to justify its judicial activism in birth status cases, since these sources provide normative standards for the preservation of existing rights and for the recognition of new rights that have no explicit textual support in the U.S. Constitution.[47] By informing the Equal Protection Clause through the external sources identified above, the Court could "provide a sound policy for protecting 'discrete and insular minorities' in relation to national power" (Christenson, p.3). Indeed, the framework provided by these instruments would "infuse ambiguous constitutional guarantees with normative content" (Park, p.1244) that "offer an alternative source of tools for arriving at principled decisions while avoiding the dangers of subjective activism" (Christenson, p.17).

By appealing to both constitutional and extra-constitutional norms to inform and strengthen its equal protection decisions, the Court would not be violating the sovereign integrity of U.S. law. It has been persuasively argued by Jordon Paust that "basic human rights are already a viable part of the constitutionally guaranteed rights of Americans" (Paust, p.243). This point is reiterated by Gordon Christenson, who asserts that "[t]he tradition of using external sources to interpret the Constitution is very strong in the United States. That tradition reflects both natural law, in which concepts such as reasonableness, experience, custom, and universal principles are used as guides to clarify constitutional ambiguities, and positivism, in which judicial activism must be grounded in text since non-textual interpretations lack legitimacy" (Christenson, p.35).

The United States is a party to the United Nations Charter, which is the first international document to promote the idea of universal human rights. Since this document is classified as a treaty and has been ratified by the U.S. Senate, the "human rights and fundamental freedoms" of all persons protected by this document should be protected by the U.S. Constitution under the Supremacy Clause (Article VI, Section 1). This is not necessarily the case, however, since it is a non-self-executing treaty—that is, it is not capable of enforcement unless Congress has passed prior implementation legislation. To discover exactly which "human rights and fundamental freedoms" might be covered under the U.N. Charter if Congress were to implement it, reference must be made to this and other United Nations documents.

In its preamble, the Charter reaffirms the United Nations' "faith in fundamental human rights, in the dignity and worth of the human person, in the equal rights of men and women and of nations large and small" (Brownlie, p.2). The United Nations commitment to the principle of equality is reiterated in Chapter I, Article 1, Clause 3, which states that the purpose of the United Nations is "[t]o achieve international cooperation in solving international problems of an economic, social, cultural, or humanitarian character, and in promoting and encouraging respect for human rights and fundamental freedoms for all" (Brownlie, p.3). Chapter 9, Article 56 ostensibly imposes an obligation on all members "to take joint and separate action in cooperation with the Organization for the achievement of the purposes set forth in Article 55."[48] Consequently, United Nations members are pledged to promote, through Chapter 9, Article 55, "universal respect for, and observation of, human rights and fundamental freedoms for all."[49]

While the Charter provisions are non-specific with regard to the rights of non-marital children and their parents, other United Nations Documents can assist in the endeavor to "unpack" the phrase "human rights and fundamental freedoms" as applied to them. These documents would include

1. *The International Bill of Rights.* Articles 1–3, 6–8, 12, 16, 20, 22, and 25 of the *Universal Declaration of Human Rights* grant non-marital children and their parents the right to non-discrimination, human dignity, life, liberty, property, recognition as persons, equality before and equal protection of the law, effective judicial remedies, privacy, association, social security, and an adequate standard of living; Articles 2(§2) and 10(§3)-12 of the *International Covenant on Economic, Social, and Cultural Rights* grant the right to non-discrimination, an adequate standard of living, and the highest possible standard of physical and mental health; and Articles 2, 6, 9–10, 14, 16–17, 22, 24, and 26 of the *International Covenant on Civil and Political Rights* grant the right to non-discrimination, life, liberty and security of person, human dignity and respect, equality before and equal protection of the law, recognition, privacy and family life, and association.

2. The *European Convention on Human Rights.* Articles 5, 8, 11–14 grant the right to liberty, respect for private and family life, association, founding a family, and effective judicial remedy.

3. The *American Convention on Human Rights.* Articles 1, 5, 7, 11, 16–19, and 24–25 grant the right to non-discrimination, physical, mental, and moral integrity, personal liberty, privacy, association, family life, a name, and protection.

4. The *Helsinki Accord*. Article VII obligates states to promote and encourage the effective exercise of civil, political, economic, social, cultural, and other rights and freedoms essential to a person's free and full development.

5. The *Convention on the Elimination of All Forms of Discrimination Against Women*. Articles 1, 12–13, and 15–16 grant the right to non-discrimination, health care, family benefits, parental rights and duties, and family planning.

6. The *European Convention of the Legal Status of Children Born Out of Wedlock*. This document grew out of the *Study of Discrimination Against Persons Born Out of Wedlock* and establishes common rules for treatment of non-marital children. In essence, the document bases maternal affiliation on the fact of birth (Article 2); and paternal affiliation on either voluntary recognition or judicial decision (Article 3); prohibits anyone from contesting a biological father's voluntary recognition of his non-marital child (Article 4); deems scientific evidence admissible in attempts to establish/disprove paternity (Article 5); recognizes equal maintenance responsibilities for both single parents (Article 6); rejects the automatic attribution of parental authority to the father when the identities of both parents have been established but allows for the transfer of parental authority in accord with international law (Article 7); grants to the parent without parental authority the right of access to the child under some circumstances (Article 8); grants non-marital children an inheritance right, equal to that of marital children, against both parents and extended families (Article 9); and allows marriage of the single parents to confer full legal status on their children (Article 10).

If the United States government's policies at either the state or federal level fail to protect the "human rights and freedoms" of non-marital children and their parents, then its policies would be in violation of the United Nations Charter and, by extension, in violation of a non-self-executing U.S. treaty. Under Article 56 of the United Nations Charter, the United States is justified and obligated to "take . . . action" against any violation; under Article 3 of the U.S. Constitution, the judicial branch is granted jurisdiction over "all cases in law and equity, arising under the Constitution, the laws of the United States and Treaties made, or which shall be made under this authority." But for the Court to consider an alleged violation of the U.N. Charter would probably require Congress to execute implementation legislation for the Charter.

This does not mean that the Court has been silent on the usage of international law. According to the U.S. Supreme Court, the appropriate sources of international law from which the law of nations may be ascertained would include: "consulting the works of jurists writing professedly on public law [not for the speculations of their authors concerning what the law ought to be, but for trustworthy evidence of what the law really is]; or by the general usage and practice of nations; or by judicial decisions recognizing and enforcing the law" (*Filartiga*, p.880). Support for the Supreme Court's choice of sources comes from the international arena in the Statute of the International Court of Justice which provides that the Court, whose function is to decide in accordance with international law such disputes as are submitted to it, shall apply (a) international conventions, whether general or particular, establishing rules expressly recognized by the contesting states; (b) international custom, as evidence of a general practice accepted as law; (c) the general principles of law recognized by civilized nations; (d) subject to the provisions of Article 59, judicial decisions and the teachings of the most highly qualified publicists of the various nations as subsidiary means for the determination of the rules of law" (*Filartiga*, p.881; *Filartiga* Memorandum, pp.6–7).

The significance of the Supreme Court's choice of international law sources stems in part from its acknowledgment that international law, rather than being frozen in time, is an ever evolving process. Thus, contemporary international laws governing a state's treatment of its own citizens are very much different from the laws existing prior to World War II. The first question that must be answered is how the Court gauges whether a treaty is in fact part of customary international law and/or the Law of Nations. Does it depend upon the number of nations willing to sign and/or ratify the document, or does it merely depend upon the various nations' implementing domestic legislation incorporating the provisions of the treaty? After this is established, it must be determined whether theory or practice takes precedence when the Court attempts to discern whether a prohibition exists according to the Law of Nations and/or customary international law.

The first question, regarding treaty ratification, is answered in Article 18 of the Vienna Convention of the Law of Treaties. This Convention states that "while the signature of a treaty on behalf of a state does not make the state a party to it, the act of signing is not devoid of legal significance. When a state has signed a treaty, it is obligated to refrain from acts that would defeat the object and purpose of the treaty until it makes its intentions clear not to become a party to it" (Blum and Steinhard, p.53). Under these circumstances, the signing states are in a very real sense both giving their assent to the contents of the treaty and obeying, or at least not violating, the treaty's provisions. If, during the interim between signing the treaty and "making its intentions clear," a state fails to refrain from prohibited acts, it would appear that the offending state would, on some level, be guilty of violating the treaty. Should this be the case, it would seem to follow that the Supreme Court (theoretically) would be justified in concluding that all of the United Nations declarations and conventions mentioned above can properly be thought of as the Law of Nations and/or as customary international law.

The Court thus possesses the potential for incorporating international law into its decisions. The practice, however, would only occur if the U.N. treaties, declarations, and conventions mentioned above were self-executing. If the Court were to consider enforcing a non-self-executing treaty, then the second question—whether theory or practice takes precedence when the Court determines what constitutes customary international law—needs to be addressed. It is not uncommon for there to exist some degree of divergence between what states say and what they actually do with regard to protecting the "human rights and fundamental freedoms" of non-marital children and their parents. Nations frequently do not honor the provisions of the treaties, declarations, and accords to which they have voluntarily assented. Enforcement of international law rests upon a nation's discretion;[50] the effectiveness of international law stems from its enforcement. Thus the actions of a nation are at least as important, if not more so, as the fictitious theory by which nations pretend to live.

It could be argued that without theory there might exist even more denial and abuse of non-marital children's and their parents' rights than currently exists. Without theory there would be no standards by which to measure a nation's performance or to prick a nation's conscience and no goal to which a nation might strive. Theory makes it possible for every nation to be evaluated, at least potentially, according to a "higher law"—a law beyond its individual formulation and narrow interests—rather than allowing each state to be "the law unto itself." In a sense, theory makes nations aware of their accountability for violations of practice.

For this reason it appears that in the long run the Court would be taking the stronger position by opting to give theory precedence over practice when deciding what constitutes customary international law. It would thus use international laws as references or guides rather than trying to enforce them through its decisions. Were the Court to prefer theory to practice in birth status cases, laws conflicting with the protection of the "human rights and fundamental freedoms" of non-marital children and their parents would be subject to strict scrutiny and quite possibly laid aside (Gunther, 1980, p.898).

By appealing to the objective authority attributed to the list of sources external to the Fourteenth Amendment's Equal Protection Clause, the Court could ground its decisions on extra-constitutional normative standards (Western, 1982; Western, 1982a; Western, 1983) and thus enhance its birth status decisions. The Court could effectively demonstrate that the substantive rights ascribed to non-marital children and their parents are among the discoverable rights contained in the U.S. Constitution and reinforced through international human rights law—that is, privacy rights, economic and property rights, family rights, and human dignity rights.[51] By grounding these rights in this manner, it becomes possible for the Court to (1) explicitly state the grounds upon which its opinion rests; (2) explain how its decisions fit into the larger social and political context and explicitly state the underlying assumptions and norms upon which its decisions rest (Karst, 1984, p.498);[52] and (3) deliver consistent, unequivocal birth status decisions. By elevating the basis for its decisions from a subtextual level, the Court would be able to avoid the problems it encounters under the first approach. It could conclusively demonstrate why one outcome is superior to another and why one governmental action is more acceptable than another.

THIRD APPROACH: IDENTIFY THE ILLUSION

Inherent in the conceptualization of equality arguments and equal protection claims under the first two approaches is the idea that non-marital children are either different from marital children or similar to them in some legally significant manner. In either case, the position of non-marital children and their parents is juxtaposed with that of marital children and their parents. While the first approach discussed above identifies the relevant characteristics for differentiating between marital and non-marital children and their respective parents, the second approach identifies the substantive rights possessed by non-marital children and their parents, which supersede legislative mandates. Consequently, in cases challenging statutes that discriminate on the basis of birth status, the focus is not on the legitimacy of the classification per se. It is on proving that the classification enacted by the legislature is flawed in a specific instance or in a particular way.

In turning from the first two approaches to the third, the nature of the discussion changes. Rather than emphasizing the establishment of similarities or differences between marital and non-marital children, the third approach focuses on whether a group experiences systematic subordination because of birth status. If enforced inferiority is at issue, as it is in birth status cases, then the offending classification must be invalidated.

The third approach questions everything—"the methods and scope of inquiry, the categories which structure how questions are framed, and the rules which both legitimize sources of information and govern modes of interpretation" (Wishik, p.68). It focuses on the underlying issues (such as domination, disadvantage, and disempowerment) which are at the crux of birth status distinctions. It requires that the unacknowledged power relations, which exist within society and are institutionalized through legislative policies, be acknowledged. It insists upon identification of the legal deprivation imposed, the persons legally deprived, the persons legally benefited, and the reasons that the legal distinction exists.[53] Ultimately, the third approach demands a rethinking of accepted norms, conferred privileges, and inflicted injuries in order to make explicit the social and judicial valuations and their reason(s) for existing.

The third approach identifies the illusion perpetuated by the existing legal system in the area of birth status classifications: that the legislative differences created between non-marital and marital children are neutral and objective. In fact, birth status classifications are neither. They are a legislative point of view that is mistaken for reality and serves specific interests: to guarantee that the heir apparent is the heir entitled, to protect private property, and to promote the traditional family. In order to accomplish these objectives, the legislators impose legal restrictions designed to perpetuate patriarchal society by controlling the sexual behavior of women.

The third approach goes beyond merely alleviating the burdens imposed on non-marital children. It also entails a broadening of the inquiry to investigate the "genderization of the world" (Scales, p.1382), which is prior to (and the foundation for) birth status discrimination. It "requires an investigation which must delve as deeply as circumstances demand into whether the challenged policy or practice exploits gender status" (Scales, p.1397).[54] In the case of birth classifications, such gender exploitation does indeed exist, as evidenced by the assumptions inherent in such classifications. At the root of birth status distinctions are the skewed power dynamics between men and women in favor of the former (and between Blacks and whites in favor of the latter). These distinctions draw upon the stereotypic social definitions of gender that subordinate women to men: "A central feature of the classical definition of femininity unquestionably is the quality of being pleasing to men. But femininity of the traditional kind means more than that; it also means submissiveness, dependence, and domesticity. These features of the construct of woman reinforce a system of control by men over the sexuality and maternity of women . . . [through] the law" (Karst, 1984, pp.456–457).

Through legislative policy and judicial decisions, women have been consistently deprived of reproductive choices[55] and have been assigned a disproportionate amount of the burden for offending the sexual mores of society. The censure inflicted upon single mothers, and by extension on their children, through legal decree reflects the social fact that a sexual double standard still exists (despite the denial of such since the "sexual revolution" of the 1960s). It also embodies the biological fact that an unwed father never exhibits physical traits that distinguish him from other males; his anonymity is assured unless he or someone else establishes his paternity. Further, this censure mirrors the legal fact that a child must be assigned a male parent in order to be eligible for those benefits and privileges restricted by paternity and birth status and the economic fact that an unwed mother has a greater potential than an unwed father to become a financial burden to the government.

Lawmakers enact policies that represent the ideology of the social order. Differentiation between marital and non-marital children simplify the question of property rights and reinforce the institutionalized structures of marriage and the traditional family (Davis, 1939). Hence, the family protection argument has shaped a large percentage of the legislative debates in the area of birth status classifications. At the heart of these arguments is the concept of consent by the male to accept the legal obligations associated with fatherhood.[56] Marriage is considered indicative of such consent and is the socially preferred method of legitimation. By relying upon marriage and the traditional family, society in general and the legislature in particular reflect theories that are inconsiderate of or insensitive to persons affected by birth status designations. The rhetoric that substantiates institutionalized biases against non-marital children and their parents breaks down into an argument of morality, administrative convenience, and/or the prevention of spurious and stale claims.

The legislature's search for the votes necessary to gain passage of a birth status discrimination bill causes it to overlook the potential impact of the statutes on persons who are not white, not middle class, and/or do not ascribe to the customs or standards of the dominant social culture (Gans).[57] In 1978 approximately "1 in 7 persons born in the United States was born out of wedlock" (Levithan & Belous, p.64); in 1983, about 1 in 5 such births occurred (*New York Times*, October 26, 1981, and December 5, 1982). The number of non-marital children continues to grow.[58] When the problems associated with non-marital children and their parents are brought to the attention of the legislature, the final result is a policy mirroring the values and mores of society's dominant segment. Their concerns are the ones reflected in both the legislative and judicial records—as reflected in the Louisiana Attorney General's brief in *Levy* wherein it was maintained that "Deviation in sexual behavior is costly to society. Illegitimacy, a by-product of sexual deviation, constitutes one of society's dilemmas; the welfare of the illegitimate is balanced against the desire of society to promote marriage as the preferable status for producing offspring" (*Levy*: Brief of Attorney General, p.9).

Regardless of the policy's guise, its primary function is to promote the official status quo.[59] Maintenance of the status quo, however, necessitates discrimination against non-marital children and their parents. While the validity of the discriminatory form has been the object of intense Supreme Court debate for more than twenty-five years, the Court still has not invalidated all distinctions on the basis of birth status.[60] Yet application of the third approach would necessitate such an invalidation.

If, at any point, the Court had utilized the third approach—and in effect elevated birth status classifications to a suspect class—in the adjudication of birth status cases, the rationale offered by the Court in support of its decisions would have been different. Regardless of which case became the Court's starting point for applying the third approach, the problems in need of analysis and the focus of its juridical sight would have been the same in each case insofar as the underlying issues at the crux of birth status distinctions would have become part of the inquiry. For example, if the third approach had been used by the Court in *Levy*, the Court not only would have established that enforced inferiority on the basis of birth status was unconstitutional, it also would have addressed the covert issues inherent in that case—race, class, and sex discrimination.

By disarming the objective reality and challenging the ruling ideology of the lawmakers, the third approach would reveal, as it challenged, the legal basis for the domination, disadvantage, and disempowerment of one group by another on the basis of race, class, or sex. As one variant of feminist jurisprudence, the third approach "brings law back to its purpose—to decide the crux of the matter in real human situations" (Scales, p.1387).

CONCLUSION

The possibility that the Court will use the second approach—appeal to international law to inform its interpretation of the Equal Protection Clause of the Fourteenth Amendment—or the third approach—transform its decisions through a feminist critique of the norms, privileges, and injuries which the legal system embodies—is slim. Several reasons can account for the Court's reluctance to change its juridical analysis. On a practical level, no attorney has ever presented a birth status argument to the Court using either the second or the third approach. But even if an attorney were bold enough to present such an argument, using either of the alternative approaches, Chief Justice Rehnquist has consistently maintained that judicial deference to legislative policy is the preferred course of action and that the rational basis test is the appropriate standard of review for equal protection challenges of birth status classifications. Moreover, conservative or moderate jurists have replaced most of the liberal justices on the Court. Finally, the legacy of the Reagan-Bush administrations has been an upsurge of right-wing activists who are firm believers in the sanctity of the traditional family.[61]

It seems the Court will continue to use the first approach in its birth status decisions, will continue to uphold discrimination against alternative family units, and may even reevaluate the rights currently enjoyed by non-marital children and their parents—a course that would *not* be possible under either the second or the third approach. While Justice Rehnquist's position reversal in the last four birth status cases is probably not a prelude to a judicial shift in attitude regarding birth status classifications, the question still remains: can the Court be convinced to alter its approach to birth status cases and heed the needs and rights of non-marital children and their parents? The search for an answer requires an analysis of the theoretical underpinnings of the respective approaches—liberalism (first approach), international law (second approach), and feminist jurisprudence (third approach).

NOTES

1. "No State shall . . . deny to any person within its jurisdiction the equal protection of the laws."

2. "The Congress shall have the power to enforce, by appropriate legislation, the provisions of this article."

3. "It is emphatically the province and duty of the judicial department to say what the law is. Those who apply the rule to particular cases, must of necessity expound and interpret that rule. If two rules conflict with each other, the courts must decide on the operation of each" (*Marbury* (1803) as cited in Gunther, 1980, p.10).

4. See also: Harris (1982); Murphy (1978).

5. See: Kairys; Tushnet (1979); Holt; Cole (1985); Kelman (1984).

6. It is argued that the Court's position on birth status discrimination is unclear because the Court is "inconsistent," "confusing," "wavering," and "unsettled" (See: Guerin; Gunther (1980), ch. 10, sec. 3; Isaacson; Note (1979); Weidner).

7. See: Baer, p.21; *Doe*; Richards; Wilkinson & White.

8. Exception: Wallach & Tenoso.

9. See: *Railway Express Agency*; *Jimenez*.

10. For example: *Reed*.

11. For example: *Trimble*.

12. See: *Weber*.

13. See also *Dandridge*, pp.546, 549 (1970), wherein the Court states: "So long as its judgments are rational, and not invidious, the legislature's efforts to tackle the problems of the poor and the needy are not subject to a constitutional straitjacket . . . [I]t is not irrational for the State to believe that the young are more adaptable than the sick and elderly . . . Whether or not one agrees with this state determination, there is nothing in the Constitution that forbids it."

14. Exception: *Morey*, overruled; *Dukes*.

15. *Schweiker* (1982); *Schweiker* (1981); *USR.R. Retirement Board*; *Dukes*; *Jefferson*; *Dandridge*; *McGowen*.

16. Justice Marshall makes this same argument in his dissenting opinion in *Dandridge*, pp.520–521: "This case simply defies easy characterization in terms of one or the other of these [equal protection] 'tests.' . . . Rather, concentration must be placed upon the character of the classification in question, the relative importance to individuals in the class discriminated against of the governmental benefits that they do not receive, and the asserted state interests in support of the classification."

17. *Craig*, p.197: "To withstand constitutional challenge, . . . classifications by gender must serve important governmental objectives and must be substantially related to achievement of those objectives." See also Justice Powell's concurrance in *Craig*, pp.210–211 n.*: "candor compels the recognition that the relatively deferential 'rational basis' standard of review normally applied takes on a sharper focus when we address a gender-based classification."

18. See, for example, the Court's decisions in the area of gender, alienage, and birth status. For articulation of some of the intermediate levels of scrutiny, see: Spece.

19. These five techniques of intermediate review are catalogued by Tribe at pp.1082–1089; *Kramer*, quoting *Williams*, p.30.

20. The concept of flexibility appears to be entailed in the fundamental rights and interests standard also, especially if the critics are correct in their claims that this standard is open-ended and dynamic and allows the Court to pick and choose

which interests are fundamental for purposes of contriving new principles. See: Gunther, 1972; *Katzenbach* (Justice Harlan's dissent); *Webster* (Justice Rehnquist's dissent); Weschler (1959); Karst (1969).

21. *Levy v. Louisiana* (1968); *Glona v. American Guarantee & Liability Co.* (1968); *Labine v. Vincent* (1971); *Stanley v. Illinois* (1972); *Weber v. Aetna Casualty & Surety Co.* (1972); *Richardson v. Davis* (1972); *Richardson v. Griffin* (1972); *New Jersey Welfare Rights Organization v. Cahill* (1973); *Gomez v. Perez* (1973); *Jimenez v. Weinberger* (1974); *Beaty v. Weinberger* (1974); *Norton v. Mathews* (1977); *Quilloin v. Walcott* (1978); *Lalli v. Lalli* (1978); *Parham v. Hughes* (1979); *Caban v. Mohammed* (1979); *Califano v. Boles* (1979); *United States v. Clark* (1980); *Mills v. Habluetzel* (1982); *Pickett v. Brown* (1983); *Lehr v. Robertson* (1983); *Reed v. Campbell* (1986); *Bowen v. Gilliard* (1987); *Clark v. Jeter* (1988).

22. While the Ninth Amendment of the Constitution grounds all fundamental rights, neither it nor any other section of the Constitution defines "fundamental rights," differentiates between fundamental and other types of rights—the right to property or the right to work, for example—or provides guidance for determining what rights are fundamental. Hence, whether a right is classified as fundamental is neither value free nor guaranteed.

23. See: Vieira (1979); Touchy, (1967); *Eakin* (Justice Gibson's dissent). Counter-arguments: rights *are* grounded in the language of the ninth and fourteenth amendments; what of people who are *not* protected because of society's preju-dices/blindness; laws are not benign, laws support the status quo and can be oppressive in order to do this. As Baer has noted, "individual rights do not get protected by majorities or by elected representatives. For them to have any mean-ing at all, a separate branch, neither accountable nor responsible in a direct manner is needed" (Baer, p.282).

24. *Levy; Glona; Stanley; Weber; Davis; Griffin; Cahill; Gomez; Jimenez; Beaty; Caban; Clark; Mills; Pickett; Reed; Bowen; Jeter.*

25. *Labine; Mathews; Fiallo; Quilloin; Lalli; Parham; Boles; Lehr.*

26. Exception: *Reed.*

27. See: Van Loan.

28. See: Berger; *Weber; Trimble* (Justice Rehnquist's dissent in *both* cases).

29. This contention is consistently made by Justice Rehnquist in almost all of the birth status cases.

30. See: Weschler, 1972, pp.42–45; Weschler (1965); Weschsler (1959); Baum; Wright; *Weber* (Justice Rehnquist's dissent); *Griswold* (Justice Black dissenting).

31. Individuals in the legislature also believed, with varying degrees of inten-sity, that slavery was justifiable—see: Bell, Jr.; Franklin; Finkelman. To concede that those judges, jurists, or scholars who thought slavery was justified were merely the products of their socio-political-historical times, and to allow that on other issues these individuals demonstrated that they possessed a conscience, does not negate their responsibility for the consequences of their actions or their beliefs.

32. See: Kairys; Tushnet (1979); Holt; Cole; Kelman; MacKinnon (1987, 1991).

33. See chapter 2 for a complete discussion of these cases.

34. *Caban; Parham; Lalli; Mathews.* For a similar analysis see: Isaacson.

35. Justice Rehnquist replaced Justice Burger as Chief Justice of the U.S. Su-preme Court in 1981.

36. But cf. Wallach and Tenoso; however, this article does not respond to Western's argument.

37. See: Western (1982); Western (1982a); Western (1983).

38. For example: the Court would still have invalidated the New Jersey statute in *Cahill*, which limited financial assistance to traditional families. However, it would have recognized that the statute at issue did not discriminate solely against non-marital children but in fact also discriminated against non-marital family units. The Court's justification for invalidating the statute would have been based on the principles that the challenged birth status classification violated the right of individuals to privacy, to create and maintain a family unit or lifestyle, and to make personal choices. By relying on these principles, the Court would have articulated an anterior standard capable of providing "a general policy statement about the permissibility or impermissibility of the classification or interest itself necessary to ensure predictability and uniformity of results" (Wallach and Tenoso, pp.23, 59n.172).

39. For example: instead of upholding the birth status classifications in *Mathews*—which, according to the Court, had as its purpose the financial protection of children financially dependent on the wage earner at his death and the prevention of spurious claims—the Court, if it had identified the substantive rights of non-marital children, would have overturned the classification on the grounds that it inflicted burdens on innocent persons who bore no responsibility for their social or legal status at birth.

40. See Chapter 2.

41. The International Bill of Human Rights is composed of (1) The Universal Declaration of Human Rights, adopted by the United Nations General Assembly on December 10, 1948; this document did not require ratification, as all members belonging to the United Nations have explicitly or implicitly accepted it; (2) The International Covenant on Economic, Social, and Cultural Rights, draft accepted by the United Nations on December 16, 1966; entered into force on February 3, 1976. Although the United States has signed this covenant, it has not yet ratified it; and (3) The International Covenant on Civil and Political Rights, draft accepted by the United Nations on December 16, 1966; entered into force on March 23, 1976; the United States has signed this covenant but not yet ratified it.

42. Ratified by the United States on August 8, 1945; entered into force on October 24, 1945.

43. Signed on November 4, 1950; entered into force on September 3, 1953; the United States did not sign this document.

44. Also known as the Pact of San José; entered into force on July 18, 1978; the United States has signed this document but has yet to ratify it.

45. The official name of this document is the Final Act of the Conference on Security and Co-Operation in Europe. This agreement was declared ineligible for registration under Article 102 of the United Nations Charter; that is, it was not accorded the status of an international treaty. The United States is a party to this agreement. See: Dowrick, p.197; Williams (1981).

46. This document entered into force on September 3, 1981. It is the outgrowth of the Declaration for the Elimination of All Forms of Discrimination Against Women [A/6716 (1967)], which was unanimously adopted by the United Nations General Assembly on November 7, 1967 in Resolution 2263 (XXII). The declara-

tion, a resolution of the General Assembly, is a comprehensive instrument and is binding on state parties. However, the United States has not signed this document and is not, therefore, legally bound by it.

47. For in-depth discussion of the applicability of human rights law to the Fourteenth Amendment see: Christenson; Park.

48. Brownlie, p.14. Although not specifically mentioning non-marital children and their parents, Chapter 10, Article 62, Clauses 1–2 provides that the Economic Security Council "may make recommendations for the purposes of promoting for, and observation of, human rights and fundamental freedoms for all" (Brownlie, p.19).

49. Brownlie, p.14. Objectives of the trusteeship system, as stated in Chapter 12, Article 76, Clause (c) are identical to those stated in Article 55.

50. The world's governments are reluctant "to establish a completely independent human rights organ, divorced from any semblance of governmental control, possessing independent powers in its own right, and with guarantees that its decisions will be accepted and complied with by governments" (Mower, p.108). The resistance of the world's governments to the creation of such an organ is evident in the implementation process of the various human rights documents and conventions emanating from the United Nations. All of the international instruments concerned, either directly or indirectly, with the rights of non-marital children and their parents are devoid of strong enforcement provisions. See for example: UN Charter, Articles 13–14, and 55–56; Universal Declaration of Human Rights, Preamble; Economic, Social, and Cultural Rights, Articles 2, 16, and 23; Civil and Political Rights, Articles 40–42; International Court of Justice, Article 59; Discrimination Against Women, Article 18—the potential strength of Article 20 is negated by Article 29(2) as well as by Article 59 of the International Court of Justice; American Declaration, Article 33; and Helsinki, section ii. The European Convention on the Legal Status of Children Born Out of Wedlock does not contain information on how this document is to be enforced, except insofar as it notes in Article 1: "Each Contracting Party undertakes to ensure the conformity of its laws with the provisions of this Convention and to notify the Secretary General of the Council of Europe of the measures taken for that purpose."

The only action allowable under the United Nations documents and conventions mentioned in the text of this work is the issuance of general recommendations—based on information and reports furnished by the state parties. Consequently, the "measures of implementation are wholly dependant upon [voluntary] state cooperation" (McDougal). While the state parties may be obligated by the provisions of a specific document or convention to *consider* the proposed recommendations, they are not *legally* bound to implement them (Galley, p.287). The degree to which specific governments in the world comply with, or agree to be bound by, the human rights standards contained in the U.N. documents and conventions is ultimately connected to its perceptions of self-interest: "the absence of any *real* enforcement prospect makes it feasible to give lip service to human rights, [even though actual compliance with the international instruments is not intended]; . . . the *theoretical* possibility of enforcement inhibits certain governments from regarding human rights as binding rules of international law [even though their governments technically comply with the proposed principles]" (Falk, p.33).

51. See: Kelsey; Corwin; Rogge; Call; Bertelsman; Kutner; Moore; Koral.

52. See also: *Weber*, and Wallach and Tenoso.

53. See: Baer; Wishik, p.68; Karst (1984), p.498; MacKinnon (1987); MacKinnon (1991); Scales. Although these scholars focus primarily on sex discrimination, their model applies equally as well to birth status discrimination.

54. Passage of the ERA would have produced this result if and only if the attitudes, preconceptions, and perceptions of the law makers and the judiciary were to be transformed.

55. Poor and uneducated women bear a disproportionate amount of the burden imposed by the deprivation of reproductive choices, since the availability of contraception and abortion is severely limited by socioeconomic conditions. The restriction of federal funds for abortions by the Hyde Amendments, which permitted only a very narrow range of exceptions—cases in which the pregnancy threatened the mother's life or were the result of rape or incest that had been "promptly reported"—was upheld by the Supreme Court in *Harris* on the grounds that "[the state] placed no obstacles—absolute or otherwise—in the pregnant woman's path to abortion. . . . By making childbirth a more attractive alternative, the state may have influenced a woman's decision, but it has imposed no restriction on access to abortion not already there. Although government may not place obstacles in the path of a woman's exercise of her freedom of choice, it need not remove those not of its creation. . . The financial constraints that restrict an indigent woman's ability to enjoy the full range of constitutionally protected freedom of choice are the product not of government restrictions on access to abortions, but rather of her indigency" (*Harris*, p.316). The Court reached this decision despite past state policies that have created the economic conditions that constrain poor women's choices and present state policies that exacerbate or perpetuate the economic conditions that restrict poor women's choices. Gender, race, and class inequalities also create, exacerbate, or perpetuate restrictions on the reproductive choices of women who carry their pregnancies to term—either from personal choice, coercion, or some other reason. According to Elizabeth Fox-Genovese, "the hard truth is that our society is not prepared to provide adequately for children, and those who oppose abortion are, in general, the least in favor of expanding social and family services" (Fox-Genovese p.81).

56. Although single fathers are legally required to support their offspring in many states, such laws are difficult to enforce and thus non-marital fathers frequently fail, in fact, to support their children. Although the federal government has attempted to guarantee state collection of child support payments, problems still persist with enforcement. See: Ginger; Casey.

57. It should be noted that this same argument could quite possibly be true for most, if not all, statutes.

58. Approximately 4,179,000 live births occurred in the United States in 1990, of which 1,094,200 (26.1 percent) were outside marriage (U.S. Department of Commerce, 1991, p. 64, 69). This is a 6.7 percent increase from 1982 when "approximately 3,681,000 live births occurred . . . [with] about 715,200 (or 19.4%) of these children [born outside marriage]. The overall percentage of non-marital children has risen dramatically since 1960 when only 5.3% of children were born outside wedlock. By 1970, the percentage had risen to 10.7% and by 1975, to 14.2%" (U.S. Dept. of Commerce (1985), as cited in Wheller, p.722 fn.84).

59. Despite the fact that the majority of families do not replicate the traditional nuclear family, it is still considered to be the norm in this society. The Supreme Court and the legal briefs filed in the birth status cases, by deemphasizing the validity of alternative family units, perpetuate the stigma against and inferior legal status accorded to non-traditional families. In addition, even in birth status cases purporting to examine the rights of non-marital parents, the Court uses as its standard the traditional, nuclear family in reaching its final decision. See also: Ehrenzweig.

60. The Supreme Court noted in *Reed* that "there is a permissible basis for some 'distinctions made in part on the basis of legitimacy'; specifically, . . . statutory provisions that have an evident and substantial relation to the State's interest in providing for the orderly and just distribution of a decedent's property at death" (*Reed*, p.855; *Mathews*, p.505; *Lalli*, p.259). The Court also erected "an impenetrable barrier that works to shield otherwise invidious discrimination" (*Fiallo*, p.813) by deliberately conceding that "Congress has license to deny fundamental rights to citizens according to the most disfavored criteria simply because the Immigration and Nationality Act is involved" (*Fiallo*, p.800).

61. This was evidenced most clearly during the Republican National Convention in 1992. Other examples include the 1992 Colorado and Oregon campaigns for Amendment 2 and Measure 9 in these respective states.

4

In the Best of All Possible Worlds . . .

INTRODUCTION

In the twenty-five cases analyzed in this study, the Supreme Court has acknowledged that the prejudice and stigma associated with birth status originated in society's attempts to preserve the traditional family, discourage promiscuity, prevent spurious claims, and ensure the orderly distribution of intestate property. The Court has maintained that despite long-held social attitudes, children should not be held responsible for the actions of their parents. Consequently, the legal rights of non-marital children have slowly expanded.

To date, the Court has eliminated most birth status discrimination. It has not, however, provided total relief for these children, nor has it adequately protected the rights of single parents or non-marital family units.[1] Through a case-by-case analysis, the authors have traced the development of the Court's rulings, examined its pattern of using the various equal protection tests, and evaluated the consistency of the Court's position. We have concluded that the tests utilized by the Court to reach its birth status decisions have been neither consistent nor clear. The Court's reluctance to declare birth status a suspect category, we have argued, deprives non-marital children and single parents of life, liberty, and property. If the Court is to properly protect the Fourteenth Amendment Equal Protection rights of non-marital children, single parents, and alternative family units, it must alter its approach to birth status cases and focus on the needs and rights of all persons affected by birth status classifications.

We have suggested that those affected by birth status classification might obtain relief and protection through the utilization of feminist jurisprudence and international normative standards. The methodology of feminist jurisprudence might well allow the Court to address the underlying issues at the crux of birth status distinctions. International normative standards, with their unambiguous recognition of human rights, could provide an extra-constitutional basis to inform the Court's interpretation of the Equal Protection Clause. By basing its birth status decisions on both feminist jurisprudence and international normative standards, the Court might be able to better protect the substantive rights of non-marital children and their parents.

In light of the above observations and arguments, the primary question remains: how might the Court be convinced to alter its approach to birth status cases and fully protect the needs and rights of non-marital children and their parents? Secondary questions derived from this first one include: What theories might challenge and restructure the Supreme Court's birth status decisions? What would an altered Supreme Court position look like, and what would be its foundation? What changes, reforms, and/or reshaping of the Court's consciousness would be necessary, and how might they be brought about?

Speculative answers to these questions would require, at a minimum, consideration of three major theories—liberal legal theory, critical legal studies, and feminist jurisprudence—which might provide the necessary theoretical foundation for an alteration of the Supreme Court's decision-making process. Because the ideas on human rights as they apply to non-marital children in two United Nations documents might make a contribution to any such speculations—but as presently stated do not, since they are encased in highly traditional approaches to gender differences and family forms—we will review them first.

INTERNATIONAL NORMATIVE STANDARDS

Normative standards expressed by the United Nations provide a statement by the international community of conditions deemed desirable for every person. The United Nations has proposed and produced many documents on human rights, two of which—*The Study of Discrimination Against Persons Born Out of Wedlock* (Saario) and *European Convention on the Legal Status of Children Born Out of Wedlock* (Council of Europe)—focus specifically on the rights of non-marital children. The goals of *The Study of Discrimination* were to be global, factual, and objective, to point out general legislative trends and developments, to educate world opinion, and to make recommendations for action (Saario, p.182). Because these documents are bound by the historical, economic, social, and political development of the countries to which its framers belong, they are limited by the blinders of the traditions, customs, and cultures of several nations.

The normative standards as written would protect the rights of non-marital children; however, they fail to adequately protect single mothers and alternative family units. While the U.N. standards provide a grounding for substantive human rights norms, they still reflect the priorities of patriarchal values. In *The Study of Discrimination Against Persons Born Out of Wedlock*, for example, Vieno Saario asserts that

the child has a fundamental right to have a father and to enjoy status in relation to him. . . .

The information gathered in this study reveals that sometimes the approval of the mother is necessary in order for the acknowledgment made by the father to be effective. This requirement constitutes an infringement upon the right of the child to have his paternal filiation established. Because this right should not be denied, the approval of the mother should never constitute a prerequisite to the acknowledgment by the father. . . .

[T]he duty to disclose the identity of the father to the competent authorities should be imposed upon all persons having such knowledge as well as direct knowledge of the pregnancy or birth (Saario, p.76).

This standard implicitly advances the idea that regardless of the circumstances surrounding a single woman's pregnancy or her wishes, a single father is entitled to establish a relationship with his child. An unmarried woman who desires to establish a family unit without interference from the biological father is thwarted by the granting of legal parenthood status on the male parent when his identity is known. This document essentially repackages the theory of "father-right." Nancy Erickson aptly pointed out that "[f]or a man, by virtue of an accidental pregnancy, to get parental rights over the objection of the pregnant woman in effect means that a woman who accidentally gets pregnant is deemed married to the source of the sperm for purposes of decisions regarding the child" (Erickson, p.455).

Saario's study affirms the legitimacy of fatherhood, whereby the power and privileges of fathers are extended beyond marriage. The document seeks to abolish fatherless families—not the legal concept of "illegitimacy," insofar as it makes clear that "some differences exist will have to remain and may not be improved upon" because of the parents' marital status (Saario, p.19)—since men are still assumed intrinsic to the family unit. By focusing on the father-child relationship, the study concentrates on the rights of unwed fathers without addressing the ways in which the establishment of "equal rights" with the single mother may be discriminatory. By assuming an apolitical perspective, the document leaves several notions unchallenged, including "the concept of the family as a natural and fundamental group unit in society" (Saario, p.18), the assumption that men are essential to a family unit, and the inherent differences that exist between the social concepts of "motherhood" and "fatherhood."

LIBERAL LEGAL THEORY

The central tenets of liberal legal theory, neutrality and objectivity,[2] are embodied in the very definition of justice. These tenets have served as the foundation for every birth status decision rendered by the Supreme Court. The Court routinely employed these concepts to reinforce the legitimacy of the judiciary and to perpetuate the dominant normative standards. The ancient Aristotelian concept of formal equality—that similarly situated individuals are to be treated similarly—was translated in liberal legal theory as entitlements of the individual. The weight and authority of centuries legitimated utilization of this theory and made it possible to dismiss the collective interests and identities of groups in favor of the individual.

Some people have challenged the existing system: a small minority of scholars and lawyers, with power and voice within our society, who believe that the perspectives and experiences of marginalized individuals and groups require consideration. They have made inroads into the dominant realm at the intellectual and scholarly level by demonstrating that behind objectivity and neutrality lurk myths and ideological constructs. What has been considered "normal," "natural," "factual," "apolitical," and "value-neutral," they persuasively argue, is actually a reflection of the beliefs and interests of the powerful. Contemporary critics have exposed the myth of legal reasoning, demonstrating how the judiciary perpetuates the notion that law is above or separate from politics. By relying on an idealized model, the judiciary is able to deny or ignore the social and political content of the law. The judicial myth, according to David Kairys, supposes that with regard to its decision-making process,

(1) the law on a particular issue is preexisting, clear, predictable, and available to anyone with reasonable legal skills; (2) the facts relevant to disposition of a case are ascertained by objective hearings and evidentiary rules that reasonably ensure that the truth will emerge; (3) the result in a particular case is determined by a rather routine application of the law to the facts; and (4) except for the occasional bad judge, any reasonably competent and fair judge will reach the "correct" decision. (Kairys, pp.1–2).

Precisely this mode of judicial decision making, which underlies almost every judicial decision, made it possible for the Supreme Court to deprive non-marital children of legally recognized personhood until 1968, and enables the Court to deny single parents and alternative family units adequate protection under the Fourteenth Amendment even today. Indeed, the Court and the legal briefs discuss and justify every birth status decision in terms of whether it adhered to or deviated from the liberal model. The gender, class, or race of the person affected by the birth status classification was considered in some of the amicus briefs, but seldom was there a discussion of the values, politics, culture, class, gender, race, or social perceptions of the justices rendering the decisions. While open articulation of these elements makes neither the justices nor their decisions necessarily more egalitarian, it might shed light on the political apsects of legal reasoning. Only in critical legal studies and feminist jurisprudence are these factors integral and essential to the theories themselves.

CRITICAL LEGAL STUDIES

Roberto Unger, in his book *Knowledge and Politics*, articulated the Critical Legal Studies thesis that "no coherent theory of adjudication is possible within liberal political thought" (1976, pp. 12, 98). Proponents of Critical Legal Studies understand and acknowledge that law is neither neutral, ahistorical, nor independent of societal power relationships. Consequently, Critical Legal Studies demonstrate "the inability of doctrinal analysis to produce results which are independent of prior predilections of the judges or academics doing that analysis" (Tushnet, 1984, p.239).

Analysis of the relationship between theory and practice, between law and politics, is central to the concept of Critical Legal Studies. As Alan Freeman asserts, in order to fully grasp the relativistic transitory nature of legal doctrine, it becomes imperative that "[o]ne . . . step outside the liberal paradigm into a realm where truth may be experimental, where knowledge resides in world views that are themselves situated in history, where power and ideas do not exist separately" (1981, p.1237).

When critical legal theorists consider the concept of equality, for example, they might automatically assume that as a product of historical development, it is incapable of transcending the time, space, or perceptions of its conceivers. These theorists might maintain that the inherent weakness of Aristotelian formal equality is self-evident. As noted in Chapter 3, whether two things are similarly situated requires a predetermination regarding the standard against which the things are to be measured—a predetermination which is extrinsic to, rather than inherent in, the equality concept. In a manner similar to statements of procedural equality, statements regarding formal equality tend to ignore or dismiss the actual inequality between competing parties. They gloss over differences judged irrelevant by the decision makers who determine what characteristics "count" for purposes of measurement.

No critical legal scholar has yet considered the issue of birth status classifications. If any such theorists were to undertake an analysis of this issue, they would necessarily attempt to "trash" the rulings of the Supreme Court. The statement made by Alan Freeman in his article "Truth and Mystification in Legal Scholarship" and cited below allows us to speculate that through the process of trashing or negative critique of the Supreme Court opinions, critical theorists might well seek to demonstrate that the

legal reasoning of the Court is ultimately indeterminate, irrational, inco-
herent, unpredictable, subjective, and ideological.[3] As Freeman points out,
"[t]he point of delegitimation [a fancier term for trashing] is to expose
possibilities more truly expressing reality, possibilities of fashioning a
future that might at least partially realize a substantive notion of justice
instead of the abstract rights, traditional bourgeois notions of justice that
generate so much of the contradictory scholarship" (pp.1230–1231).

Following this line of thought, the birth status decisions rendered by the
Supreme Court could be explained if and only if birth status cases were
placed in historical, social, and political contexts. This manner of contextu-
alization would require recognition of Kairys's claim that "the law and the
state [are not] neutral, value-free arbiters, independent of and unaffected
by social and economic relations, political forces, and cultural phenomena"
(Kairys, p.4). It would also necessitate acknowledging that the Court's
members are influenced by their social, political, economic, cultural, and
life experiences—factors that do not evaporate merely because the justices
don black robes.

In an alternative visioning of the world, a critical inquiry into birth status
cases would focus on the substance and social significance of the Court's
decisions. The inquiry would then note the degree of institutional violence,
in the form of social control and enforcement, perpetuated by the Court's
various decisions. Finally, a determination would be made regarding the
extent to which the Court's decisions maintained and legitimated the status
quo.

Ideally, Critical Legal Studies demand that law be studied as part of the
sociopolitical institution, as opposed to being analyzed within the existing
social structures that reflect the values and interests of the ruling class. It
thus seeks to expose the contradictions and incoherence of liberal legal
theory (Unger, 1986, pp.12–13), to develop a social policy that would enable
individuals to reach beyond exploitative hierarchical institutions (Note,
1982, p.1681 n.80), and to create a transformative legal vision (Unger, 1983a,
p.561; Unger, 1986, pp. 19, 22, 25).

Although a common objective and similar themes are woven into Critical Legal Studies works, the approaches espoused by various theorists to
achieve their goal are widely dissimilar (Unger, 1986, pp.121–122; Gordon,
pp. 281, 290–291; Kelman, 1987). Critical Legal Studies theorists and prac-
titioners are committed to "radical legal scholarship" (Kennedy, 1981,
p.1275) and "transformative activity" (Unger, 1986, p.109), insofar as they
agree that law is a product of politics and offer a critique of the liberal legal
system. But they disagree on methodology. According to Duncan Kennedy
and Karl Klare, the reason for this difference, is that "C[ritical] L[egal]
S[tudies] scholarship has been influenced by a variety of currents in contemporary radical social theory, but does not reflect any agreed upon set of
political tenets or methodological approaches" (Kennedy and Klare, p.461).

J. Stuart Russell (pp.4–5), for example, has identified three primary schools of philosophy within Critical Legal Studies: the Frankfurt School of Marxist Criticisms, whose membership includes Jugen Habermas and Theodor Adorno, as well as a faction that encompasses Kennedy and Mark Kelman; "Orthodox" or "Scientific" Marxism, whose membership includes Mark Tushnet, Robert Gordon, Karl Klare, and some constituents of the National Lawyers Guild; and the Law and Social Science Perspective, whose affiliation includes members of the Law and Society Association. It should be noted, however, that these schools are not mutually exclusive and that many scholars, such as Richard Parker, William Simon, Katherine Stone, and Roberto Unger, do not fit neatly into any of them.

Unger is the only critical legal theorist who has provided a detailed theoretical model of a liberal society transformed. His writings, in the opinion of Hugh Collins, "provide the only credible basis for the [Critical Legal Studies] Movement's critique of the ruling ideas of contemporary legal systems" (p.388). Cornell West maintains that Unger is "often considered a guru to C[ritical] L[egal] S[tudies]" (p.757); and Robin West refers to Unger as "premiere spokesperson for the communitarian left" (West, p.2). Primary emphasis here will be placed on his ideas, rather than on the diverse and multifarious nature of Critical Legal Studies.

Unger maintains that the ideal society would consist of small organic groups "established . . . by an initially distinct set of common experiences and shared purposes" (Unger, 1986, p.279), whose decisions and behavior would be guided by "the communion of ends" (Unger, 1986, p.262). His ideal society would ultimately eliminate hierarchical orderings and concentrate on equality of condition, power, and participation (Unger, 1986, p.26). As Unger conceptualizes the reconstruction of society, all direct personal connections would be made free from constrictive divisions or hierarchies; opportunities and experiences currently available to only some individuals would be available to all; and neither social, class, nor gender contrasts would be fixed or preassigned (Unger, 1986, pp.23, 26). Every individual would be allowed to develop their talents and capacities, since such development embodies the essence of the "theory of the self" (Unger, 1986, p.239).

This theory has at its core "the idea that the good consists in the manifestation and development of individual and universal human nature" (Unger, 1986, p.239). Thus Unger's communitarian perspective necessitates that any tension between group and individual rights, needs, and relations must be balanced (Unger, 1986, pp.279–280). This social ideal would give rise to an empowered democracy wherein economic distribution would follow the socialist maxim ("from each according to ability, to each according to need"), and decisions would follow democratic principles (Unger, 1986, pp.267–274).

In the society Unger envisions, rights and freedoms of individuals would be guaranteed by both governing units—the organic groups and the state. On the one hand, the organic group would legally protect the right of individuals to freely join or leave any community, express their opinions on communal goals, and choose the character of their work (Unger, 1986, p.279). The state, on the other hand, would establish peace among the organic groups, oversee the protection of individual rights, and imitate the relationship of the individual and the group with regard to the state and the groups (Unger, 1986, pp.282–283).

In the United States this utopian vision could be realized through "the law and doctrine of destabilization rights" (Unger, 1986, p.52). As Unger explains, "[t]he central idea of the system of destabilization rights is to provide a claim upon governmental power obliging government to disrupt those forms of division and hierarchy that, contrary to the spirit of the constitution, manage to achieve stability only by distancing themselves from the transformative conflicts that might disturb them" (Unger, 1986, p.53). The system of destabilization rights would require a commitment to transformative activity. At a minimum, this would entail disruption of "the tacit connection between the currently available set of institutional alternatives and any underlying scheme of practical or moral imperatives" (Unger, 1986, p.109); engagement in revolutionary reform by replacing "the elements of a formative institutional or imaginative structure piecemeal rather than all at once" (Unger, 1986, p.110); implementation of "the devices for reproducing society [as] the tools of social disruption" (Unger, 1986, p.111); and discovery of "ways to override the contrast between the politics of personal relations and the politics of the large-scale institutional structure" (Unger, 1986, p.116).

The realization of Unger's transformed society would offer much to those persons or groups currently dominated and oppressed. But it would not explicitly offer protection to all members of a familial unit. For instance, Unger deems the family the prime example of the ideal private community (Unger, 1986, p.65), "a structure of power, ennobled by sentiment" (Unger, 1986, pp.65–66). Unger fails, however, to analyze or challenge the underlying male dominance in the family structure:

The nineteenth-century bourgeois family or its diluted successor constitutes a certain structure of power. Like all structures of power, it calls upon its members to accept the legitimacy of gross inequalities in the distribution of trust. In the most pristine versions, the husband had to be allowed wide powers of supervision and control over his wife and children, as if discretion in their hands would endanger the family group. The fluidity of entitlements seems consistent with the maintenance and prosperity of the family only because there is an authority at the head capable of giving direction to the team. (Unger, 1986, p.65)

Unger's seeming acceptance of male rule in the family suggests that scholars using his work might be unable to extirpate themselves from the patriarchal values embedded in it to sufficiently challenge or restructure the Court's position on either birth status classifications or alternative families. As Kennedy has pointed out, "the very structures against which we rebel are necessarily within us as well as outside of us" (Kennedy, 1979, p.212). If Unger, and by extension Critical Legal Studies, sought to reach beyond these structures—no longer reduced to his plaintive cry of "Speak, God" (Unger, 1986, p.295)—he might find the insights offered by feminist analyses enlightening.

FEMINIST JURISPRUDENCE

Feminist jurisprudence shares Critical Legal theory's conviction that law is neither neutral, objective, nor universal. Both acknowledge the political nature of law and rail against legal domination and oppression. Both attempt to transcend the institutional limitations that confine roles and behavior of individuals. Both denounce "hierarchy, passivity, depersonalization, and decontextualization" (Menkel-Meadow, p.61). Both were influenced by post-World War II philosophical currents that found old ways of thinking in serious need of revision. Both, along with anthropology, history, literary criticism, and other disciplines, began questioning formerly unassailable truths and reached the conclusion that definitions of reality were largely dependent upon the perspective of the observer. To most radicals, the notion of a reality separate from all perspective became an illusion.

Despite these similarities, however, Critical Legal Studies and feminist jurisprudence are not identical. The difference between them is explicitly delineated by Carrie Menkel-Meadow:

The main difference between the two ways of looking at the world is that the feminist critique starts from the experiential point of view of the oppressed, dominated, and devalued, while the critical legal studies critique begins—and some would argue, remains—in a male-constructed, privileged place in which domination and oppression can be described and imagined but not fully experienced. . . . [T]he feminist critique . . . originates not only in conceptual constructs but in experience—in *being* dominated, not just in thinking about domination. (Menkel-Meadow, p.61)

The social position of women has rarely exceeded that accorded second-class citizens. Women have been and continue to be widely denigrated, exploited, abused, stepped over, and ignored. Feminist jurisprudence exerts continual efforts to prevent gender subordination from remaining invisible or disappearing once more from view. To this end, the seven questions raised by Heather Wishik (and discussed in Chapter 1) is one attempt to focus a feminist inquiry regarding the relationship between law and society

(Wishik, pp.72–75). Consistent reference to these questions might lead to a fundamental restructuring of society's institutions and policies.

The goal of feminist jurisprudence is to develop an alternative legal system that is neither patriarchal, binary, nor static. Such a system would acknowledge the tensions and strife that might arise from the multiple conflicting layers of a society guaranteeing "the non-oppression of all women." It would not, according to Clare Dalton, presume to *replace* male or masculinist theory; it would merely *displace* it (Dalton, p.7). Feminist jurisprudence might require that the Court step outside liberal legal theory—a theory that has guided its decisions since the court of John Marshall—and find "a place to stand, close to but not engulfed by" existing legal theory which would encourage its receptivity to a new legal philosophy. The theoretical perspective offered by feminist jurisprudence would result in an alteration of the Supreme Court's reasoning in birth status cases.

At the core of its legal analysis, feminist jurisprudence recognizes that points of view are essentially that—angles of vision which belong to some individual or group and thus reflect their perspective and preconceptions.[4] Feminist jurisprudence elevates to the plane of intellectual respectability the commonplace truism that point of view affects both how the world is seen and how it is experienced by the individual. Martha Minow identifies three prerequisites for infusing popular knowledge with academic credence: (1) it is necessary to transcend the limits of one's own viewpoint; (2) it is impossible to reach beyond one's own perspective unless one becomes cognizant of the perspective of others; and (3) it is difficult to gain an understanding of multiple points of view unless one's own position, assumptions, values, and points of reference are subjected to an in-depth analysis (Minow, 1987). If one is willing to meet these antecedent conditions, it becomes exceedingly difficult to mistake one's own reality or truth as Reality or Truth itself.

Acceptance of Minow's position would result in intellectual humility. It would require acknowledgment that while a feminist analysis is essential to a self-reflexive social critique, it is not the only analytical perspective capable of "transformative activity." As David Cole has noted:

Self-reflection requires one to recognize one's position in the social structure along all imaginable axes. The limiting case of self-reflection is omniscience; it would entail the ability to see a totality without reducing its multiplicity. While this is probably unattainable, we can be true to its ideal by refusing to universalize our perspective while simultaneously seeking to communicate with and understand the perspectives of those who are differently situated in the social structure. (Cole, 1985, pp.80–81 n.86)

Remembrance of humility might serve those who practice or who are willing to explore the merits of feminist thinking. Suspended judgment might allow this alternative approach to receive a fair hearing.

Catharine MacKinnon's formulation of how to transform the law was cited in Chapter 1 because she is among the most widely known codifiers of feminist thinking in the legal system. She asserts that the primary method of feminist jurisprudence is consciousness raising, or the acquisition of self-consciousness—the "quintessential expression" (MacKinnon, 1982, p.535) of the aphorism "the personal is political." The process of becoming fully cognizant of the extent to which "the personal is political" required women of the 1960s to follow Adrienne Rich's advice:

To question everything. To remember what it has been forbidden to even mention. To come together telling our stories, to look afresh at, and then to describe for ourselves, the frescoes of the Ice Age, the nudes of "high art," the Minoan seals and figurines, the moonlandscape embossed with the booted print of a male foot, the microscopic virus, the scarred and tortured body of the planet Earth. (Rich, p.66, quoted by Scales, p.1384).

Feminist jurisprudence is committed to principled self-reflection and self-criticism. It is also committed to hearing the multiple viewpoints that issue from all quarters of the globe simultaneously, but especially from those who have been and are "marginalized." A tall order. But not impossibile, especially if one maintains the stance of intellectual humility noted above.

Joan Scott adapts the work of Jacques Derrida to the needs of feminist theory—one of the sources of feminist jurisprudence—explaining that

[d]econstruction involves analyzing the operations of difference in texts, the ways in which meanings are made to work. The method consists of two related steps: the reversal and displacement of binary oppositions. This double process reveals the interdependence of seemingly dichotomous terms and their meaning relative to a particular history. It shows them not to be natural but constructed oppositions, constructed for particular purposes in particular contexts. (Scott, pp.37–38)

The deconstructive technique allows one to employ a set of legal terms while exposing their hidden interdependence; to work within the sociopolitical structure while attempting to dismantle it; to adopt a position under a specific set of circumstances while seriously challenging the validity of that position.

Tracing and assessing the historical circumstances surrounding an issue, feminist jurisprudence attempts to keep conscious awareness of the politics of the legal system in the forefront. It submits any law, policy, practice, or doctrine under challenge to an ultimate test—a determination of whether systematic subordination exists because of sex. According to MacKinnon, this test is to ascertain "whether [the law, policy, practice, or doctrine] integrally contributes to the maintenance of an underclass or a deprived position because of gender status" (MacKinnon, 1979, p.117). The doctrine resulting from a new philosophy of law might resemble a feminist reading and readjustment of international human rights standards.

Feminist jurisprudence frames legal questions in a manner that represents and expresses a woman-centered point of view. It takes seriously the urging of Audré Lorde, a prominent poet and literary critic, that it lay aside "the master's tools" (Lorde, pp.110–114); tools that can only allow for either a complete reversal of or conformity to the existing order. Neither reversal nor conformity, however, is relevant to the aims of feminist jurisprudence, which daringly reaches beyond the confines of the existing legal vocabulary, epistemology, psychology, and political theory.

CONCLUSION

A necessary prerequisite to any Supreme Court commitment to eliminating current discriminatory birth status classifications would require, at a minimum, the use of available statistical data regarding who are affected by birth status classifications and how they are affected, in conjunction with an in-depth analysis of the values, assumptions, and interests promoted by such classifications. If the Court were to adopt a feminist, as opposed to a non-feminist critical legal analysis, its inquiry would necessarily be so focused.

In view of the majority of the Court's birth status decisions, such a focus would primarily affect the reasoning, but not necessarily the outcome, of these cases. For example, the *Lehr* decision would remain the same—Lehr might still have been denied the power to veto the adoption of his daughter by the biological mother's husband. The Court might have pointed out that in the patriarchal society of the United States, the social power and privilege invested in males perpetuates sexual inequality and sexual discrimination against women. It also might have recognized that unwed fathers are not seeking equal status with single mothers when they claim their non-marital children over the objections of the biological mother; they are in fact seeking equal status with married fathers, who are unfettered by the desires or wishes of their children's mother. Finally, the Court might have questioned why the existence of a father in a family unit is deemed essential.

The Court cannot raise, let alone answer, these concerns or questions by appealing solely to international normative standards. Although the two U.N. documents regarding the rights of non-marital children are firmly committed to a legal and social principle of birth status non-discrimination, they do not focus adequately on the needs and rights of all persons affected by birth status classifications. In order to address a global community, they were framed in sweeping terms. Consequently, they lack the depth of analysis necessary to serve as the sole guides to the Supreme Court's interpretation of the Equal Protection Clause.

The only theory that seriously addresses the gender issues underlying birth status distinctions is feminist jurisprudence. International standards, nevertheless, might assist the Court in identifying and protecting the rights of all persons affected by birth status classifications—if the Court substituted feminist jurisprudence for liberal legal theory as a theoretical mode.

NOTES

1. See Chapters 2 and 3.
2. See: Wechsler, 1959; Dworkin, 1978; Nozick; Ackerman; Cole, 1984; Unger, 1976, 1983a; Tushnet, 1980; MacIntyre; Sagoff.
3. See: Gabel and Kennedy; Kelman, 1984.
4. The information regarding points of view and their inherent subjectivity is drawn from Minow (1987).

References

BOOKS AND PERIODICALS

Abbott, Grace. *The Child and the State, Volume 4: The Dependent Child and the Delinquent Child: The Child and the Unmarried Parents: Selected Documents with Introductory Notes.* Chicago: University of Chicago Press, 1938.

Ackerman, Bruce. *Social Justice in the Liberal State.* New Haven, CT: Yale University Press, 1980.

Adams, Abigail. "Selected Letters from the Adams Family Correspondence (March 31, 1776)," as quoted in Alice S. Rossi (ed.), *The Feminist Papers: From Adams to deBeauvoir.* New York: Bantam, 1973.

Adams, John. "Selected Letters from the Adams Family Correspondence (April 14, 1776)," as quoted in Alice S. Rossi (ed.), *The Feminist Papers: From Adams to deBeauvoir.* New York: Bantam, 1973.

Arditti, Rita, Renate Duelli Klein, and Shelley Minden. *Test-Tube Women: What Future for Motherhood?* London, Boston, Melbourne, & Henley: Pandora Press, 1984.

Auwers, Linda. "Equal Protection and the Illegitimate Child." 21 *Houston Law Review* 229 (1984).

Ayer, Joseph Cullen, Jr. "Legitimacy and Marriage." 16 *Harvard Law Review* 22 (1902).

Baer, Judith. *Equality Under the Constitution: Reclaiming the Fourteenth Amendment.* Ithaca, New York, and London: Cornell University Press, 1983.

Baum, Lawrence. *The Supreme Court.* Washington, DC: Congressional Quarterly Press, 1981.

Beitzinger, A. J. *A History of American Political Thought.* New York: Harper & Row, 1972.

Bell, Derrick A., Jr. *Race, Racism, and American Law.* 2d ed. Boston: Little, Brown, 1980.

Berger, Raul. *Government by the Judiciary.* Cambridge, MA: Harvard University Press, 1977.

Berger, Brigitte, and Peter L. Berger. *The War Over the Family*. New York: Doubleday, 1983.

Bertelsman, William O. "The Ninth Amendment and Due Process of Law—Toward a Viable Theory of Unenumerated Rights." 37 *University of Cincinnati Law Review* 777 (1968).

Black, Henry Campbell." *Black's Law Dictionary*. 4th ed. rev. St. Paul, MN: West, 1968.

"The Black Family: 1986." 17 *The Black Scholar* (special issue) (September/October 1986).

Blackstone, William. *Commentaries on the Laws of England: Vol. 1*. London: W. Kerr, 1857.

Blum, Jeffrey M., and Ralph G. Steinhard. "Federal Jurisdiction over International Human Rights Claims: The Alien Tort Claims . . ." 22 *Harvard Law Journal* 53 (1981).

Blustein, Jeffrey. *Parents and Children: The Ethics of the Family*. New York and Oxford: Oxford University Press, 1982.

Bodenheimer, Bridgitte M. "New Trends and Requirements in Adoption Law and Proposals for Legislative Change." 49 *Southern California Law Review* 10 (1975).

Breckinridge, Sophonsiba P. *The Family and the State*. Chicago: University of Chicago, 1934; Reprint. New York: Arno Press, 1972.

Brennan, Teresa, and Carole Pateman. "Mere Auxiliaries to the Commonwealth: Women and the Origins of Liberalism." 27 *Political Studies* 183 (1979).

Breslin, H. Paul. "Notes: Liability of Possible Fathers: A Support Remedy for Illegitimate Children." 18 *Stanford Law Review* 859 (1966).

Brophy, Julia, and Carol Smart. "From Disregard to Disrespect: The Position of Women in Family Law," in Elizabeth Whitelegg, et. al. (eds.), *The Changing Experience of Women*. Oxford: Basil Blackwell & The Open University, 1982, 1984.

Brownlie, Ian (ed.). *Basic Documents in International Law*. 2nd ed. Oxford: Clarendon Press, 1967, 1972.

Butler, Melissa A. "Early Liberal Roots of Feminism: John Locke and the Attack on Patriarchy." 72 *American Political Science Review* 135 (1978).

Bysiewicz, Shirley Raissi. Foreword, *The Laws Respecting Women*. Reprinted from the J. Johnston edition, London, 1777. Dobbs Ferry, NY: Oceana Publishers, 1974.

Call, Joseph L. "Federalism and the Ninth Amendment" 64 *Dickinson Law Review* 121 (1960).

Casey, Timothy. "The Family Support Act of 1988: Molehill or Mountain, Retreat or Reform?" 23 *Clearinghouse Review* 930 (1989).

Center for the Study of Social Policy. *Flip Side of Black Families Headed by Women: The Economic Status of Black Men*. Washington, DC: Center for the Study of Social Policy, 1984.

Chesler, Phyllis. *Mothers on Trial: The Battle for Children and Custody*. Seattle: Seal Press, 1986, 1987.

Children's Defense Fund. *Black and White Children in America: Key Facts*. Washington, DC: Children's Defense Fund, 1985.

Christenson, Gordon A. "Using Human Rights Law to Inform Due Process and Equal Protection Analysis" 52 *University of Cincinnati Law Review* 3 (1983).

Clark, Anna. *Women's Silence, Men's Violence: Sexual Assault in England, 1770–1845.* London & New York: Pandora Press, 1987.

Clark, Helen I. *Social Legislation.* New York: Irvington, 1957.

Clark, Lorenne M. G. "Women and Locke: Who Owns the Apples in the Garden of Eden?" in Lorene M. G. Clark and Lynda Lange (eds.), *The Sexism of Social and Political Theory: Women and Reproduction from Plato to Nietzsche.* Toronto: University of Toronto Press, 1979.

Claude, Richard P. *The Supreme Court and the Electoral Process.* Baltimore: John Hopkins University Press, 1970.

Cohen, Marie Prince. "Equal Protection for Unmarried Parents." 65 *Iowa Law Review* 679 (1980).

Cole, David. "Getting There: Reflection on Trashing from Feminist Jurisprudence and Critical Theory." 8 *Harvard Women's Law Journal* 59 (1985).

———. "Strategies of Difference: Litigating for Women's Rights in a Man's World." 2 *Law & Inequality: Journal of Theory and Practice* 33 (1984).

Collins, Hugh. "Roberto Unger and the Critical Legal Studies Movement." 14 *Journal of Law and Society* 387 (1987).

Comer, Lee. "Monogamy, Marriage and Economic Dependence," in Elizabeth Whitelegg et al. (ed), *The Changing Experience of Women.* Oxford: Basil Blackwell & The Open University, 1982, 1984.

Comment. "The Equal Protection Clause and Illegitimacy—What Standard of Review?" 28 *University of Kansas Law Review* 140 (1979).

Corea, Gena. *The Mother Machine: Reproductive Technologies from Artificial Insemination to Artificial Wombs.* New York: Harper & Row, 1985.

Corwin, Edward. "The 'Higher Law' Background of American Constitutional Law: Parts 1–2." 42 *Harvard Law Review* 149 (1928–1929).

Council of Europe. European Committee on Legal Cooperation. *European Convention on the Legal Status of Children Born Out of Wedlock [European Treaty Series No. 85].* Strasbourg: Council of Europe, 1975.

Current Population Reports. Series P-20. No. 433. *Marital Status and Living Arrangements: March 1988.* Washington, DC: Government Printing Office, 1989.

Dalton, Clare. "Commentary: Where We Stand: Observations on the Situation of Feminist Legal Thought." 3 *Berkeley's Women and Law Journal* 1 (1987/1988).

Davis, Angela Y. "The Black Women's Role in the Community of Slaves." 3 *Black Scholar* 7 (1971).

Davis, Angela Y., and Fania Davis. "The Black Family and the Crisis of Capitalism." 17 *Black Scholar* 33 (1986).

Davis, Kingsley. "Illegitimacy and the Social Structure." 45 *American Journal of Sociology* 215 (1939–1940).

De Crow, Karen. *Sexist Justice.* New York: Vintage Books, 1974.

"Developments in the Law: The Constitution and the Family." 93 *Harvard Law Review* 1156 (1980).

DeWar, Diana. *Orphans of the Living: A Study of Bastardy.* London: Hutchinson, 1968.

Donovan, Josephine. *Feminist Theory: The Intellectual Traditions of American Feminism*. New York: Ungar, 1985.

Douthwaite, Graham. *Unmarried Couples and the Law*. Indianapolis: Allen Smith, 1979.

Dowrick, F. E. *Human Rights: Problems, Perspectives, and Texts*. Westmead, U.K. Saxon House, 1979.

Dworkin, Ronald. "Liberalism" in Stuart Hampshire (ed.), *Public and Private Morality*. New York: Cambridge University Press, 1978.

_____ . *Taking Rights Seriously*. Cambridge, MA: Harvard University Press, 1977.

Dwyer, John M. "Equal Protection for Illegitimate Children Conceived by Artificial Insemination." 21 *San Diego Law Review* 1061 (1984).

Eastwood, Mary. "The Double Standard of Justice: Women's Rights Under the Constitution." 5 *Valparaiso University Law Review* 281 (1971).

Ehrenzweig, Albert A. "The 'Bastard' in the Conflict of Laws—A National Disgrace." 29 *University of Chicago Law Review* 498 (1962).

Eisenstein, Zillah R. *Capitalist Patriarchy and the Case for Socialist Feminism*. New York & London: Monthly Review Press, 1979.

_____ . *Feminism and Sexual Equality: Crisis in Liberal Feminism*. New York: Monthly Review, 1984.

_____ . *The Radical Future of Liberal Feminism*. New York: Longman, 1981.

Eisler, Riane Tennehaus. *Dissolution: No-Fault Divorce, Marriage, and the Future of Women*. New York: McGraw-Hill, 1977.

Elshtain, Jean Bethke. *Private Man, Private Woman: Women in Social and Political Thought*. Princeton, NJ: Princeton University Press, 1981.

Ely, John Hart. *Democracy and Distrust: A Theory of Judicial Review*. Cambridge, MA: Harvard University Press, 1980.

Erickson, Nancy S. "The Feminist Dilemma Over Unwed Parents' Custody Rights: The Mother's Rights Must Take Priority." 2 *Law and Inequality: A Journal of Theory and Practise* 447 (1984).

Falk, Richard. *Human Rights and State Sovereignty*. New York: Holmes & Meier, 1981.

Felsenthal, Carol. *Phyllis Schlafly: The Sweetheart of the Silent Majority*. Chicago: Regnery Gateway, 1981, 1982.

Finkelman, Paul. *The Law of Freedom and Bondage: A Casebook*. New York: Oceana, 1986.

Finley, Lucinda. "Breaking Women's Silence in Law: The Dilemma of the Gendered Nature of Legal Reasoning." 64 *Notre Dame Law Review* 886 (1989).

_____ . "Choice and Freedom: Elusive Issues in the Search for Gender Justice." 96 *Yale Law Review* 914 (1987).

_____ . "Transcending Equality Theory: A Way Out of the Maternity and the Workplace Debate." 86 *Columbia Law Review* 1118 (1986).

Fox-Genovese, Elizabeth. *Feminism Without Illusions: A Critique of Individualism*. Chapel Hill: University of North Carolina Press, 1991.

Franklin, John Hope. *From Slavery to Freedom: A History of Negro Americans*. 3d ed. New York: Vintage, 1947, 1967.

Frazier, E. Franklin. *The Negro Family in the United States*. Chicago: University of Chicago Press, 1939, 1969.

Freeman, Alan. "Truth and Mystification in Legal Scholarship." 90 *Yale Law Review* 1229 (1981).

Freeman, Jo. "The Legal Basis of the Sexual Caste System." 5 *Valparaiso University Law Review* 203 (1971).

French, Marilyn. *Beyond Power: Women, Men, and Morals*. New York: Ballantine Books, 1985.

Friedmann, Wolfgang Gaston. *Law in a Changing Society*. New York: Columbia University Press, 1972.

Fuchs, Lawrence. *Family Matters*. New York: Warner, 1971.

Furman, Nelly. "The Politics of Language: Beyond the Gender Principle?" in Gayle Greene and Coppelia Kahn (eds.), *Making a Difference: Feminist Literary Criticism*. New York: Methuen, 1985.

Gabel, Paul, and Duncan Kennedy. "Roll Over, Beethoven." 36 *Stanford Law Review* 1 (1984).

Galley, Margaret. "Promoting Non-Discrimination Against Women: The UN Commission on the Status of Women." 23 *International Studies Quarterly* 285 (1979).

Gans, Herbert J. "The Negro Family: Reflection on the Moynihan Report" in Lee Rainwater and William L. Yancey (eds.), *The Moynihan Report and the Politics of Controversy*. Cambridge, MA: MIT Press, 1967.

Gibbs, Jewelle Taylor, et al. (eds.). *Young, Black, and Male in America: An Endangered Species*. Dover, MA: Auburn House Publishing, 1988.

Giddings, Paula. *When and Where I Enter: The Impact of Black Women on Race and Sex in America*. New York: Bantam Books, 1984.

Ginger, Ann Fagan. "Enforcing the Hidden U.S. Equal Rights Law." 20 *Golden Gate University Law Review* 385 (1990).

Ginsburg, Ruth Bader. "Gender and the Constitution." 44 *University of Cincinnati Law Review* 1 (1975).

Goldman, Sheldon, and Austin Sarat (eds.). *American Court Systems: Readings in Judicial Process and Behavior*. San Francisco: W. H. Freeman, 1978.

Goldstein, Leslie Friedman. *The Constitutional Rights of Women: Cases in Law and Social Change*. 2d ed. Madison: University of Wisconsin Press, 1988.

Goldstein, Leslie Friedman (ed.). *Feminist Jurisprudence: The Difference Debate*. Lanham, MD: Rowman & Littlefield, 1992.

Gordon, Robert W. "New Developments in Legal Theory," in David Kairys (ed.), *Politics of Law*. New York: Pantheon Books, 1982.

Greenwalt, Kent. "How Empty Is the Idea of Equality?" 83 *Columbia Law Review* 1167 (1983).

Grey, Thomas C. "Do We Have An Unwritten Constitution?" 27 *Stanford Law Review* 703 (1975).

Gruberg, Martin. *Women in American Politics*. Oshkosh, WI: Academia Press, 1968.

Guerin, Jane. "Illegitimacy and Equal Protection: *Lalli v. Lalli*—A Retreat from *Trimble v. Gordon*." 57 *Denver Law Journal* 3 (1980).

Gunther, Gerald. *Constitutional Law: Cases and Materials*. Mineola, New York: Foundation Press, 1980.

———. "The Supreme Court, 1971 Term—Forward: In Search of Evolving Doctrine on a Changing Court: A Model for a Newer Equal Protection." 86 *Harvard Law Review* 1 (1972).

Gutman, Herbert. *The Black Family in Slavery and Freedom: 1750–1925.* New York: Pantheon Books, 1976.

Hamilton, John R. "The Unwed Father and the Right to Know of His Child's Existence." 76 *Kentucky Law Journal* 949 (1987–1988).

Harris, Robert J. *The Quest for Equality: The Constitution, Congress, and the Supreme Court.* Baton Rouge: Louisiana State University Press, 1960.

Harris, William. "Bonding Word and Polity: The Logic of American Constitutionalism." 76 *American Political Science Review* 34 (1982).

Harrison, Cynthia. "A Richer Life: A Reflection on the Women's Movement," in Sara E. Rix (ed.) for the Women's Research & Education Institute, *The American Woman, 1988–1989: A Status Report.* New York: Norton, 1988.

Haskins, Frank. "Illegitimacy." 7 *Encyclopedia of the Social Sciences* 579 (1939).

Helmholz, R. H. "Support Orders, Church Courts, and the Rule of *Filius Nullius*: A Reassessment of the Common Law." 63 *Virginia Law Review* 431 (1977).

Hill, Stacey Lynn. "Putative Fathers and Parental Interests: A Search for Protection." 65 *Indiana Law Journal* 939 (1990).

Hirsch, Fred. *Social Limits of Growth.* Cambridge, MA: Harvard University Press, 1976.

Holt, Wayne. "Tilt." 52 *George Washington Law Review* 280 (1984).

Holy Bible. King James Version. New York: New American Library, 1974.

Hooper, Winifred. *The Law of Illegitimacy.* London: Sweet & Maxwell, 1911.

Horton, Carroll, and Jessie C. Smith. *Statistical Record for Black America.* 2d ed. Detroit: Gale Research, 1993.

Isaacson, Scott E. "Equal Protection for Illegitimate Children." 1980 *Brigham Young University Law Review* 142 (1980).

Jacobs, A. C. "Illegitimacy, Legal Aspects." 7 *Encyclopedia of Social Sciences*, Edwin R. A. Seligman, editor-in chief. New York: Macmillan, 1934.

Jefferson's Correspondence, Vol. 4, as cited in Harriett Martineau, *Society in America.* Edited, abridged, with an introductory essay by Seymour Martin Lipset. Garden City, NY: Doubleday, 1962.

Jehlen, Myra. "Archimedes and the Paradox of Feminist Criticism." 6 *Signs* 575 (1981).

Kairys, David (ed.). *The Politics of Law: A Progressive Critique.* New York: Pantheon Books, 1982.

Karst, Kenneth. " 'A Discrimination So Trivial': A Note On Law and the Symbolism of Women's Dependency." 49 *Los Angeles Bar Bulletin* 499 (1968).

_____. "Invidious Discrimination: Justice Douglas and the Return of the Natural-Law-Due-Process Formula." 16 *UCLA Law Review* 716 (1969).

_____. "Women's Constitution." 1985 *Duke Law Journal* 447 (1984).

Kay, Richard S. "The Equal Protection Clause in the Supreme Court, 1873–1903." 29 *Buffalo Law Review* 667 (1980).

Kay, Herma Hill. *Sex-based Discrimination: Text, Cases, and Materials.* 3d ed. St. Paul, MN: West, 1988.

Kelman, Mark. *A Guide to Critical Legal Studies.* Cambridge, MA: Harvard University Press, 1987.

_____. "Trashing." 36 *Stanford Law Review* 293 (1984).

Kellner, Mark. "Ideology, Marxism, and Advanced Capitalism." 42 *Socialist Review* 38 (1978).

Kelly, Joan. "Early Feminist Theory and the *Querelle des Femmes*, 1400–1789." 8 *Signs* 4 (1982).

Kelley, James F. "The Uncertain Renaissance of the Ninth Amendment." 33 *University of Chicago Law School* 814 (1966).

Kelsey, Knowlton H. "The Ninth Amendment of the Federal Constitution." 11 *Indiana Law Journal* 309 (1936).

Kennedy, Duncan. "Cost-Reduction Theory as Legitimation." 90 *Yale Law Journal* 1275 (1981).

———. "The Structure of Blackstone's Commentaries." 28 *Buffalo Law Review* 205 (1979).

Kennedy, Duncan, and Karl Klare. "A Bibliography of Critical Legal Studies." 94 *Yale Law Journal 461 (1984).*

Koral, Mark Allen. "Ninth Amendment Vindication of Unenumerated Federal Rights." 42 *Temple Law Quarterly* 46 (1968).

Kramer, Rita. *In Defense of the Family*. New York: Basic Books, 1983.

Krause, Harry D. "Equal Protection for the Illegitimate." 65 *Michigan Law Review* 477 (1967).

———. *Illegitimacy: Law and Social Policy*. Princeton, NJ: Princeton University Press, 1971.

———. "The Supreme Court 1976 Term Forward . . . " 91 *Harvard Law Review* 1 (1977).

Kutner, Luis. "The Neglected Ninth Amendment: The 'Other Rights' Retained by the People." 51(2) *Marquette Law Review* 121 (1967).

Ladner, Joyce. *Tomorrow's Tomorrow: The Black Woman*. New York: Doubleday, 1971.

Laqueur, Walter, and Barry Rubin (eds.). *The Human Rights Reader: A Unique Sourcebook and Documentary History on the Issue of Human Rights*. New York: New American Library, 1977.

Lasch, Christopher. *Haven in a Heartless World*. New York: Basic Books, 1977.

Laslett, Paul, Karla Oosterveen, and Richard M. Smith (eds.). *Bastardy and Its Comparative History*. Cambridge, MA: Harvard University Press, 1980.

Law, Sylvia. "Rethinking Sex and the Constitution." 132 *University of Pennsylvania Law Review* 952 (1984).

Leavitt, Ruby R. "Woman in Other Cultures," in Vivian Gornick and Barbara K. Moran (eds.), *Woman in Sexist Society: Studies in Power and Powerlessness*. New York: Basic Books, 1971.

Levithan, Sar A., and Richard S. Belous. *What's Happening to the American Family?* Baltimore: John Hopkins University Press, 1981.

Lindgren, J. Ralph, and Nadine Taub. *The Law of Sex Discrimination*. St. Paul, MN: West, 1988.

Locke, John. *The Two Treatises of Government*. Introduction and notes by Peter Laslett. Cambridge: Cambridge University Press, 1960, 1963.

Lorde, Audré. "The Master's Tools Will Never Dismantle the Master's House," in Audré Lorde, *Sister Outsider: Essays and Speeches*. Trumansburg, NY: Crossing Press, 1984.

MacFarlane, Alan. "Illegitimacy and Illegitimates in English History," in Peter Laslett, Karla Oosterveen, & Richard M. Smith (eds.), *Bastardy and Its Comparative History*. Cambridge, MA: Harvard University Press, 1980.

MacIntyre, Alasdair. *After Virtue: A Study in Moral Theory*. Notre Dame, IN: University of Notre Dame, 1984.

MacKinnon, Catharine A. "Feminism, Marxism, and the State: An Agenda for Theory." 7 *Signs* 515 (1982).

_____. "Feminism, Marxism, and the State: Feminist Jurisprudence." 8 *Signs* 635 (1983).

_____. *Feminism Unmodified: Discourses on Life and Law*. Cambridge, MA: Harvard University Press, 1987.

_____. "Reflections on Sex Equality Under Law." 100 *Yale Law Review* 1281 (1991).

_____. *Sexual Harassment of Working Women: A Case of Sex Discrimination*. New Haven, CT: Yale University Press, 1979.

_____. *Toward a Feminist Theory of State*. Cambridge, MA: Harvard University Press, 1989.

Malinowski, Bronislaw. "Kinship." 13 *Encyclopedia Britannica*, 14th ed. (London and New York, 1929).

Maltz, Earl A. "The Concept of Equal Protection of the Laws—A Historical Inquiry." 22 *San Diego Law Review* 499 (1985).

Martineau, Robert J., Jr. "Interpreting the Constitution: The Use of International Human Rights Norms." 5 *Human Rights Quarterly* 87 (1983).

McDougal, Myres S., Harold D. Lasswell, and Lung-chu Chen. "Human Rights and the United Nations." 50 *American Journal of International Law* 531 (1964).

Menkel-Meadow, Carrie. "Feminist Legal Theory, Critical Legal Studies, and Legal Education or 'The Fem-Crits Go to Law School.' " 38 *Journal of Legal Education* 61 (1988).

Mill, James. "Government," as quoted in Susan Groag Bell and Karen M. Offen (eds.), *Women, the Family, and Freedom: The Debate in Documents, Volume 1, 1750–1880*. Stanford, CA: Stanford University Press, 1983.

Mill, John Stuart. "The Subjection of Women," in John Stuart Mill and Harriet Taylor-Mill, *Essays on Sex Equality*, (ed.) Alice S. Rossi. Chicago: University of Chicago Press, 1970.

Miller, Casey, and Kate Swift. *The Handbook of Non-sexist Writing: For Writers, Editors, and Speakers*. New York: Harper & Row, 1980.

_____. *Words and Women: New Language in New Times*. New York: Doubleday, 1976.

Millet, Kate. *Sexual Politics*. New York: Doubleday, 1970.

Minow, Martha. *Making All the Difference: Inclusion, Exclusion, and American Law*. Ithaca, NY: Cornell University Press, 1990.

_____. "The Supreme Court 1986 Term—Foreword: Justice Engendered." 101 *Harvard Law Review* 10 (1987).

Moore, Terence J. "The Ninth Amendment—Its Origins and Meaning." 7 *New England Law Review* 215 (1972).

Morais, Nina. "Sex Discrimination and the Fourteenth Amendment: Lost History." 97 *Yale Law Journal* 1153 (1988).

Morgan, Robin. "Introduction: Planetary Feminism: The Politics of the 21st Century," in Robin Morgan (ed.), *Sisterhood Is Global: The International Women's Movement Anthology*. Garden City, NY: Anchor Press/Doubleday, 1984.

Morris, Herbert. "Persons and Punishment" in A. I. Melden (ed.), *Human Rights*. Belmont, CA: Wadsworth, 1970.

Mower, Glenn A., Jr. "Implementing United Nations Covenants" in Abdul Aziz Said (ed.), *Human Rights and World Order*. New York: Praeger, 1978.

Moynihan, Daniel P. *The Negro Family: The Case for National Action*. Washington, DC: U.S. Department of Labor, 1965; reprinted in Lee Rainwater and William L. Yancey. *The Moynihan Report and the Politics of Controversy*. Cambridge, MA: MIT Press, 1967.

Murphy, Walter F. "Constitutional Interpretation: The Art of the Historian, Magician or Statesman?" 87 *Yale Law Journal* 1752 (1978).

_____ . *Elements of Judicial Strategy*. Chicago: University of Chicago Press, 1964.

National Center for Health Statistics. *Vital Statistics of the U.S., 1988, Vol. 1, Natality*. DHHS Pub. #(PHS) 90–1100. Washington, DC: Public Health Service, GPO, 1990.

National Urban League. *The State of Black America, 1985*. New York: National Urban League, 1985.

New World Translation of the Holy Scriptures. New York: Watchtower Bible and Tract Society, 1961.

Nicholi, Armand, Jr. "The Fractured Family" in Arthur S. DeMoss (ed.), *The Rebirth of America*. Philadelphia: Arthur S. DeMoss Foundation, 1986.

Noonan, John T., Jr. "The Family and the Supreme Court." 23 *Catholic University of America Law Review* 255 (1973–74).

Norton, A. S. and P. C. Glick. "One Parent Families: A Social and Economic Profile." 35 *Family Relations* 9 (1986).

Notes. " 'Round and 'Round the Bramble Bush: From Legal Realism to Critical Legal Scholarship." 95 *Harvard Law Review* 1669 (1982).

Notes. "The Rights of Illegitimates Under Federal Statutes." 76 *Harvard Law Review* 337 (1962).

Nozick, Robert. *Anarchy, State, and Utopia*. New York: Basic Books, 1974.

Okin, Susan Molkin. *Women in Western Political Thought*. Princeton, NJ: Princeton University Press, 1979.

Otto, Herbert A. (ed.). *The Family in Search of a Future: Alternative Models for Moderns*. New York: Appleton-Century-Crofts, 1970.

Park, Ann I. "Human Rights and Basic Needs: Using International Human Rights Norms to Inform Constitutional Interpretation." 34 *UCLA Law Review* 1195 (1987).

Pateman, Carole. *The Disorder of Women: Democracy, Feminism and Political Theory*. Cambridge, U.K.: Polity Press, 1989.

Paust, Jordon J. "Human Rights and the Ninth Amendment: A New Form of Guarantee." 60 *Cornell Law Review* 231 (1975).

Pearce, Diana. "The Feminization of Poverty: Women, Work, and Welfare." 11 *Urban and Social Change Review* 28 (1978).

Perrin, Porter G., George H. Smith, and Jim W. Corder. *Handbook of Current English*. 3d ed. Glenview, IL: Scott, Foresman, 1968.

Petchesky, Rosiland Pollack. *Abortion and Woman's Choice: The State, Sexuality, and Reproductive Freedom*. Boston: Northeastern University Press, 1985.

Pines, Burton. *Back to Basics: The Traditionalist Movement That Is Sweeping Grass-Roots America*. New York: Marrow, 1982.

Pinkney, Alphonso. *Black Americans*. 4th ed. Englewood Cliffs, NJ: Prentice Hall, 1993.

Pogrebin, Letty Cottin. *Family Politics: Love and Power on an Intimate Frontier*. New York: McGraw-Hill, 1983.

Pollock, Sylvia, and Jo Sutton. "Fathers' Rights, Women's Losses." 8 *Women's Studies International Forum* 593 (1985).

Ramazanoglu, Caroline. *Feminism and the Contradictions of Oppression*. London and New York: Routledge, 1989.

Reagan, Ronald. "Untitled." In Arthur S. DeMoss (ed.), *The Rebirth of America*. Philadelphia: Arthur S. DeMoss Foundation, 1986.

Redenius, Charles. *The American Ideal of Equality: From Jefferson's Declaration to the Burger Court*. Port Washington, NY: Kennikat Press, 1981.

Rehnquist, William. "The Notion of a Living Constitution." 54 *Texas Law Review* 693 (1976).

Rich, Adrienne. "Natural Resources," in Adrienne Rich, *The Dream of a Common Language: Poems, 1974–1977*. New York: Norton, 1978.

———. *Of Woman Born: Motherhood as Experience and Institution*. New York: Bantam Books, 1976.

Richards, David A. J. "Sexual Autonomy and the Constitutional Right to Privacy: A Case Study in Human Rights and the Unwritten Constitution." 30 *Hastings Law Journal* 957 (1979).

Rifklin, Janet. "Toward a Theory of Law and Patriarchy." 3 *Harvard Women's Law Journal* 83 (1980).

Rix, Sara E. (ed.) for the Women's Research & Education Institute. *The American Woman, 1988–1989: A Status Report*. New York: Norton, 1988.

Robbins, Horrace H., and Francis Deak. "The Familial Property Rights of Illegitimate Children: A Comparative Study." 30 *Columbia Law Review* 308 (1930).

Robertson, John A. "Procreative Liberty and the Control of Contraception, Pregnancy, and Childbirth." 69 *Virginia Law Review* 405 (1983).

Rogge, O. John. "Unenumerated Rights." 47 *California Law Review* 787 (1959).

Rosaldo, Michele Zimbalist, and Louise Lamphere (eds.). *Woman, Culture, and Society*. Stanford, CA: Stanford University Press, 1974.

Rubin, Gayle. "The Traffic in Women: Notes on the 'Political Economy' of Sex," in Rayna R. Reiter (ed.). *Toward an Anthropology of Women*. New York: Monthly Review Press, 1975.

Russell, J. Stuart. "The Critical Legal Studies Challenge to Contemporary Mainstream Legal Philosophy" 18 *Ottawa Law Review* 1 (1986).

Saario, Vieno Voitto. *The Study of Discrimination Against Persons Born Out of Wedlock*. New York: United Nations, 1967.

Sagoff, Mark. "Liberalism and Law," in Douglas MacLean and Claudia Mills (eds.). *Liberalism Reconsidered*. Totowa, NJ: Rowman & Allanheld, 1983.

Sapiro, Virginia. *Women in American Society: An Introduction to Women's Studies*. Palo Alto, CA: Mayfield, 1986.

Satir, Virginia. *People Making*. Palo Alto, CA: California Science & Behavior Books, 1972; as quoted by John A. Robertson, "Procreative Liberty and the Control of Contraception, Pregnancy, and Childbirth." 69 *Virginia Law Review* 405 (1983).

Scales, Ann. "The Emergence of Feminist Jurisprudence: An Essay." 95 *Yale Law Review* 1373 (1986).

Schneider, David M., and Kathleen Gough (eds.). *Matrilineal Kinship*. Berkeley, CA: University of California Press, 1961.

Schrim, Allen L., James Trussell, Jane Menken, and William R. Grady. "Contraceptive Failure in the US: The Impact of Social, Economic, and Demographic Factors." 14 *Family Planning Perspectives* 68 (1983).

Scott, Joan W. "Deconstructing Equality-Versus-Difference: Or, the Uses of Poststructuralist Theory for Feminism." 14 *Feminist Studies* 33 (1988).

Sidel, Ruth. *Women and Children Last: The Plight of Poor Women in Affluent America*. New York: Penguin Books, 1986.

Smith, Patricia T. (ed.). *Feminist Jurisprudence*. New York: Oxford University Press, 1993.

Smith, Raymond T. "The Nuclear Family in Afro-American Kinship." 1 *Journal of Comparative Family Studies* 57 (1970).

Spece, Roy G. "The Most Effective or Least Restrictive Alternative as the Only Intermediate and Only Means-focused Review in Due Process and Equal Protection." 33 *Villanova Law Review* 111 (1988).

Spender, Dale. *Man Made Language*. London, Boston, Henley: Routledge & Kegan Paul, 1980, 1985.

Stack, Carol B. *All Our Kin: Strategies for Survival in a Black Community*. New York: Harper & Row, 1974.

Standard, Una. *Mrs. Man*. San Francisco: Germainbooks, 1977.

Staples, Robert. *The Black Family: Essays and Studies*. Belmont, CA: Wadsworth, 1971.

———. "The Political Economy of Black Family Life." 17 *Black Scholar* 2 (1986).

Stone, Olive M. "Illegitimacy and Claims to Money and Other Property: A Comparative Study." 15 *International and Comparative Law Quarterly* 505 (1966).

Stroud, Michael B., Teril Bundrant, and D. Leo Galindo. "Paternity Testing: A Current Approach." 16 *Trial* 46 (1980).

Teichman, Jenny. *Illegitimacy: An Examination of Bastardy*. Ithaca, NY: Cornell University Press, 1982.

Terasaki, Paul I. "Resolution by HLA Testing of 1,000 Paternity Cases Not Excluded by ABO Testing." 16 *Journal of Family Law* 543 (1978).

Thorne, Barrie. "Feminist Rethinking of the Family: An Overview," in Barrie Thorne with Marilyn Yalom (eds.), *Rethinking the Family: Some Feminist Questions*. New York: Longman, 1982.

Touchy, Hugo A. "The New Legality." 53 *American Bar Association Journal* 544 (1967).

Tribe, Lawrence. *American Constitutional Law*. Mineola, NY: Foundation Press, 1978.

Trubek, Mark. "Where the Action Is: Critical Legal Studies and Empiricism." 36 *Stanford Law Review* 575 (1984).

Tushnet, Mark. "Darkness on the Edge of Town: The Contribution of John Hart Ely to Constitutional Theory." 89 *Yale Law Journal* 1037 (1980).

———. "Perspective on Critical Legal Studies: Introduction." 52 *George Washington Law Review* 239 (1984).

_____. "Truth, Justice, and the American Way: An Interpretation of Public Law Scholarship in the Seventies." 57 *Texas Law Review* 1307 (1979).

Tussman, Joseph, and Jacobs tenBroek. "The Equal Protection of the Laws." 37 *California Law Review* 341 (1949).

Unger, Roberto. "Critical Legal Studies Movement." 96 *Harvard Law Review* 561 (1983a).

_____. *The Critical Legal Studies Movement*. Cambridge, MA: Harvard University Press, 1983b, 1986.

_____. *Knowledge and Politics*. New York: Free Press, 1976.

U.S. Bureau of the Census. Current Population Reports. Series P-60. No. 181. *Poverty in the United States: 1991*. Washington, DC: Government Printing Office, 1992.

U.S. Bureau of the Census. Current Population Reports. Series P-20. No. 461. *Marital Status and Living Arrangements: March 1991*. Washington, DC: Government Printing Office 1992.

U.S. Bureau of the Census. Current Population Reports. Series P-20. No. 380. *Marital Status and Living Arrangements: 1983*. Washington, DC: Government Printing Office, 1983.

U.S. Bureau of the Census. Current Population Reports. Series P-60. No. 174. *Money Income of Households, Families, and Persons in the U.S., 1990*. Washington, DC: Government Printing Office, 1991.

U.S. Bureau of Labor Statistics. *Employment and Earnings*. Washington, DC: Government Printing Office, January 1987.

"U.S. Commission on Interstate Child Support." 18 *Family Law Reporter* 2001 (3 March 1992).

U.S. Department of Commerce. Bureau of the Census. *Statistical Abstract of the United States: 1986*. 106th ed. Washington, DC: Government Printing Office, 1985.

U.S. Department of Commerce. Bureau of the Census. *Statistical Abstract of the United States: 1992*. 112th ed. Washington, DC: Government Printing Office, 1991.

Van Loan, Eugene, III. "Natural Rights and the Ninth Amendment." 48 *Boston University Law Review* 1 (1968).

VanZile, Philip, III. "Reaching Equal Protection Under Law: Alternative Forms of Family and the Changing Face of Monogamous Marriage." 1975 *Detroit College of Law Review* 95 (1975).

Vieira, Norman. "Rights and the United States Constitution: The Declension from Natural Law to Legal Positivism." 13 *Georgia Law Review* 1395 (1979).

Viguerie, R. A. "The Pro-Family Movement and the New Right," in R. A. Viguerie (ed.), *The New Right: We're Ready to Lead*. Falls Church, VA: Viguerie, 1980.

Vincent, Clark E. "Illegitimacy," in David L. Sills (ed.), 7 *International Encyclopedia of Social Science*. New York: Macmillian & Free Press, 1968.

_____. *Unmarried Mothers*. New York: Free Press, 1961.

Wallach, Aleta. "Musings on Motherhood, Marshall, Molecules: A Passage Through the Heart of Maternal Darkness from God's Creation to Man's." 6 *Black Law Journal* 88 (1978–1979).

Wallach, Aleta, and Patricia Tenoso. "A Vindication of the Rights of Unmarried Mothers and Their Children: An Analysis of the Institution of Illegitimacy, Equal Protection, and the Uniform Parentage Act." 23 *University of Kansas Law Review* 23 (1974).

Walzer, Michael. *The Company of Critics*. New York: Basic Books, 1988.

———. *Interpretation and Social Criticism*. Cambridge, MA: Harvard University Press, 1987.

Webster's New Collegiate Dictionary. Springfield, MA: G & C Merriam, 1977.

Weidner, Paul A. "The Equal Protection Clause: The Continuing Search for Judicial Standards." 57 *University of Detroit Journal of Urban Law* 867 (1980).

Werner, Oscar. *The Unmarried Woman in German Literature*. New York: Columbia University Press, 1972.

Wechsler, Herbert. "The Courts and the Constitution." 65 *Columbia Law Review* 1001 (1965).

———. "Neutral Principles of Constitutional Adjudication v. Purposive Jurisprudence" in David F. Forte (ed.), *The Supreme Court in American Politics: Judicial Activism v. Judicial Restraint*. Lexington, MA: D. C. Heath Co., 1972.

———. "Toward Neutral Principles of Constitutional Law." 73 *Harvard Law Review* 1 (1959).

West, Cornell. "CLS and a Liberal Critic." 97 *Yale Law Journal* 757 (1988).

West, Robin. "Jurisprudence and Gender." 55 *University of Chicago Law Review* 1 (1988).

Western, Peter. "The Empty Idea of Equality." 95 *Harvard Law Review* 537 (1982).

———. "On 'Confusing Ideas': Reply." 91 *Yale Law Journal* 1153 (1982a).

———. "To Lure the Tarantula from Its Hole: A Response." 83 *Columbia Law Review* 1186 (1983).

Westin, Jeanne. *The Coming Parent Revolution*. Chicago: Rand-McNally, 1981.

Wheller, Ann Minnick. "A Father's Right to Know His Child: Can It Be Denied Simply Because the Mother Married Another Man?" 20 *Loyola of Los Angeles Law Review* 705 (1987).

White, Deborah Gray. *Ar'n't I a Woman?: Female Slaves in the Plantation South*. New York: W. W. Norton, 1981.

White, G. Edward. *The American Judicial Tradition: Profiles of Leading American Judges*. New York: Oxford University Press, 1976.

Whitelegg, Elizabeth, Madeline Arnot, Else Bartes, Veronica Beechley, Lynda Birke, Susan Himmelweit, Kiana Leonard, Sonja Ruehl, and Mary Anne Speakman (eds.). *The Changing Experience of Women*. Oxford: Basil Blackwell & The Open University, 1982, 1984.

Wilkinson, J. Harvey, III, and G. Edward White. "Constitutional Protection for Personal Lifestyles." 62 *Cornell Law Review* 563 (1977).

Williams, Paul (ed.). *The International Bil of Human Rights*. Glen Ellen, CA: Entwhistle Books, 1981.

Williams, Wendy W. "The Equality Crisis: Some Reflections on Culture, Courts, and Feminism." 7 *Women's Rights Law Reporter* 175 (1983).

Wilson, William J. "The Urban Underclass" in Leslie J. Dunbar (ed.), *Minority Report*. New York: Pantheon Books, 1984.

Wishik, Heather. "To Question Everything: The Inquiries of Feminist Jurisprudence." 1 *Berkeley Women's Law Journal* 64 (1985).

Wolgast, Elizabeth H. *Equality and the Rights of Women*. Ithaca, NY: Cornell University Press, 1980.

Wright, J. Skelly. "Judicial Review and the Equal Protection Clause." 15 *Harvard Civil Rights–Civil Liberties Law Review* 1 (1980).

Zingo, Martha T. "Equal Protection for Illegitimate Children: The Supreme Court's Standard for Discrimination." 3 *Antioch Law Review* 59 (1985).

_____." 'Nameless Persons': Legal Discrimination Against Non-Marital Children in the United States." Ph.D. dissertation, University of Michigan, Ann Arbor, 1989.

Zuckerman, Karl D. "Social Attitudes and the Law." In National Council on Illegitimacy (ed.), *The Double Jeopardy, The Triple Crisis—Illegitimacy Today.* New York: National Council on Illegitimacy, 1969.

INTERNATIONAL DOCUMENTS

American Convention on Human Rights (also known as: The Pact of San Jose). No. 22, 1969, O.A.S.T.S. No. 36, Organization of American States Official Record. OEA/Ser. L/V/II.23 doc. 21 rev. 6 (1979). Reprinted in Laqueur and Rubin, pp.248–260.

Charter of the United Nations: OPI/511; 59 STAT 1031 (1945). Reprinted in Brownlie, pp.1–31.

Convention on the Elimination of All Forms of Discrimination Against Women: E/5451 (E/CN/.6/589) (1974).

European Convention for the Protection of Human Rights and Fundamental Freedoms: E.T.S. No.5. Reprinted in Brownlie, pp.206–232.

European Convention on the Legal Status of Children Born Out of Wedlock [European Treaty Series No. 85]. Strausbourg: Council of Europe.

Helsinki Accords [also known as: the Helsinki Agreement; Official Name—Final Act of the Conference on Security and Co-Operation in Europe]: 1 August 1975, Dep't State Pub. No. 8826 (Gen'l For. Pol. Ser. 298). Reprinted in Laqueur and Rubin, pp.282–292.

International Bill of Human Rights is composed of (1) The Universal Declaration of Human Rights—U.N. Doc. A/811; reprinted in Brownlie, pp.144–149; (2) The International Covenant on Economic, Social, and Cultural Rights—reprinted in Brownlie, pp.151–161; and (3) The International Covenant on Civil and Political Rights—reprinted in Brownlie, pp.162–180; Laqueur and Rubin, pp.216–224.

Study of Discrimination Against Persons Born Out of Wedlock: General Principles on Equality and Non-Discrimination in Respect of Persons Born Out of Wedlock: Sub-Commission on Prevention of Discrimination and Protection of Minorities of the Commission on Human Rights, United Nations Economic and Social Council, U.N. Doc. E/CN. 4 Sub. 2/L. 453. New York: United Nations, 1967.

LEGAL CASES

Beaty, see *Weinberger v. Beaty.*
Beaty v. Weinberger, 478 F.2d 300 (1973).
Baugh v. Maddox, 266 Ala. 175, 95 So. 2d 268 (1957).

Boles, see *Califano v. Boles*.
Bolling v. Sharpe, 347 U.S. 497 (1954).
Bowen v. Gilliard, 483 U.S. 587 (1987).
Bradwell v. Illinois, 16 Wall. 130 (1873).
Bradwell v. Illinois, Transcript of Record, Opinion of the Court Denying Application.
Brown v. Board of Education, 347 U.S. 488 (1954).
Caban v. Mohammed, 441 U.S. 380 (1979).
Califano v. Boles, 443 U.S. 282 (1979).
Carolene, see *United States v. Carolene Products*.
City of New Orleans v. Dukes, 427 U.S. 297 (1976).
Clark, see *United States v. Clark*.
Clark v. Jeters, 486 U.S. 456 (1988).
Craig v. Boren, 429 U.S. 190, 197 (1976).
Dandridge v. Williams, 397 U.S. 471 (1970).
Davis, see *Richardson v. Davis*.
Doe v. Commonwealth's Attorney General for Richmond, 425 U.S. 901 (1976), aff'd 403
    F. Supp. 1199 (E.D. Va. 1975).
Doughty v. Engler, 112 Kan. 583 (1923).
Dukes, see *City of New Orleans v. Dukes*.
Eakin v. Raub, 12 S&R 330 (Pa 1825).
Fiallo v. Bell, 430 U.S. 787 (1977).
Filartiga v. Pena-Irala, 630 F.2d 876, 880 (2d Cir. 1980).
Filartiga v. Pena-Irala, "Memorandum for the U.S. as *Amicus Curiae*."
Geduldig v. Aiello, 417 U.S. 484 (1974).
Griffin, see *Richardson v. Griffin*.
Griswold v. Connecticut, 381 U.S. 479 (1965).
Glona v. American Guarantee & Liability Co., 391 U.S. 73 (1968).
Goesaert v. Cleary, 335 U.S. 464 (1948).
Goldberg v. Kelly, 397 U.S. 254 (1970).
Gomez v. Perez, 409 U.S. 535 (1973).
Harris v. McRae, 448 U.S. 297 (1980).
Hogan, see *Mississippi University for Women v. Hogan*.
Houghton v. Dickinson, 82 N.E. 481 (Mass. 1907).
Hoyt v. Florida, 368 U.S. 57 (1961).
Jefferson v. Hackney, 406 U.S. 535 (1972).
Jeters, see *Clark v. Jeters*.
Jimenez v. Weinberger, 417 U.S. 628 (1974).
Katzenbach v. Morgan, 384 U.S. 641 (1966).
Korematsu v. United States, 323 U.S. 214 (1944).
Kotzke v. Kotzke's Estate, 171 N.W. 442 (1908).
Kramer v. Union School District, 345 U.S. 621 (1969).
Labine v. Vincent, 401 U.S. 532 (1971).
Lalli v. Lalli, 439 U.S. 259 (1978).
Lehr v. Robertson, 463 U.S. 248 (1983).
Levy v. Louisiana, 391 U.S. 68 (1968).
Levy v. Louisiana, "Brief of Attorney General."
Lindsley v. Natural Carbine Gas, 220 U.S. 60 (1911).
Little v. Streater, 452 U.S. 1 (1981).

Lochner v. New York, 198 U.S. 45 (1905).
Loving v. Virginia, 388 U.S. 1 (1967).
Mager v. Grima, 49 U.S. 490, 493 (8 How. 1890).
Martin v. Claxton, 274 S.W. 77 (Mo. 1925).
Mathews v. Lucas, 427 U.S. 495 (1976).
McGowen v. Maryland, 366 U.S. 420 (1961).
Memorial Hospital v. Maricopa County, 415 U.S. 250 (1974).
Michael M. v. Superior Court, 450 U.S. 464 (1981).
Mills v. Habluetzel, 456 U.S. 91 (1982).
Minor v. Happersett, 88 U.S. (21 Wall.) 162 (1875).
Mississippi University for Women v. Hogan, 102 S.Ct. 3331 (1981).
Mitchell, see *Oregon v. Mitchell*.
Morey v. Doud, 354 U.S. 457 (1957), overruled.
Mosley, see *Police Dept. of Chicago v. Mosley*.
Muller v. Oregon, 208 U.S. 412 (1908).
New Jersey Welfare Rights Organization v. Cahill, 411 U.S. 619 (1973).
New Orleans v. Dukes, 427 U.S. 297 (1976).
Nolan Breedlove v. Suttles, Tax Collector, 302 U.S. 277 (1937).
Norton v. Mathews, 427 U.S. 524 (1975).
Norton v. Weinberger, 364 F. Supp. 1117, 1128 (Md. 1973).
Oregon v. Mitchell, 400 U.S. 112 (1970).
Parham v. Hughes, 441 U.S. 347 (1979).
Pfeifer v. Wright, 41 F.2d 464 (10th Cir. 1930).
Pickett v. Brown, 462 U.S. 1 (1983).
Plessy v. Ferguson, 163 U.S. 537 (1896).
Poe v. Ullman, 367 U.S. 497 (1961).
Police Dept. of Chicago v. Mosley, 408 U.S. 92 (1972).
Pyler v. Doe, 457 U.S. 202 (1982).
Quilloin v. Walcott, 434 U.S. 246 (1978).
Quong Wing v. Kirkindall, 223 U.S. 62 (1912).
Railway Express Agency v. New York, 336 U.S. 106 (1949).
Reed v. Campbell, 476 U.S. 852 (1986).
Reed v. Reed, 404 U.S. 71 (1971).
Richardson v. Davis, 409 U.S. 1069 (1972), aff'd 342 F. Supp. 588 (D. Conn. 1972).
Richardson v. Griffin, 409 U.S. 1069 (1972), aff'd 346 F. Supp. 1226 (1972).
Rodriguez, see *San Antonio Independent School District v. Rodriguez*.
Rodriguez-Fernandez v. Wilkinson, 654 F.2d 1382 (10th Cir. 1981).
Roe v. Wade, 410 U.S. 113 (1973).
Royster Guano Co. v. Virginia, 253 U.S. 412, 415 (1920).
Salfi, see *Weinberger v. Salfi*.
San Antonio Independent School District v. Rodriguez, 41 U.S. 1 (1973).
Schweiker v. Hogan, 457 U.S. 569 (1982).
Schweiker v. Wilson, 450 U.S. 221 (1981).
Shapiro v. Thompson, 394 U.S. 618 (1969).
Skinner v. Oklahoma, 316 U.S. 535 (1942).
Slaughter-House Cases, 83 U.S. (16 Wall.) 36 (1873).
Smith v. Organization of Foster Families for Equality Reform, 431 U.S. 816 (1977).
Stanley v. Illinois, 405 U.S. 645 (1972).

Thompson v. Vestal Lumber & Mfg. Co., 16 So. 2d 594, 596 (La. Ct. App. 1943), reversed on other grounds, 22 So. 2d 842 (1944).

Trimble v. Gordon, 430 U.S. 762 (1977).

Turnmine v. Mayes, 114 S.W. 478 (Tenn. 1908).

United States v. Carolene Products, 304 U.S. 144 (1938).

United States v. Clark, 445 U.S. 23 (1980).

USR.R. Retirement Board v. Fritz, 449 U.S. 166 (1980).

Vance v. Bradley, 440 U.S. 93 (1979).

Weber v. Aetna Casualty & Surety Co., 406 U.S. 164 (1972).

Weinberger v. Beaty, 418 U.S. 901 (1974), aff'd 478 F.2d 300 (5th Cir. 1973).

Weinberger v. Salfi, 422 U.S. 749 (1975).

Wengler v. Druggists Mutual Insurance Co., 100 S.Ct. 1540 (1980).

Williams v. Rhodes, 393 U.S. 23 (1968).

Williamson v. Lee Optical, 348 U.S. 483 (1955).

Wisconsin v. Yoder, 406 U.S. 205 (1972).

Yoder, see *Wisconsin v. Yoder*.

Index

About the Authors

MARTHA T. ZINGO is an Assistant Professor of Political Science at Oakland University in Michigan.

KEVIN E. EARLY is an Assistant Professor of Sociology at Oakland University and is the author of *Religion and Suicide in the African-American Community* (Greenwood, 1992).

ISBN 0-275-94711-4

9 780275 947118

HARDCOVER BAR CODE